Decoding Entrepreneurial Vision

Modern China Series

Decoding Entrepreneurial Vision

Fan Xiaoping

North American Business Press

Decoding Entrepreneurial Vision

ISBN: 978-1-948915-32-8

North American Business Press
Atlanta, Georgia
Miami, Florida
New York, New York
Toronto, Canada

FIRST PRINTING, 2023

About Modern China Series

As one of the oldest civilized regions globally, China has emerged as a "new world" because it embraces its essence and heritage and links them to viable economic strategies. In the last 25 years, China has made tremendous strides. The country and its people have every right to take pride in these accomplishments. Many Chinese leaders and intellectuals anticipate continuing growth with these successes. Furthermore, China's plans and strategies are often based on this premise.

The U.S. has tremendous interest in the Chinese economy and business environment. China has emerged as a global superpower, and scholars and business people in the U.S. are keenly interested in learning how this will affect them and do business with China. In response to growing interest from international and Asian scholars, North American Business Press is pleased to announce our Modern China Series (MCS) books. It is the first book series about modern China in the U.S., garnering tremendous interest in the U.S. and worldwide. With our first book reaching stores in September 2011, this initiative develops relationships between NABP and Chinese scholars. They desire to promote their academic and applied business writings to the rest of the world.

We have had an overwhelming demand for the Modern China Series from authors who would like to publish in the series and people who would like to read the books. The books have been viewed by thousands of people from the U.S. and the rest of the world. There are currently ten books published in the series, and we have a couple of dozen books that we are considering for the series.

We have published books on several areas revolving around the Chinese business environment. We have a few that focus on the best practices in marketing in China; some are compared to "best practices" in doing business in China, and a few are on the outlook of the Chinese economy. The market for the Modern China Series is enormous. There are tens of thousands of scholars who are keenly interested in the continued growth of the Chinese economy and the implications that it will have on the business world. Even more significant are the millions of business people interested in the impact that China will continue to have on the global economy. It is difficult to pinpoint the exact demand for the series, but it Is enormous.

We have big plans for growing the Modern China Series. It can be one of the most significant economic/business series ever produced. We are very selective with the books we will add to the collection, but we encourage scholars who think they have unique and exciting perspectives on China to submit their book manuscripts. From the readers' perspective, we are committed to producing high-quality books regularly, so readers should expect a steady stream of insightful books to come out for many years.

This initiative is headed by Dr. Robert Tian, a renowned researcher and academic. He spearheads our efforts in partnering with foreign authors and administering the day-to-day operations of this series. Dr. Tian, the Vice-President of North American Business Press and Editor of this series, spends much of his time in Beijing, Shanghai, and other Chinese cities, focusing on developing and managing our interests with authors and universities. Below is the list of the books we have published:

Enterprise Strategy: New Horizon, authored by Zhang Xiuyu
Governance of Private Enterprises in Modern China, authored by Zhong Qin
The Art of War and Enterprise Strategy Management, authored by Fu Shouzhi
Marketing Issues in Modern China, edited by Robert Guang Tian et al.
The Footprints of the Academician, authored by Fu Zhouzhi
Marketing and Economics in Modern China (I) edited by Xiaoguang Qi et al.
Marketing and Economics in Modern China (II) edited by Wang Tianjin et al.
An Islamic Heritage in China, authored by Ma Zhanming
China Environmental Anthropology authored by Wang Tianjin, Tian Guang, and Ma Jianfu
Can China Rule the New World? Authored by Tian Guang and Chen Gang

Critiques on Pan-marketization authored by Li Cunlin, Liu Hongfei, and Tian Guang
Economic and Business Anthropology in China, edited by Xiaoguang Qi and Tian Guang
China-Mongolia Economic Corridor authored by Eerdun Taoketao, Zhang Zhe, Wang Gang, and Wei Lisi
Anthropology of Chinese Foodways authored by Tian Guang and Chen Gang
Urbanization of Rural China, authored by Li Taohong
Child Rearing in Rural China by Jiang Youchun and Yang Yunyi
Belt and Road vs. China and World by Tian Guang and Chen Gang
Modernization of China by Tian Guang, Luo Kanglong and Chen Qian
Abnormal School Behaviors: China vs. South Korea by Yu Yanyan
Shi Zhengyi and Chinese Ethnological Economics by Tian Guang and Zhong Ni
Decoding Entrepreneurial Vision by Fan Xiaoping

Table of Contents

Preface

The Origin of Entrepreneurial Vision

French writer Victor Hugo remarked,

"There is one spectacle grander than the sea, that is the sky;

there is one spectacle grander than the sky: the interior of the soul."

However, the breadth of a person's soul varies greatly from one individual to another. From the top of a mountain:

Some see the dust on the ground,

Some see the green grass,

Some see the flowers on the trees,

Some see colorful clouds in the sky.

What determines all this is a person's vision.

Vision has been given rich connotations in the traditional oriental culture. In the book *From the Soil: The Foundations of Chinese Society*, Fei Xiaotong elaborated on Chinese interpersonal relations, an egocentric differential pattern with differences in affinity. Vision is figuratively described as the distance between "ego" and "other." A big deal may no longer be the same "big deal" when viewed ten years later, across the whole country or the global community!

Since its inception, the word vision has carried rich connotations and a special historical mission. It has deeply influenced every aspect of Chinese people's lives. As a professional manager and investor, I have led and coached more than ten companies to get listed in the capital market. I have served as director, board secretary, vice president, president and chairman of nearly ten listed companies. Over the past 30 years of management, I have bonded with the terms "vision" and "entrepreneur's vision." Looking back on my experience of knowing, understanding and working with "vision," I sometimes feel delighted with a heartfelt smile and thrilled like walking on thin ice.

Here are two cases: one is pleasant, and the other is thrilling.

Case 1: In early 2000, I traveled south from Sichuan to Guangdong to look for a job. I met the owner of a company in Foshan. The company was small, and the owner was straightforward. We had a relatively frank and cordial conversation. Furthermore, I could only get an average image of this company. After the meeting, the company's car sent me to the airport. While chatting with the driver, I asked him what he thought of his boss. The driver answered immediately that his boss was very nice and had a broad vision. I was surprised that a driver would describe his boss with the word "vision." I asked him why he thought his boss had a broad vision. The driver replied that he and his boss used to drive for others, but his boss went from being a driver to trading and opened his factory. His boss knew nothing about technology or production, but he would distribute his shares in the company, so many people joined the company. Six Zen masters have told us that those of low status often have superior true wisdom, while those of high status have times when their wisdom is buried. The driver's simple description enlightened me. So, I started to learn more about the company. Ultimately, I gave up the larger companies offering higher salaries and joined this company in Foshan. It is Dymatic Chemicals, Inc., and the owner is surnamed Huang.

I was mainly responsible for managing the business and facilitating the company's IPO. In the standardization of business management, I inevitably ran into the interests of those with vested interests, but it also increased the cost of operation. In addition, China launched the split share structure reform and the company's IPO was suspended. I had difficulties taking a step forward, and the company's listing was heavily impeded.

At this time, President Huang prevailed over all dissenting views and steadfastly supported the standardization of management and listing. He said everything went as planned, and even if they failed, they could start again. They did not have to worry about anything. Huang's vision, heart and vigor were transformed into a driving force for the company when it struggled to move forward. My colleagues and I were very confident and enthusiastic. After China's split share structure reform, the first listed company was Dymatic Chemicals (002254). My experience at Dymatic Chemicals has made me realize that an entrepreneur's vision directly affects the development of a company. It has been an enjoyable journey. I have been very close to the leadership and staff of Dymatic Chemicals, although I left the company more than ten years ago. The company still pays me a monthly five-figure salary.

Case 2: One day, I was invited to dinner by a government leader, and he requested me during the meal. A company in the district has patented technologies with a large scale and considerable benefits. The leader hoped I could help expand and strengthen this company and launch it to the capital market. I later reviewed the company's profile and found the fundamentals satisfactory. Then, I met with the owner of the company. The owner was humble and repeated that he would do whatever I wanted as long as I joined his company. So, I accepted the leader's invitation.

A few friends of mine live where this company is located. When they heard I was joining this company, they were unanimously against it, and they all said that the boss was too stingy and short-sighted. My heart jolted when I heard the word "vision." Nevertheless, I could not go back on my promise.

I joined the company as the CEO. At first, the owner treated me respectfully and fully supported my work. We worked together to develop the company's strategic goals, improve the organizational structure, and clarify the management process. We also issued a decentralization manual and brought in key and much-needed professionals. The market environment was also favorable, and the company's earnings were growing exponentially, with profits in just seven months exceeding those of the previous year. At the same time, the company's IPO proceeded smoothly. We reported to the regulator, and it started the counseling and acceptance. However, the owner suddenly turned hostile when the company was booming and promising. He destroyed the company's organizational division of labor for no apparent reason, denied the system of related responsibilities and authority, and began to command and manage beyond his authority. The general manager's authority to approve funds was reduced from RMB 500,000 to RMB 3,000. The owner even controlled the recruitment of an ordinary. The company's management became chaotic and disorganized, and purchasing, production and sales were seriously affected. After repeated conversations, I realized that the owner wanted to manage the company personally because of the good performance and the increased market capitalization. He told me that if someone else were in charge of the company, he would feel uneasy even when eating and sleeping.

At that moment, I remembered my friends' comments that the owner was stingy and short-sighted. We could not reach a consensus because of the different levels of cognition. I had no choice but to resign. After I left, the core management and key employees left the company, and the company went downhill quickly.

These two contrasting experiences made me interested in vision and entrepreneurship. I started to review all kinds of materials and literature. The result was disappointing and exciting as there was no systematic research. Thus, during my five years of study, I conducted comprehensive and in-depth research on entrepreneurial vision and enterprise growth through a scientific and rigorous methodology. I initiated in-depth interviews with familiar companies and entrepreneurs. I was surprised to find that the vision and the entrepreneurial vision are like a mysterious gold mine. The vision is rooted in the long and splendid Chinese culture. It has survived the political economy and secular life over a long history. It has colorful connotations and vast extensions. Through studying human vision and entrepreneurial vision, I have found new answers to the laws of the rise and fall of countless private enterprises in the past forty years of reform and opening up. My research is different from the traditional paradigm of organization theory, which is based on the resource and institutional perspectives. It returns to Penrose's appeal in his masterpiece *The Theory of the Growth of the Firm*, as entrepreneurial ability is the helmsman of enterprise growth, and we should not and cannot ignore entrepreneurs' unique ability. Entrepreneurial vision is integral to entrepreneurial ability in the Eastern Confucian cultural genes. It is even more important to Chinese entrepreneurs than Schumpeter's theory of entrepreneurship based on Western studies.

Moreover, it is indispensable for explaining the rapid growth of China's private economy during the transition period. In my research, I am committed to addressing entrepreneurial vision, how it can be scientifically measured, and how it affects enterprise growth. With the systematic interpretation of these questions, I hope to contribute to management practitioners' and policymakers' understanding of the mystery of China's economic growth and enterprises' development.

Acknowledgement

In the autumn of 2017,
with great ambition for business,
I came to Université Paris-Dauphine, PSL,
where I got learnings from my kindhearted teachers,
and from distinguished masters.
Looking back to those old days,
I found the shimmering Ganges on the other bank.
To see the world in a grain of sand,
I'm just a worm,
glimmering with a faint glow...
My great ambition for business
all turned into a thin leaf.
The leaf ignites a small fire.
Make a pot of coffee
for life changers.
A drop of aroma
connects to the boundless world,
and to the future of memory.

First of all, I would like to extend my sincere thanks to Professor Fan Yushun!

My gratitude goes to my teachers, Professor Herve Alexandre, Professor Jean-Pierre Segal, Professor Horacio Ortiz, Professor Nicolas Berland, and Professor Jean-François Chanlat. Thanks also go to Professor Dongcheng Hu, Professor Zhishu Yang, Professor Ke Tang, Professor Wuxiang Zhu, Professor Rongsheng Qin, Professor Qinglong Zhang, Professor Jianxing Chen, and Professor Runtian Jing.

Thank you, my teachers, Zhang Yingjun, Niu Liqun, Yang Yindi, Li Kangning, and others from the faculty team!

Thank you, my senior and junior schoolmates!

Lastly, thank my family and friends for their support and help!

Foreword

Stand Tall Atop Lofty Mountains; Ponder Deeply Across Countries

Fan Yushun, Tsinghua University

One hundred thirty years ago, Alfred Marshall proposed a fourth factor, entrepreneurship, beyond the three factors of land, capital and labor that drive economic growth in classical economics. In his distribution theory, he expanded the earlier concept (labor wages, land rent, capital interest, and entrepreneurship profits). At the same time, he attributed organizational profit to management profit from entrepreneurship. Since then, entrepreneurship studies have long been regarded as the core of research on organization theories. However, in terms of management practice, the history of domestic enterprises in China over the past 150 years has shown that the rise and fall of private enterprises, an important component of China's economy, has always been closely related to the entrepreneurial capabilities of their leaders. Moreover, it is independent of the great changes in the enterprise's scale, technology and industry and the drastic changes in the external political, legal and other formal institutions.

Ph.D. Fan Xiaoping, with his rich practical experience in management and solid theoretical foundation, profoundly analyzes entrepreneurship in the transition economies under the Confucian cultural circle in East Asia from his unique perspective. In his book Decoding Entrepreneurial Vision, he tries to take entrepreneurial vision, a key component of local entrepreneurship in China, as an entry point. He explores the components of entrepreneurial vision and their influence on business growth. Readers can more comprehensively understand the importance of entrepreneurial vision to enterprise growth. Thus, they can gain a deeper insight into the differences in the growth trajectories of different private enterprises in China's economic transition. Also, it allows for a more scientific and precise prediction of the possible evolution of Chinese private enterprises in the transition from family-oriented to professional-oriented. The book's theoretical contributions are mainly reflected in the following three aspects: First, the grounded theory and scale development techniques are used to identify the connotations and dimensions of entrepreneurial vision. The localization of strategic leadership has long been a focus of academic research. Based on theoretical analysis and practical observation, it develops the concept and connotation of entrepreneurial vision in the Chinese context. It systematically develops a scale of entrepreneurial vision, providing an essential and fundamental instrument for studying it in local contexts. In addition, it clarifies the structure and measurement scale of entrepreneurial vision in the Chinese context. It reveals the differences in strategic leadership focus between China and the West. Thus, it can guide the subsequent cross-cultural comparative research on strategic leadership. Second, it reveals the mechanisms by which entrepreneurial vision affects enterprise performance. Two decision logics (causation and effectuation) are introduced, and the dual dynamics of entrepreneurial vision on enterprise performance through different decision logics are confirmed. This study confirms for the first time the impact of entrepreneurial vision, a localized form of strategic leadership in China, on enterprise performance, deepening and expanding the research on strategic leadership. More importantly, it reveals the influence mechanisms of causation and effectuation in this process. This finding provides a deeper source of how entrepreneurial vision affects enterprise performance and further deepens and expands the research on causation and effectuation. Third, it extends the study on the impact of entrepreneurial vision on enterprise performance from the perspective of industrial dynamics. The impact of entrepreneurial vision on enterprise performance depends to some extent on the industry's dynamic environment facing the firm. It introduces industrial complexity and dynamics to portray the importance of industrial dynamics in influencing the relationship between entrepreneurial vision and enterprise performance. This finding somewhat bridges the paradox of strategic leadership research on enterprise performance. It also responds to the debates in strategic leadership research about the usefulness of simple mental models versus more complex mental models in strategic decision-making.

Currently, China's private enterprises are in a critical period of promoting industrial transformation, upgrading, and economic development with high quality, meeting unprecedented and severe challenges. The book addresses the important practical problems in the practice of private enterprises. It emphasizes the unique contextual factors in China while adhering to the general rules of the evolution of enterprise growth patterns worldwide. The conclusions and perspectives can undoubtedly provide useful insights and suggestions for private entrepreneurs to boost their confidence, elevate their visions and practice long-term values. They also help optimize enterprises' external development environment by government agencies. Therefore, this book has great theoretical and practical significance in the present and the medium and long term. We should stand tall atop lofty mountains and ponder deeply across countries.

Abstract

The reform and opening-up, which started in 1978, has transformed China's economy from a rigid and single-plan system to a diversified market system, from rapid development to high-quality development. Entrepreneurs, as the "genes" and "souls" of enterprises, have contributed greatly to the recovery of the Chinese economy and social development. The general public has highly recognized entrepreneurs as the focus of practitioners and theorists for a long time. With the rapid development of science and technology, the business model has changed dramatically, and enterprises' internal and external environments are complicated and changeable. As the helmsman and final decision-maker of an enterprise, entrepreneurs are crucial to sustainable and healthy development because of their attributes, spirit and mindset. The study of entrepreneurial strategic leadership has been the focus of strategic management research since the 1980s. Researchers have paid extensive attention to the critical impact of entrepreneurial strategic leadership on enterprise performance. However, most studies are based on Western management contexts, and no studies have been conducted on entrepreneurial strategic leadership in China's unique institutional and cultural contexts.

In contemporary management practice, "entrepreneurial vision" is often found in people's discourse. Many management practitioners gradually emphasize entrepreneurial vision and consider it a key variable affecting the survival and development of enterprises. It is a potential factor that causes differences in business growth and is an essential condition for the success of entrepreneurial endeavors. We should consider what entrepreneurial vision is, what it entails, how it affects the development of a company, and what factors make up this concept widely used in the industry. Also, we should consider how to evaluate entrepreneurial vision and cultivate it consciously. The topic of strategic leadership, which originated in China's unique cultural context, has received widespread attention from practitioners and reformers. However, rigorous and systematic academic research on this topic is lacking. Hence, this study examines entrepreneurial vision as a unique aspect of strategic leadership and explores its dimensions and measurements. Furthermore, it examines the underlying mechanisms of entrepreneurial vision affecting enterprise performance. It answers three key scientific questions (what entrepreneurial vision is, how it is measured, and how it influences enterprise performance).

Based on the qualitative and quantitative data analysis, this study mainly draws the following conclusions: (1) It identifies the characteristics and dimensions of entrepreneurial vision in the Chinese context. It is widely recognized in traditional Chinese Confucian culture and Chinese management practices that entrepreneurial vision has a crucial impact on organizational management practices. However, there is no clear definition of entrepreneurial vision. Based on the related research on strategic leadership and the rooted analysis of entrepreneurs, this study refines the nine dimensions of entrepreneurial vision (modesty, calmness, promise-keeping, perspective, courage and insight, profound research, aspiration, win-win cooperation, and patriotism). (2) It develops and tests a scale of entrepreneurial vision in China. This study constructs an initial scale of entrepreneurial vision by combining the dimensions extracted from the grounded research with the literature on strategic leadership. The initial scale is used for the questionnaire survey and exploratory factor analysis, and the scale is further optimized into 18 items in six dimensions (aspiration, modesty, win-win cooperation, promise-keeping, calmness and patriotism). A confirmatory factor analysis of the new scale shows that the new scale has good structural validity and reliability, with satisfactory discriminant validity. (3) It explores the mechanism of entrepreneurial vision influencing enterprise performance. Entrepreneurial vision is an important embodiment of entrepreneurial strategic leadership in the Chinese context. Management practitioners have observed the significant impact of entrepreneurial vision on organizational management, but they lack systematic and rigorous evidence to support this speculation. This study finds that entrepreneurial vision boosts enterprise performance through a survey of 298 SMEs. It is mainly based on two different decision logics: causation and effectuation. Through rigorous empirical analysis, this study confirms for the first time the critical impact of entrepreneurial vision on enterprise performance in the Chinese context and its underlying mechanisms. (4) It reveals the significant impact of industrial complexity and industrial dynamics on the relationship between entrepreneurial vision and enterprise performance. The industry environment is a critical condition for entrepreneurs to make decisions. The effectiveness of any given decision-making process or strategic initiative largely depends on its fit with the industry environment. This study reveals that the relationship between entrepreneurial vision and enterprise performance is also influenced by industrial complexity and industrial dynamics. Industrial complexity reinforces the facilitating (inhibiting) effects of causation (effectuation) on enterprise performance. Industrial dynamics weakens the facilitating (inhibiting) effects of causation (effectuation) on enterprise performance. The boundary conditions of the relationship between entrepreneurial vision and enterprise performance are further clarified by analyzing the factors of the industry environment.

Based on the above summary, this study develops the entrepreneurial vision scale for the first time in the Chinese context and conducts systematic tests. It explores the mechanisms and boundaries of entrepreneurial vision affecting enterprise performance. It deepens the interpretation and cognition of entrepreneurial vision in the Chinese context. Moreover, it extends the analytical framework of strategic leadership to provide effective suggestions for improving management practices in the Chinese context.

Chapter 1
Introduction

This chapter first elaborates on the background and significance of the topic and presents the research questions. Second, it defines the research object and main concepts for the research questions, outlines the logical framework, and addresses the significance and innovations. Finally, it gives a detailed description of the technical route, research methodology and content arrangements.

Realistic Background

Since implementing the reform and opening-up policy in China, the economic pattern and enterprise structure in China have been shaped by institutional transformation and market creation. From a constructivist point of view, these two forces are not given but have contributed to the generation and construction of an entrepreneurial economic system in the market-oriented and internationalized process. Studies of transition economies have emphasized the institutional transition from planned to market, but the entrepreneurship unleashed by institutional and market changes has been somewhat underestimated. China's entrepreneurial spirit (government as an entrepreneur) from the central to local governments and the creative power of the market, where administrative control is constantly being relaxed, are the fundamental drivers of China's rapid economic growth. One of the factors that cannot be ignored in market creation is the entrepreneurial community. Since the beginning of reform and opening up in 1978, China has been pushing forward the liberalization of its market and the internationalization of its enterprises. It has been transformed from the simple mode of three-processing and one compensation trade (namely, commission processing, processing with supplied designs and samples, assembly with supplied parts and compensation trade) to strategic alliance cooperation and international entrepreneurship. It can be argued that the entrepreneurial ability demonstrated by Chinese entrepreneurs is an indispensable strategic guideline for the growth of Chinese enterprises. Management practitioners and researchers are aware of the crucial role of entrepreneurial ability. Because of this, the study of strategic leadership has become a core topic in strategic management research. For quite a long time, researchers have been devoted to explaining performance differences among organizations from the perspective of managers' competencies (Crossland & Hambrick, 2007; Krause et al., 2019).

With the advent of the digital economy, entrepreneurial strategic leadership is becoming increasingly important to organizations. The digital economy is rapidly changing all aspects of the economy and society. It is developing faster, radiating more widely and influencing more deeply. Moreover, the digital economy is becoming a key driving force in reorganizing global factor resources, reshaping global economic structure and updating global competition patterns. First, the digital economy is based on the Internet of Everything. The digital economy involves more elements than traditional economic activities, and the correlations between the elements are diversified. Therefore, the digital economy is more complex. Second, the digital economy combines digital elements and modular resources. Compared with the traditional economy, the digital economy is more flexible, resulting in faster replacement. Finally, the digital economy breaks the industry's boundaries, so the competition rises from the competition between peer enterprises to the competition at the ecological level. It also means that the form of competition is enriched, and the definition of competitors is more difficult, greatly enhancing the ambiguity of the digital economy. As a result, the digital economy creates a more uncertain market environment for enterprises with higher complexity, faster replacement and stronger ambiguity.

Strategic leadership refers to the ability to anticipate, visualize, remain flexible, and motivate others to make needed strategic changes. Entrepreneurial strategic leadership is key in helping companies cope with uncertainty and thus sustain their business. First, entrepreneurs with strategic leadership tend to be far-sighted, thus guiding their enterprises on the right track amidst the fog. Second, entrepreneurs with strategic leadership are often more resilient and can maintain vitality in setbacks and conflicts, laying the foundation for sustainable development. Finally, entrepreneurs with strategic leadership better coordinate relationships and resources, thus adapting to potential uncertainty through greater network flexibility.

To summarize, the strategic leadership of entrepreneurs is of crucial value and significance in helping enterprises to overcome uncertainty. It also plays an increasingly important role in business management under the development trend of the digital economy. As the helmsman and final decision-maker of an enterprise, entrepreneurs are crucial to sustainable and healthy development because of their attributes, spirit and mindset. In contemporary management practice, "entrepreneurial vision" is often found in people's discourse. Many management practitioners gradually emphasize entrepreneurial vision and consider it a key variable affecting the survival and development of enterprises. It is a potential factor that causes differences in business growth and is an essential condition for the success of entrepreneurial endeavors. We should consider what entrepreneurial vision is, what it entails, how it affects the development of a company, and what factors make up this concept widely used in the industry. Also, we should consider how to evaluate entrepreneurial vision and cultivate it consciously. All these questions urgently require systematic and intensive research.

Its long history makes Chinese culture one of the world's most influential and longest-standing cultural genres. Over the past 40 years of reform and opening up, China has grown rapidly to become the world's second-largest economy in a relatively short time, backed by a huge local market, a strong government drive, and a diverse and specialized industrial base. China ranks first in the world regarding the number of Fortune 500 companies, rising from 10 in the early 2000s to 143 in 2021. China's rapid economic and social development, especially in the context of the growing influence of the digital economy globally, has attracted the attention of Chinese and Western scholars. Regarding the rapid development of Chinese enterprises, Chinese entrepreneurs, based on China's real-life situation and cultural background, integrate Western management experience, make bold explorations and innovations, and ultimately explore a path of innovation with Chinese features from catching up with the West to surpassing the West (Sheng et al., 2021). Digging deeper into the characteristics of entrepreneurial strategic leadership in China's unique institutional and cultural settings is conducive to providing enterprises with effective theoretical tools to cope with uncertainty. It is also an important attempt to gradually build a management theory paradigm and discourse system with Chinese features.

Theoretical Background

Enterprise growth is the root cause of economic growth, but early neo-classical economics ignored the crucial role of entrepreneur ability in entrepreneurial growth. The optimal production scale theory of neoclassical economics and the transaction cost theory of new institutional economics suggest that the power sources of enterprise growth can be categorized into endogenous and exogenous power sources. Exogenous power emphasizes that the source of power that determines the growth of an enterprise is mainly the external factors (institutional environment, market structure, social environment). Enterprises cannot control or influence these factors and can only passively adapt to them for growth. On the other hand, endogenous power emphasizes that the source of power that determines the growth of an enterprise is mainly its internal heterogeneous resources. Only enterprises that fully utilize and develop heterogeneous resources can achieve sustainable growth. Exogenous power always treats the enterprise as a "black box." However, endogenous power unlocks this "black box" and makes the research of enterprise growth theory operational. The evolution of the perspective reflects that researchers' understanding of the firm has changed from static to dynamic and from passive to active.

In the studies on the micro-foundations of the theory of the firm's growth, especially Penrose's, *The Theory of the Growth of the Firm* is regarded as the key to systematically revealing the firm's growth. For Penrose, growth means a developmental process that results in quantitative growth or qualitative improvement. Similar to natural biological processes, a series of internal changes interact and cause an organism to increase in size and change in features. Hence, her theory of the firm's growth seeks to answer the question of "whether there is some internal factor that both facilitates and necessarily limits the rate of growth of a firm." Unlike transaction cost theory, which defines a firm as a collection of contracts, Penrose defines a firm as a collection of resources bound to a regulatory framework. According to this definition, the firm will continue to grow until it reaches a corporate boundary where managerial coordination and authoritative communication are no longer viable.

Contrary to general economic theory, Penrose argues that firms keep expanding to increase their profits in the long run rather than maximizing short-term profits. Firms expand to take advantage of opportunities that they believe are profitable. Regardless of the marginal return on investment, entrepreneur ability is a key determinant of firm growth.

As the focus of research has returned to entrepreneurs, their strategic leadership has been the "jewel" of the spotlight. Many research results have been accumulated on strategic leadership (Neely et al., 2020; Hambrick, 2007). However, as the digital economy develops rapidly, industrial environments, business models, and the patterns of market competition have undergone rapid and drastic changes (Jafari-Sadeghi et al., 2021; Wang et al., 2021). The uncertainties associated with these new industrial, business, and competitive models have posed new challenges to traditional entrepreneurial leadership research (Zhang et al., 2020). In response to these new challenges, breaking the organizational boundaries of existing entrepreneurial leadership research and actively engaging in dialogue with the literature on strategic management is imperative. Thus, a theoretical bridge can be built between leadership and responses to corporate uncertainty (Benitez et al., 2022; Bennis, 2013).

Management is a discipline that originates from practice, and the most up-to-date and contemporary management theories are necessarily derived from the regions and cultures with the fastest developments in management practices. As Chinese enterprises become more and more internationally oriented and digitized, scholars and practitioners worldwide have been paying attention to the adaptability and leadership of Chinese enterprises in the new economic environment (Gao et al., 2022; Li et al., 2020). In this context, entrepreneurial strategic leadership with Chinese features, as an integral part of the management system with Chinese features, is a valuable field to explore (Chen et al., 2011; Pan et al., 2021). However, related research lacks a theoretical foundation with Chinese features, thus limiting its theoretical significance.

Existing leadership research has been widely explored around the connotation of strategic leadership and its different types presented in different contexts. Furthermore, numerous types of leadership with different functions have been condensed, such as strategic leadership, responsible leadership, platform leadership, and supply chain leadership (Simsek et al., 2015; Vera & Crossan, 2004; Li & Tang, 2022; Wang et al., 2022; Zhang et al., 2020). However, the current research on strategic leadership focuses more on how leadership balances different logical conflicts within an executive team or an organization(Zhang, 2021). Fewer studies have addressed the underlying mechanisms of how Chinese entrepreneurs' unique strategic leadership affects enterprise performance.

Research Questions

In the face of the impacts and opportunities of the digital economy, Chinese firms have fully grasped various opportunities and effectively resisted the impacts of external uncertainties, even though they have no internationally leading technology and market capabilities. Also, they have demonstrated stronger economic resilience. Based on this, the core research question of this paper is how entrepreneurial strategic leadership affects firm growth in China's unique cultural and institutional settings. In this paper, the core question is broken down into three sub-questions. We construct a theoretical model of how entrepreneurial vision with Chinese features affects enterprise performance by answering each sub-question separately.

First, what are the concepts, characteristics and dimensions of entrepreneurial vision in China? As mentioned earlier, Chinese entrepreneurs have demonstrated much greater vigor and efficiency than their counterparts in other countries when facing the challenges and opportunities from emerging technologies and economic forms such as digital technology and digital economy (Oliveira et al., 2014; Shinkle & Kriauciunas, 2012). Exploring the concepts, characteristics and dimensions of the entrepreneurial vision with Chinese features and constructing a model of the entrepreneurial vision with Chinese features is of great theoretical and practical value for fostering more productive entrepreneurs and telling the Chinese story (Du & Sun, 2022; He et al., 2021; Zhou et al., 2021). Therefore, the first sub-study will focus on the concepts, characteristics and dimensions of the entrepreneurial vision with Chinese features. Based on numerous biographies and interviews of Chinese entrepreneurs, we attempted to condense the conceptual model of entrepreneurial vision in China by utilizing grounded theory.

Second, how can the entrepreneurial vision with Chinese features be scientifically measured? Existing research lacks a theoretical overview of the entrepreneurial vision with Chinese features. It can hardly measure the entrepreneurial vision in China and further examine its relevance to various aspects of firm performance (Li et al., 2020; Pan et al., 2021). Therefore, the second sub-study will focus on "how to measure the entrepreneurial vision with Chinese features." Based on the classical scaling method, the scale of the entrepreneurial vision with Chinese features is developed according to the grounded theory analysis to justify the measurement of the related concepts.

Third, how does entrepreneurial vision affect enterprise performance in China? Current leadership research has mainly investigated the mechanisms by which strategic leadership affects the internal micro-levels of organizations, such as organizational cohesion, loyalty, and multi-variate logical synergies (Neely et al., 2020; Li & Tang, 2022; Wang et al., 2022). Insufficient attention has been paid to how strategic leadership can help firms break the constraints of environmental uncertainty to achieve sustainable performance. Hence, the existing strategic leadership theories cannot explain how entrepreneurial leadership in the Chinese context helps Chinese firms achieve favorable performance under uncertainties (Zhang, 2021). Therefore, the third sub-study will analyze how entrepreneurial vision affects enterprise performance in the Chinese context. Combined with empirical analysis, it will refine the process and mechanism by which entrepreneurial vision affects enterprise performance in China.

Research Objects and Main Concepts

Research Objects

The research object is entrepreneurs influenced by Chinese culture and the enterprises under their leadership. Unlike entrepreneurs who grew up in Western individualistic cultures, Chinese culture emphasizes the qualities of "harmony" and "relationship building" (Lu & Sun, 2013). Culture is an essential factor in creating the leadership traits of a particular group of entrepreneurs (Tierney, 2004; Li, 2021). Because of this, the leadership traits of Chinese entrepreneurs differ significantly from those in mainstream Western research. Such differentiated leadership reveals unique strengths in increasingly uncertain management activities. To further highlight the leadership traits of Chinese entrepreneurs, this paper focuses on large and complex business organizations, digital start-ups or large multinationals. These companies are selected for the following reasons:

First, large and complex business organizations, digital start-ups, and large multinationals face extreme uncertainty due to complicated business, ambiguity of emerging businesses, and volatility from different institutions. The leadership traits of entrepreneurs who have sustained their businesses despite extreme uncertainty are more valuable to explore in-depth than those of other entrepreneurs. Second, large and complex business organizations, digital start-ups and large multinationals feature typical experiences. Studying their experiences is instructive for the companies. In addition, the findings can provide lessons for other types of enterprises. Third, the sample of enterprises comes from various industries, including hardware technology, digital information, education and training, and relatively traditional chemical industries. The diversity of sample sources can guarantee the reliability and validity of the conclusions.

Main Concepts

Entrepreneurial vision: Entrepreneurial vision involves collecting personal traits and personality elements such as entrepreneurial insight, mindfulness, and ideological height that influence the entrepreneur's innovation, coordination, and performance improvements. Entrepreneurial vision is the specific presentation of entrepreneurial leadership in China.

Decision logic: Decision logic refers to the specific practice and symbolic structure that constitutes an actor's information processing mode and thinking habit in the decision-making process. This paper mainly examines two types of decision logic: causation and effectuation. Causation means that the decision-maker first determines the target market, formulates a plan, determines the strategy for maximizing profitability, and then continuously adjusts the means for implementation. Effectuation indicates that from analyzing the existing means, the decision-maker determines what to do on this basis, actively interacts with acquaintances, and thus secures the commitment of stakeholders, generates new means or purposes, and expands their resources continuously.

Industrial complexity: Complexity refers to the uncertainty of causality and development trends arising from different connections between elements within a thing. Industrial complexity specifically refers to the many possibilities and trends attributed to the richness of elements within the industry.

Industrial dynamics: Industrial dynamics refers to the differences in the form, content and status of the consistency of the enterprise's macroeconomic environment, industrial environment, internal environment, social environment and other environments over time.

Enterprise performance refers to operating efficiency and operator performance in a specific period. The level of enterprise business efficiency is mainly manifested in profitability, asset operation level, solvency and subsequent development ability.

Innovations

This paper centers on the central question of how the entrepreneurial vision with Chinese features affects enterprise performance. Through case studies and large-sample empirical tests, it attempts to provide a panorama of entrepreneurial leadership with Chinese features to lead Chinese enterprises to achieve good performance in uncertainty. Based on this foundation, the innovations are mainly reflected in the following three areas:

First, the grounded theory and scale development techniques are utilized to identify the connotations and dimensions of entrepreneurial vision. The localization of strategic leadership has long been a focus of academic attention. The localization of strategic leadership can greatly expand the explanatory power of strategic leadership for management practice. More critically, it is essential to contribute to management knowledge in China. In China's long history, many political, social, and economic management experiences and various management and leadership models have been accumulated. With the rapid rise of China's economy, conducting an in-depth and systematic study of China's unique strategic leadership from a local perspective is significant. Compared with "paternalistic leadership," which is a highly localized leadership style, there is little research on the characteristics of local strategic leadership (Cao & Li, 2010). Based on theoretical analysis and practical observation, this study develops the concept and connotation of entrepreneurial vision in the Chinese context.

Moreover, a scale of entrepreneurial vision is systematically developed, providing an important basic tool for local research on entrepreneurial vision. Current researchers on entrepreneurial vision remain in theoretical discourse and conceptual presentation. They do not extract theoretical concepts for practical applications or conduct empirical testing of conceptual frameworks. Based on China's unique cultural and institutional background and the reality of corporate practice, this study establishes and validates a measurement scale for entrepreneurial vision. It provides a measurement tool for subsequent quantitative research on entrepreneurial vision. Further, it lays the foundation for a comparative study of strategic leadership in cross-cultural contexts, clarifying the structure and measurement scale of entrepreneurial vision in local Chinese culture. Moreover, it reveals the differences in the focus of strategic leadership between China and the West, guiding the subsequent cross-cultural comparative study of strategic leadership.

Second, the dual mechanisms of entrepreneurial vision affecting enterprise performance are revealed. It is unclear how vision, as an important component of entrepreneurial strategic leadership, affects enterprise performance. The Upper Echelons Theory suggests that entrepreneurs' attributes affect enterprise performance through information-seeking and decision-making, but there is no further evidence from existing research (Crossland & Hambrick, 2007). In this study, two different types of decision logic (causation and effectuation) are introduced, and the dual effect of entrepreneurial vision on enterprise performance is confirmed through different decision logic. This study confirms for the first time the impact of entrepreneurial vision, a localized form of strategic leadership in China, on enterprise performance. It deepens and extends related research on strategic leadership. More importantly, it reveals this process's dual influence mechanism of causation and effectuation. The conclusion offers a deeper understanding of how entrepreneurial vision affects enterprise performance. Although causation and effectuation are the most popular new theories in decision-making research in recent years, there is no in-depth comparative research on how they affect performance. It has been widely recognized that causation and effectuation positively affect enterprise performance (Brettel et al., 2012; Smolka et al., 2018). However, this study reveals differences in the effects of two types of decision logic on enterprise performance through comparison. It confirms the theoretical differences between the two types of decision logic. More importantly, it further deepens and expands the research on causation and effectuation.

Third, it extends the research on the impact of entrepreneurial vision on enterprise performance from the perspective of industrial dynamics. There has been consensus on how strategic leadership affects the performance of an enterprise for a long time. Because of this, strategic leadership research has been criticized (Wangrow et al., 2015). These seemingly contradictory views of strategic leadership provide a new way of thinking about how entrepreneurial vision affects entrepreneurial performance that the external environment may impact. We introduce a perspective on industrial dynamics and confirm the conjecture that the impact of entrepreneurial vision on enterprise performance depends to some extent on the industrial dynamics environment faced by the company. The industrial dynamic environment is a critical condition for companies to make decisions. The effectiveness of any given decision-making process or strategic initiative depends largely on its fit with the industry environment (Dean & Sharfman, 1996; Judge & Miller, 1991). Industrial complexity and dynamics are introduced to portray the significant impact of the dynamic industrial environment on the relationship between entrepreneurial vision and enterprise performance. This conclusion partly bridges the paradox of strategic leadership research on enterprise performance. That is, the effectiveness of any strategic leadership is not stable but is affected by the dynamics of the external industry environment. At the same time, the introduction of industrial dynamics further enriches the scenarios of entrepreneurial vision-related research. It also responds to the current debate in strategic leadership research about the usefulness of simple mental models versus more complex mental models in strategic decision-making (Wooldridge & Cowden, 2020).

Roadmap

This paper is centered on the basic question of how entrepreneurial leadership with Chinese features affects enterprise performance. Starting from the relevant theoretical foundations and empirical investigations, it will specifically explore the characteristics of entrepreneurial leadership with Chinese features, the relevant measurement methods, and the internal logic of its impact on enterprise performance. The roadmap is shown in Figure 1-1.

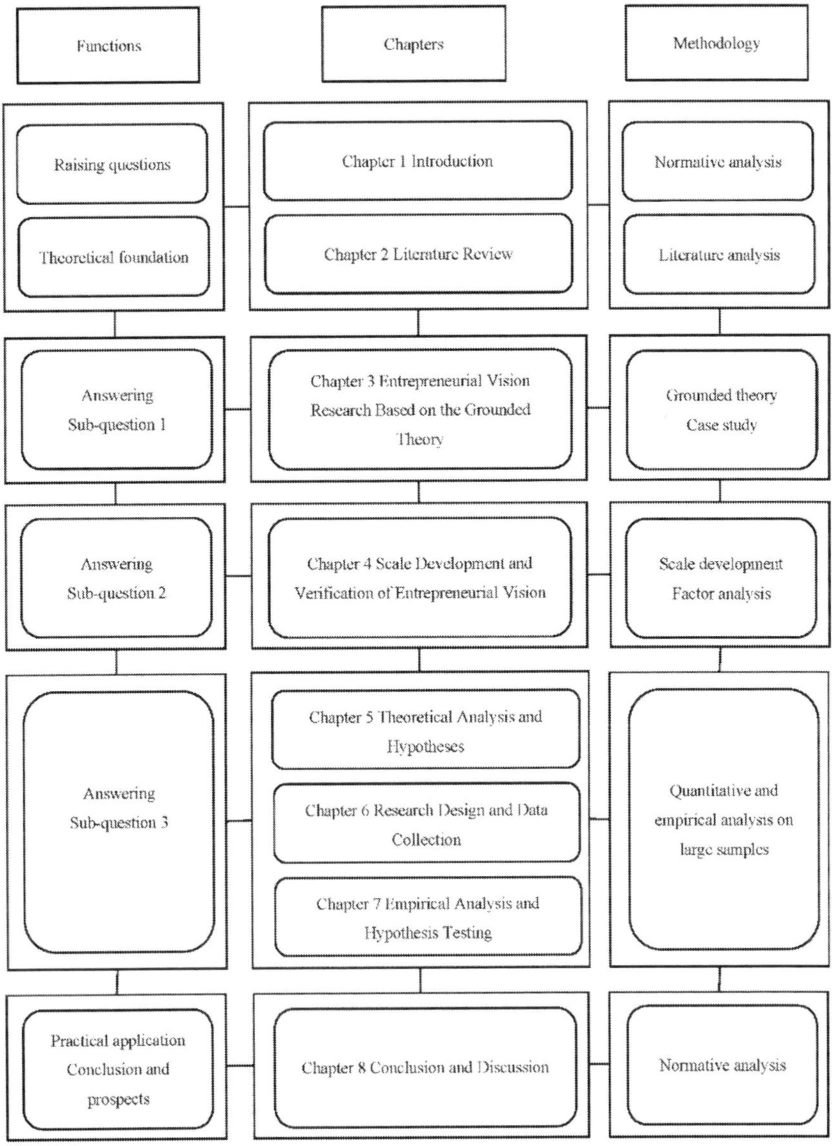

Figure 1-1 Roadmap

Source: Organized by the author

Chapter 1 is the introduction. Starting from the practical background, it will raise the research questions on the theoretical progress and gaps, briefly design the logical framework and research content to address the research questions and elaborate on the possible innovations.

Chapter 2 is a literature review. It will comprehensively sort out the origin, development and research hotspots of entrepreneurial leadership, entrepreneurial decision logic and enterprise performance, which are closely related to the research topic. Then, it will summarize the progress and shortcomings of the above studies through systematic reviews, laying a solid theoretical foundation for the subsequent research.

Chapter 3 analyzes Sub-question 1, "What are the concepts, characteristics and dimensions of the entrepreneurial vision with Chinese features." The case study based on the grounded theory digs deeper into the entrepreneurial vision's concept, features and dimensions.

Chapter 4 analyzes Sub-question 2, "How to measure the entrepreneurial vision with Chinese features." The classic scale development method is adopted. The scale is first developed based on the dimensions sorted out in Study 1. Then, exploratory and confirmatory factor analyses are conducted to test the goodness of fit of the scale to complete the scale design.

Chapters 5 to 7 analyze Sub-question 3 on "How entrepreneurial vision affects enterprise performance in the Chinese context" using quantitative empirical analysis. Chapter 5 is mainly designed for theoretical analysis and hypothesis formulation, Chapter 6 presents the research design and data collection process, and Chapter 7 presents the empirical analysis and hypothesis testing.

Chapter 8 is the conclusion and discussion. It summarizes the main conclusions of all the sub-studies and presents a relatively comprehensive answer to "How the entrepreneurial vision with Chinese features affects enterprise performance." On this basis, it discusses the theoretical contributions and practical significance, summarizes the limitations and proposes areas for future research.

Chapter 2
Literature Review

Entrepreneurial Leadership

Strategic leadership is at the core of organizational strategy research, and researchers have long been concerned about improving entrepreneurial leadership and effectively identifying efficient leadership models. As early as the beginning of the 20th century, Frederick Winslow Taylor, the father of scientific management, tried to summarize the behavioral patterns of effective leaders in his masterpiece *The Principles of Scientific Management*. Subsequently, Chester I. Barnard, the founder of the social system school, further suggested that "leadership is a function between the leader, the followers, and the external environment." These early insightful explorations provided profound inspiration for advancing the scientific study of strategic leadership. They also influenced the systematic study of leadership through psychology and sociology in the mid-to-late 20th century. There are four main perspectives in the study of leadership effectiveness: the trait theory of leadership, the behavioral theory of leadership, the situational theory of leadership and the power and process theory of leadership. From different angles, these four systematic perspectives analyze leadership effectiveness's structural, process and situational factors. Despite the differences and even conflicts between the angles of view, the debate and analysis between the angles of view have greatly enriched and promoted leadership research. These four systematic perspectives on leadership have laid the foundation for leadership research.

Trait Theory of Leadership

The trait theory of leadership began due to a long-standing debate in management research about whether great leaders are developed or born. In the 1920s and 1930s, psychologists studied the phenomenon of leadership using the trait theory of leadership. The trait theory of leadership suggests that (1) Leadership depends on the leader's personal qualities (Judge et al., 2002), which are either innate or inherited (Zaccaro, 2007). (2) For organizations, the key is selecting the right leaders through the trait theory rather than developing non-leaders into leaders (Jenkins, 1947). Early leadership researchers attempted to capture the common traits in leaders with exceptional leadership. It went through two stages.

In the first stage, researchers examined the explicit traits of leaders. Studies in this category are mainly represented by cognitive psychologists such as Bray et al. (1974). They believe that an individual's hereditary factors, physical characteristics, vigor, endocrine factors, gender differences, and neurological factors are all key determinants of their leadership. The trait of gender has been consistently validated, and the traits of dominance, masculinity, and femininity can significantly predict leadership (Lord et al., 1986). In strategic decision-making, male CEOs are willing to take higher risks than female CEOs (Faccio et al., 2016). Judge et al. (2002) qualitatively reviewed and meta-analyzed traits in leadership research. The results indicate that the Big Five Traits are a valid basis for examining personality predictors of leadership. Conscientiousness (0.29) and extraversion (0.27) are the most consistent with leadership.

The second stage is the focus on the implicit traits of leaders. The strategic decision-making school in management research, especially Herbert Alexander Simon's view that "management is decision-making," has had a widespread impact. Researchers represented by Robbins (1998) et al. have conducted in-depth studies on the implicit traits of effective leaders. They have identified cognitive ability (cognitive flexibility and cognitive complexity), decision-making ability, personality traits, self-regulation and values as key determinants of individual leadership. Moreover, they believe implicit traits are more critical in determining an individual's leadership than explicit traits because they directly reflect a leader's thinking and decision-making patterns and influence their behavioral patterns. Intelligence, adaptability, and extraversion positively affect leadership (Mann, 1959).

The third stage is the focus on mixed traits of leaders. Zaccaro et al. (2018) define leader traits as integrating relatively stable and coherent personal traits. These traits can elicit consistent patterns of leadership performance across various group and organizational contexts. Zaccaro(2007) clarifies the following three points: (1) Leader traits should not be considered in isolation but rather as attributes that influence leader performance. (2) Traits are an encompassing set of personal qualities that contribute to the stability of leadership effectiveness. They include explicit traits such as personality and gender and implicit traits such as cognitive abilities and values. (3) Leadership traits are enduring and stable, producing cross-situational stability in leadership effectiveness.

The trait theory of leadership has greatly advanced the perception of leadership effectiveness research. However, Carter et al. (1951) investigated the continuity of leadership in different task situations through laboratory experiments. They find that the ability to be a leader depends on the nature of the task, not the leader's traits. With similar studies, the development of the trait theory of leadership has been highly challenged. First, leadership is a process of social influence rather than a fixed state of being (Hollander & Julian, 1969). The trait theory of leadership cannot demonstrate that certain universal traits predict leadership effectiveness in all contexts. Second, the trait theory cannot explain the causal relationship between leadership traits and effectiveness. Are leaders born with leader traits, or are their latent traits stimulated after they become leaders? Overall, the trait theory of leadership fails to identify a consistent set of traits that predict the emergence and effectiveness of leadership. It has served as a stimulus for subsequent research on leadership behavior. As a result of recent improvements in personality measurement and assessment instruments, researchers have re-emphasized the trait theory.

Behavioral Mode of Leadership

In the late 1940s, leadership researchers became concerned with the behavioral mode of leadership, arguing that effective leadership behaviors can be acquired through acquired training and focusing on what effective leadership behaviors are. The behavioral theory of leadership was first studied at The Ohio State University in the late 1940s. Stogdill's (1948) exploration of leadership behavior initiated the behavioral theory of leadership. He believes that leaders engage in two behaviors: initiating structure and consideration. Initiating structure is to make subordinates aware of what they should do, to clarify performance standards, to plan tasks, and to supervise subordinates' compliance with rules and regulations. Consideration is to be amiable to subordinates, to treat them fairly, to value the well-being of employees, and to make leaders themselves approachable. It seems too simplistic that effective leaders act only with high levels of consideration and initiating structure (Kerr et al., 1974). The University of Michigan further developed leadership behavior's people-oriented and task-oriented dimensions. People-oriented leadership behavior is committed to improving team cohesion and ensuring that employees are satisfied with their work. Task-oriented leadership behavior involves employees' work, explaining work processes and working to improve work performance. The earliest research from Ohio State University has been questioned, and the theory has been criticized for failing to consider situational variables. The dimensions of consideration and initiating structure coexist in practice and are influenced by other contextual factors such as subordinate consideration, supervisor consideration, and task consideration (Kerr et al., 1974). Therefore, contextual factors should be considered to interpret leadership effectiveness. The two-dimensional theory developed at the University of Michigan also suggests that people-oriented and task-oriented leadership behaviors are at opposite ends of a horizontal line and cannot coexist. There are limitations to this viewpoint. The Ohio State University and the University of Michigan initiated researchers' exploration of the behavioral theory of leadership. The typical leadership styles include transformational leadership, authentic leadership, ethical leadership, and paternalistic leadership.

Transformational leadership. Historian Burns (1978) first proposes and compares transformational and transactional leadership to describe the behavior of political leadership. Bass(1985) introduces transformational leadership and transactional leadership into management. He argues that transformational leadership consists of four dimensions: idealized influence, inspirational motivation, intellectual stimulation, and individual consideration, emphasizing the direct influence of individuals on followers. However, early research has neglected the analytic hierarchy of transformational leadership and has not reached consistent conclusions about whether it is an individual- or team-level phenomenon.

Moreover, the multi-factor questionnaire for measuring transformational leadership (Antonakis et al., 2003) is not optimal for measuring group-level transformational leadership behaviors. Subsequently, scholars propose a two-tiered model of transformational leadership, arguing that the two dimensions of transformational leadership (intellectual stimulation and individual consideration) are tailored to the needs and capabilities of individual followers. It expects a connection between the leader and the follower that is more likely to manifest at the individual level. The other two dimensions (idealized influence and inspirational motivation) emphasize the group's identity, linking the followers' self-concept to the group's shared values. They are more likely to be expressed at the group level (Kark & Shamir, 2002; Wu et al., 2010).

Further, Wang and Howell(2010) develop team-focused and individual-focused transformational leadership styles. Furthermore, they have developed a two-tier transformational leadership scale. Team-focused transformational leadership has three dimensions: emphasizing group identity, communicating group vision, and team building. Individual-focused transformational leadership has four dimensions: communicating high expectations, leader following, intellectual stimulation, and individual recognition.

Transformational leadership is the paradigm in the behavioral mode of leadership that has dominated leadership research in recent years. In their review, Meuser et al. (2016) found that transformational leadership is frequently cited in strategic leadership research through a social network analysis. The center of the transformational leadership network is connected to the trait theory and the cognitive clusters of leaders and followers of team leadership. It suggests that transformational leadership belongs to the behavioral mode of leadership. However, researchers are still concerned with the key question of the trait theory (what traits make a person a great leader). The research gaps in transformational leadership are that: (1) The "dark side" of transformational leadership, or "pseudo-transformational leadership," has not been well integrated into existing research. (2) There are still no studies on cross-cultural aspects of transformational leadership, emergence and development of transformational leadership. (3) Some dimensions of transformational leadership may apply to individual and team levels. Thus, it is necessary to identify which dimensions of leadership can exist across levels and which are specific to a single level.

Authentic leadership. Authentic leadership has received great attention over the past decade (Banks et al., 2016), possibly stemming from a crisis of public trust in government and leaders. In the early days, there was no clear distinction between authentic leadership, psychological capital and transformational leadership (Gardner et al., 2011). Later, authentic leadership was defined as a process that involves authentic leaders and followers. Followers follow the leader for authentic reasons, thus forming an authentic relationship (Shamir & Eilam, 2005). According to Wong et al. (2011), authentic leaders can only enhance followers' identification with their work if followers first identify with the leader. As validated by validity tests, authentic leadership is widely accepted as having self-awareness, showing openness and clarity about who they are, and always disclosing and acting in line with their values, beliefs, motivations, and emotions. Authentic leadership has four dimensions: self-awareness, relational transparency, balanced processing, and internalized moral perspective (Walumbwa et al., 2008). Of these four dimensions, Kernis and Goldman(2006) consider self-awareness as the core of authentic leadership. Subsequently, Walumbwa et al. (2008) developed a questionnaire on authentic leadership.

Less research has been conducted on the antecedent variables of authentic leadership. Jensen & Luthans (2006a) suggest that optimistic, resilient, and hopeful PCA (Psychological Capital Appreciation) positively correlates with authentic leadership. Among the studies on the consequences of authentic leadership, both the mediating and dependent variables have been emphasized in more empirical studies. Most of the studies on the dependent variables reveal positive effects, such as the effects of authentic leadership on leader trust (Gardner et al., 2009), follower job satisfaction and organizational commitment (Avolio et al., 2004), and job performance (Chan et al., 2005). Regarding research on its mediating variables, Walumbwa et al. (2011) confirm that individual identification with supervisors fully mediates the relationship between authentic leadership and job involvement.

Gaps in authentic leadership research: (1) For authentic leadership, efforts should be made to expand its network of laws and consider specific situational and individual differences, i.e., to test the gap between theoretical and empirical research frameworks (Gardner et al., 2011). Jensen and Luthans(2006b) explicitly examine the antecedent PCA of authentic leadership, providing the basis for developing the situational leadership theory. (2) The importance of leaders in authentic leadership has been empirically tested. Authentic followers were also emphasized at the outset, but no study has clarified the role played by authentic followers (Gardner et al., 2011). (3) Existing research methods overemphasize survey measures, cross-sectional designs, and single data sources. Future researchers should employ more extensive methods, such as experimental designs and qualitative methods (Gardner et al., 2011). (4) Authentic leadership conceptually overlaps with other leadership styles. Banks et al. (2016) compare authentic and transformational leadership through a meta-analysis. They discover structural redundancies and overlaps between authentic leadership and transformational leadership. The outcomes more closely related to transformational leadership (task performance, leader effectiveness, follower job satisfaction, and follower satisfaction with leader) reflect individual-level concerns. The outcomes more closely related to authentic leadership (organizational performance and team and organizational performance) reflect group-level concerns.

Ethical leadership. Leaders should be their subordinates' primary source of ethical guidance (Brown et al., 2005). Brown et al. (2005) identify the difference between ethical and transformational leadership regarding honesty, consideration for followers and fair treatment. They argue that ethical leadership is unique. Moreover, social learning theory defines ethical leadership as "demonstrating normatively appropriate behaviors through personal behavior and interpersonal relationships and promoting such behaviors to followers through two-way communication, reinforcement, and decision-making." At the same time, they build the measurement scale of ethical leadership. In a follow-up study, Bouckenooghe et al. (2015) concluded that ethical leadership contains two dimensions. The first dimension is the moral person, consistent with the moral dimensions of transformational and authentic leadership, characterized by honesty, integrity, and trustworthiness. The second dimension is the moral manager, who actively seeks to influence the behavior of the ethical leader.

Ethical leadership is stable (Walumbwa & Schaubroeck, 2009). Ethical leadership reduces unethical behaviors and harmful behaviors of followers (Mayer et al., 2009). Previous research has argued that the positive impact of ethical leadership on employee performance is influenced by the quality of the relationship between leaders and followers (Walumbwa et al., 2011). Relationship quality ignores motivational resources at the individual level: psychological capital. Bouckenooghe et al. (2015) argue that ethical leaders as role models influence the behavior of their followers using the logic of social learning. They examine the effects of ethical leadership on subordinates' performance and its mechanisms of action.

Moreover, they demonstrate that ethical leadership positively affects subordinates' in-role performance by mediating psychological capital and aligning subordinate-leader goals. Walumbwa and Schaubroeck (2009) provide an in-depth discussion of the antecedents of ethical leadership. They suggest that individuals with high agreeableness are more likely to help and be considerate of others using constructive strategies, a component of ethical leadership. Individuals with high conscientiousness are more likely to communicate principles and standards of ethical behavior to their subordinates. That is, agreeableness and conscientiousness can significantly predict ethical leadership behaviors. At the same time, although ethical leadership behavior is stable, it is also stated in the article that the external work environment may affect ethical leadership, which requires future explorations.

Paternalistic leadership. The above-mentioned transformational leadership and ethical leadership are leadership styles that originated in the West. In contrast, paternalistic leadership is based on the local Chinese context and was explicitly proposed by Fan & Zheng (2000) based on relevant studies by Silin (1976), Redding (1990), Zheng (1995), and Westwood (1997). Fan and Zheng (2000) indicate that paternalistic leadership is a style that reveals strict discipline and authority, fatherly benevolence and moral integrity in a humanistic atmosphere. It consists of three dimensions: authoritarianism, benevolence and morality. Regarding cultural roots, paternalistic leadership is a distinctive leadership style formed under the Chinese bloodline-based patriarchal system (Liu & Liu, 2017). Paternalistic leadership originated in Chinese family firms. However, recent empirical research samples have shown that in addition to Chinese organizations in China and Taiwan, paternalistic leadership is also prevalent in other countries or regions such as South Korea (Chai et al., 2020), Turkey (Erben & Güneşer, 2008), Arabia (Siddique et al., 2020), the United States (Pellegrini et al., 2010), and Pakistan (Soomro et al., 2020). Thus, paternalistic leadership's cross-cultural attributes and widespread presence are emphasized (Cheng et al., 2014).

The consequences of paternalistic leadership are mainly based on the individual, team and organizational levels, focusing on the effects of employee performance, employee innovation, team performance and team behavior. However, the three dimensions of paternalistic leadership do not have the same effect in different contexts. As an example of the effect of authoritarian leadership or paternalistic leadership on individual-level performance, three contradictory results emerge from empirical studies on the effect of authoritarian leadership on employee job performance: negative effect (Chan et al., 2013; Schaubroeck et al., 2017), no significant correlation (Yu et al., 2017), positive effect (Zhang & Ling, 2016). The same results are found for the effects of paternalistic leadership on team-level performance (Chiang et al., 2021; Zhang et al., 2009). This paper suggests that contextual factors, such as power distance and organizational norms in different organizations, may contribute to the different results. Regarding the interaction of the three dimensions, Wang et al. (2018) argue that benevolence and authoritarianism are the most effective leadership styles and are positively related to subordinate performance. It echoes how leaders affect subordinate performance by combining benevolence with authoritarianism.

Generally speaking, the research on paternalistic leadership still has the following problems: (1) Compared with the research on the individual and team levels, paternalistic leadership has not been studied intensively at the organizational level and cross-level comparisons. (2) Most studies address paternalistic leadership's consequences, but its formation's antecedent mechanisms are insufficiently explored (Wang et al., 2020). Therefore, there is still much room for exploring and improving the formation process of paternalistic leadership. (3) Most studies examine the impact of each dimension of paternalistic leadership and its mechanism of action. Although it can enrich the research results of paternalistic leadership, it might be detrimental to developing paternalistic leadership research in the long run.

The behavioral theory also has limitations, as no behavior can consistently predict the effects of leadership. Leaders play different roles at different stages of team development. They must clarify the rules in the early stages of team development and motivate employees later.

Situational Mode of Leadership

The trait theory of leadership suggests that leadership is effective because leaders have certain traits, and the behavioral theory of leadership suggests that effective leadership behavior can be acquired through training. However, many great leaders have not received any leadership training in practice. Theoretical studies have also found that leadership is not necessarily improved after training. Nevertheless, does this mean that leadership training is ineffective? Since the late 1950s, leadership research has shifted more toward leadership situations, and the situational mode of leadership has emerged. The situational mode of leadership suggests that (1) A leader's qualities, characteristics, and skills depend highly on the demands of the situation in which the leader works (Stogdill, 1948). Leadership in one context may not be effective in another (Fleishman, 1953). (2) Leader traits are elicited, valued, and responded to varying degrees depending on the group and their needs (Hollander & Julian, 1969). They are generated through the interaction between the leader and the followers. Also, the choice of any leadership mode is attributed to the team's task, composition, and culture (Mann, 1959).

The situational mode of leadership highlights the study of leaders in different environments, particularly with different organizational tasks and structures (Hollander & Julian, 1969). Situations may dramatically alter the effectiveness of cognitive complexity in decision-making. CEO cognitive complexity improves firm performance in more complex, stable, and diverse industry environments. However, CEO cognitive complexity diminishes firm performance in simpler, more volatile, resource-constrained environments (Malhotra & Harrison, 2022). The main point of the situational theory of leadership is to identify which leadership styles or behaviors are more effective in a given situation. Leadership styles and effectiveness must vary in response to situational factors. Situational theory researchers have made great strides in recent years, and it can be divided into the following phases:

Contingency theory. The contingency theory suggests that the performance of an organization or group depends on the interaction between leadership traits and the situation. That is, the leader's motivation must be aligned with the situation in control and influence over the outcome of their decisions. It reveals the relationship between a leader's decision-making style and organizational performance, classifying leadership styles as "task-oriented" and "relationship-oriented" (Fiedler, 1971). Task-oriented leadership styles are effective in highly favorable and unfavorable situations, while relationship-oriented leadership styles are more effective in moderately favorable situations.

Path-goal theory. The path-goal theory is derived from the inconsistency between the effects of consideration and initiating structures (proposed by Ohio State University) on enterprise performance in the behavioral mode of leadership. House (1971) views the role of the leader as creating the path to success for subordinates. The leadership style creates the path, and the effectiveness of that path (leadership style) depends on the specific situation. It consists of the subordinate's traits (competence and control) and the environment's traits (the extent to which the task is structured). The contribution of this theory is to suggest that leaders should adjust their behaviors according to the situation and the characteristics of their subordinates. It also proposes the concept of participative leadership.

Power and Process Mode of Leadership

LMX (leader-member exchange). Graen and Uhl-Bien (1995) classify leadership research into research on leaders, followers, and the dichotomous relationship between leaders and subordinates (LMX). This dichotomous relationship is the core of LMX theory, unlike the trait and behavioral theories of leadership that place more emphasis on the characteristics, style, and behaviors of the leader or follower (Martin et al., 2018) and view the follower as a passive recipient (Anand et al., 2011). LMX is not limited to material transactions in transactional leadership but includes psychological and social exchanges between leaders and subordinates. A leader's relationships with subordinates in his/her team in different qualities are called LMX differentiation (Martin et al., 2018). Such differentiation is the essence of LMX, in which leaders form high-quality relationships with only a few followers (Liden et al., 2006). High-LMX relationships include tangible rewards (e.g., challenging tasks and training opportunities) and intangible rewards (e.g., the leader's trust and respect). The LMX theory suggests that the source of leadership is the relationship between the leader and subordinates. Leaders differentiate subordinates into insiders and outsiders based on subordinates' competence, trustworthiness, and sense of responsibility. The insiders take the initiative to take on more responsibility and put in more effort. Accordingly, leaders are more concerned about them. Outsiders do the day-to-day work and maintain a basic working relationship with their supervisors, and the leader manages them with only legal authority. LMX is both transactional and transformational. It starts with a limited number of "transactions" but is most effective when based on change. Scholars have tried to explain the mechanisms of LMX in different cultural contexts. Anand et al. (2011) categorize these studies into two types: (1) those that apply LMX to other national or regional cultures and (2) those that examine the relationship between various dimensions of culture and LMX.

Abusive supervision. All previous studies are about positive leadership behaviors, such as transformational and ethical leadership. However, abusive supervision exposes the dark side of leadership styles. Abusive supervision originated in the United States, but a growing body of empirical evidence suggests that abusive supervision is widespread (Martinko et al., 2013). Tepper (2007) defines abusive supervision as: "subordinates' perceptions of the extent to which supervisors engage in the sustained display of hostile verbal and nonverbal behaviors, excluding physical contact." Subordinates can have two opposite motives for abusive supervision - to cause harm or enhance performance. Based on social learning theory, Liu et al. (2012) conducted a cross-sectional study on team leader behavior and individual employee performance. They conclude that departmental abusive supervision inhibits employees' intrinsic motivation for creativity through team leaders' abusive supervision. When departmental leaders impose abusive and critical behaviors on their team leader, the team members may be dissatisfied with their work and question their contribution to the organization. Thus, the employees may become less creative in their performance.

Furthermore, they verify that two different motivational attributions of subordinates to abusive supervision affect their creativity performance differently through attribution theory. By conducting a meta-analysis of abusive supervision, Mackey et al. (2017) argue that there is no unified theoretical framework for studying abusive supervision, resulting in many theories emerging in theoretical studies. However, they use the main explanatory framework of equity theory, in which subordinates' perceived unfairness is triggered by leaders' abusive supervision behaviors

(Klaussner, 2014). Based on this, they find that perceptions of supervisory unfairness are antecedents of abusive supervision. Perceptions of supervisory fairness and abusive supervision evolve based on social exchange relationships between leaders and subordinates.

The emergence of various leadership theories has greatly enriched leadership research. Nevertheless, how many theories are needed to cover the full range of leadership? Numerous leadership theories should be weeded out to reach the essence of leadership. By integrating the current research in leadership theory, Meuser et al. (2016) investigate 49 leadership approaches/theories used in papers published in 10 top journals from 2000 to 2013. They find that the six most commonly used leadership approaches are transformational leadership, charismatic leadership, strategic leadership, leadership and diversity, participative/shared leadership, and trait theory. Banks et al. (2016) suggest that when introducing a new leadership structure, they should assess whether it has inconsistent validity with other leadership styles in predicting important outcomes. It is also one of the dilemmas arising from developing leadership theories. According to the above analysis, when new leadership theories emerge, researchers seem overly interested in testing their validity while ignoring the antecedent variables of various leadership styles, such as authentic and paternalistic leadership. Researchers should pay attention to what factors lead to various behavioral modes of leadership in the future.

Entrepreneurial Leadership and Enterprise Performance

Strategic leadership is concerned with the leadership of an organization, not the leaders in the organization. Its research primarily targets high-level organizational leaders, such as CEOs and TMTs. In the 1970s and 1980s, there was a great deal of debate among scholars about the impact of leadership on performance. The debate centers on the effectiveness of leadership as to whether strategic leadership is related to enterprise performance. Sociologists are skeptical about leadership, arguing that leadership behavior has less impact on organizational performance than organizational and environmental factors (Hannan & Freeman, 1977; Salanick & Pfeffer, 1977). However, supportive scholars argue that leaders significantly influence organizational performance (Child, 1972; Thomas, 1988). Three schools of leadership research have been developed in response to leadership skepticism.

The first is the upper echelon theory. Hambrick and Mason (1984) propose the upper echelon theory, suggesting that an organization represents the top management's perceptions and values. Managerial background characteristics such as functional background, education, and tenure can partially predict strategic choices and performance levels. The upper echelon theory has drawn the attention of strategic leadership researchers to top management's characteristics. Psychosocial theories have been used in strategic leadership research and have become one of the most influential perspectives in recent years. Researchers have focused on top management's strategic decision-making behaviors through the upper-echelon theory, greatly influencing the understanding of organizational processes and outcomes. Research on the upper echelon theory examines the impact of leaders on firm behavior and performance from two main perspectives: (1) It focuses on the heterogeneity of top management's background or job characteristics, such as their tenure, age, and educational background. Henderson et al. (2006) indicate that the relationship between CEO tenure and firm performance shows an inverted U-shaped pattern due to changes in the external environment. In stable and dynamic environments, the effect of CEO tenure on firm performance increases with time but then decreases. However, in turbulent environments, the effect of CEO tenure on firm performance is manifested more quickly. Although this study demonstrates the validity of the upper echelon theory, the effectiveness of strategic leadership, as explained by the theory, can vary in strength upon changes in external factors. Similarly, King et al. (2016) find that CEOs' education and quality affect bank performance, demonstrating that banks with CEOs who have MBA degrees outperform their peers. (2) The focus is on the heterogeneity of traits, such as personality traits and behavioral styles of top management from individuals to teams. Chatterjee and Hambrick (2007) show that narcissistic traits of CEOs lead them to make risky and eye-catching strategic moves in their strategic decisions, resulting in either excellent or terrible firm performance outcomes. However, researchers in upper echelon theory have also recognized that top management is not consistently effective for organizational performance. On the one hand, effectiveness in the management process may depend on their discretion, i.e., whether or not their decisions are constrained in the organization (Hambrick & Finkelstein, 1987). On the other hand, empirical evidence suggests that leadership effectiveness may also depend on the external environment and extreme traits.

The upper-echelon theory improves the strategic leadership framework, and the demographic characteristics that reflect leaders' perceptions and values are objective and measurable. However, 20 years ago, it was suggested that researchers of strategic leadership theory should stop using demographic variables as a substitute for psychosocial constructs (Boal & Hooijberg, 2000). Relying on demographic variables as proxies for cognitive styles and values is limiting and fails to measure subjective concepts (Carter & Greer, 2013). Researchers are constantly exploring the psychological characteristics and decision-making tendencies of top management. On the premise that the research is supported by psychological and empirical evidence (Zhu, 2021), the psychological characteristics of top management should be rigorously demonstrated.

The second is full-range leadership theory. Historian Burns (1978) first proposes and contrasts transformational and transactional leadership to describe the behavior of political leadership. Transformational leadership is the interaction between leaders and followers. In this interaction, leaders and followers elevate each other to a higher level of ethics, morality, and motivation. Transactional leadership is a more traditional leadership process in which leaders show their followers how to achieve their personal goals by adopting specific behavioral patterns. In short, transactional leaders tell their followers which behaviors will be rewarded—a transactional leader exchanges one thing for another with their followers. Introducing transformational leadership and transactional leadership into management, Bass (1985) argues that transformational leadership consists of idealized influence, inspirational motivation, intellectual stimulation, and individual consideration. Transactional leadership consists of randomized rewards and intervention management. Although transformational and transactional leadership have conceptual differences, they are not opposites. A leader may utilize both transformational and transactional leadership at the same time (Bass & Avolio, 1997). L laissez-faire leadership means leaders rarely instruct their followers. Bass places laissez-faire leadership in a hierarchical comparison with transformational and transactional leadership. It highlights the legitimacy of transformational and transactional leadership.

The full-range leadership theory involves laissez-faire, transactional, and transformational leaders.

Based on the above theoretical analysis, subsequent researchers have continuously explored the effectiveness of transformational and transactional leadership. Numerous empirical studies have shown through mediating or moderating mechanisms that transformational leadership is effective at the individual, team, and company levels. Ng (2017) examined more than 600 papers with empirical research on transformational leadership. He finds that transformational leadership positively affects task performance, citizenship behavior, and innovation behavior at the individual, team, and organizational levels through five core mechanisms (emotion, motivation, identification, social exchange, and justice enhancement). Elenkov et al. (2005) find that transformational strategic leadership behaviors significantly positively affect product market and administrative innovations using data from a six-country survey of three cultures. TMT tenure heterogeneity moderates the relationship between strategic leadership behaviors and administrative innovations in the product market and administrative innovations. Sociocultural moderates this relationship only in administrative innovations. As for the consequences of transactional leadership, some consider them favorable and some harmful.

Those who believe them favorably argue that transactional leaders exchange benefits with subordinates. The leadership's incentive to subordinates can be used as an incentive signal to motivate subordinates to innovate and improve performance. However, those who believe them detrimental argue that transactional leadership emphasizes the process of reward and punishment. Employees may lack autonomy, diminishing their motivation to improve performance or innovate. Many empirical studies have been conducted on both leadership styles, but most focus on individual leaders. However, the interactions between leaders and organizational and social factors have rarely been addressed in depth.

The third is visionary leadership. The full-range leadership theory explains that leaders must take action to make a difference in organizational change but neglects the discussion of the organization's vision that the leader communicates. Vision is a vibrant "verbal picture" of what the organization wants. Visionary leadership refers to leaders communicating the organization's vision verbally or in writing to their subordinates to inspire them to contribute to that vision (Nutt & Backoff, 1997). Researchers of visionary leadership emphasize the importance of vision, and the effectiveness of strategic leadership is reflected in the ability to construct a vision. If an organization's leaders can communicate its vision to their subordinates, the organization may be differentiated. Otherwise, there is a high probability that organizational goals cannot be achieved (Elenkov et al., 2005). There are two main levels of research on the effects of visionary leadership on performance: (1) at the individual level, scholars have explored the positive effects of visionary leadership on subordinates. Carton et al. (2014) demonstrate that visionary leadership behaviors improve subordinate performance. Stam et al. (2014) find that visionary leadership changes subordinates' cognitive leadership process; leaders' vision communication may cause subordinates to create a collective self-concept, and subordinates strive to achieve the organizational vision through self-concept enhancement. (2) At the team level, scholars have investigated the positive effects of visionary leadership on team effectiveness. Eseryel et al. (2021) investigate self-managed virtual teams and find that visionary leadership can contribute to team success by establishing shared mental models and normative convergence. On the other hand, regarding the effectiveness of visionary leadership, some scholars have also studied the conceptual connotation of visionary leadership. They reveal that visionary leadership overlaps with idealized influence and inspirational motivation in transformational leadership. Further research is needed to determine whether there are differences and commonalities between visionary and transformational leadership. The effect of different leadership styles on performance varies significantly, and the effect of the same leadership style on performance also varies to some extent. Performance includes task performance and innovation performance. This paper deals with performance in a broader sense. Performance types falling under this category are examined in this paper.

The research on the relationship between strategic leadership and performance mainly explores CEO, TMT, board attributes and enterprise performance. Using the Meta-Analytic Structural Equation Modeling (MASEM), Bergh et al. (2016) re-examine the relationship between strategic leadership and performance through 208 articles. They discover that the relationship between the board of directors and TMT supports the agency theory but rarely impacts performance. However, the board of directors mediates the relationship between TMT and performance. There are two conclusions: (1) board size positively affects TMT size, and TMT size contributes to higher performance. (2) Board leadership is associated with TMT size, while TMT size is associated with performance. The endogeneity test found that shorter CEO tenure, longer TMT tenure, greater TMT diversity, and greater TMT size positively affect the board of directors. In turn, directors are associated with higher levels of performance. Using the MASEM approach, researchers can gain insight into the relationship between the dichotomous variable of strategic leadership and performance. They can also recognize the boundaries of the theoretical model, such as the mediating and moderating effects.

Review of Leadership Research

This chapter systematizes the research related to the four schools of strategic leadership research (the trait theory of leadership, the behavioral theory of leadership, the situational theory of leadership, and the power and process theory of leadership). It reviews the research on the impact of strategic leadership on enterprise performance. The main conclusions are as follows: (1) the proponents of the trait theory of leadership cannot identify a set of inherent traits. Furthermore, it cannot solve the endogenous problem of whether a leader possesses leadership traits before becoming a leader or whether the traits are stimulated after they become leaders. (2) This paper reviews the behavioral patterns of leadership using transformational, authentic, ethical, and paternalistic leadership as examples. Sophisticated dimensions and measurement tools have been developed for these four leadership styles. (3) The situational mode of leadership considers that the selection of leader traits and modes is based on the leader's surroundings and the mode of leader-follower interaction. (4) Leadership's power and process mode is based on the interaction between leaders and subordinates. (5) Theorists do not agree on the relationship between strategic leadership and performance, as the same leadership style may lead to contradictory conclusions.

A literature review on leadership effectiveness in various schools of leadership theory reveals the following shortcomings in leadership research: First, there are two major problems in the research on the behavioral mode of leadership. On the one hand, researchers have addressed whether leadership styles are effective or not while ignoring what contributes to such leadership styles. In other words, leadership research lacks an in-depth investigation of the antecedent mechanisms (Wang et al., 2020). The study of antecedent mechanisms contributes significantly to our understanding of leadership formation. On the other hand, leadership styles keep emerging, and researchers seem overly concerned with the effectiveness of new leadership styles without emphasizing their structural and conceptual overlap with other leadership styles. In the long run, it is not conducive to leadership research. Second, there is no leadership research in China's unique context. Strategic leadership research is an important school of leadership research. In most leadership studies, the leadership style generated in the Western context is placed in the Chinese context to test the leadership model with Chinese data samples. Third, demographic variables should be used with caution in studying the trait theory of leadership.

However, strategic leadership research seems to rely too much on demographic variables as proxies for cognitive styles and values (Carter & Greer, 2013). In measuring Confucian culture, current research tends to measure the cultural factor by using the Confucian cultural climate in the birthplace of CEOs and chairpersons (the number of Confucian institutes within a 200-kilometer and 300-kilometer radius of the birthplace). This cultural factor is valid at the regional level, but its use at the individual level is questionable (Zhang, 2021). Fourth, current research approaches to leadership styles overemphasize survey measures, cross-sectional designs, and single data sources. Chatterjee & Hambrick (2007b) measure CEO narcissism with external secondary data such as the CEO's photo size in the company's annual report. However, few scholars measure a particular leadership style using measures of secondary data. Future researchers should use various methods, such as experimental design and qualitative methods (Gardner et al., 2011).

Strategic leadership is a hot research topic and will remain so in the future (Zhang, 2021). Krause et al. (2019) find that chairs of Chinese companies play a greater role than those in Germany, the UK, and the US. The chairperson in the Chinese context will outweigh the macroeconomic, industry, and organizational factors. It suggests that strategic leadership determines firms' competitive advantage in the Chinese institutional context (Li, 2021). In a review of research on leadership localization in

China, Cao and Li (2010) outline three stages of leadership research in China. They are (1) the non-local stage to validate the application of Western leadership theories in China; (2) the comparatively and weakly local stage to compare and revise the Western theories and try to develop leadership research with Chinese features; and (3) the strongly local stage to construct a new type of leadership theories based on Eastern features. The theory of paternalistic leadership typifies this stage. The review of strategic leadership research shows that strategic leadership development still stagnates in the third stage. Furthermore, the most typical paternalistic leadership remains sluggish (Li et al., 2020).

By analyzing the development and effectiveness of strategic leadership, this paper proposes the following areas for future attention. First, attention should be paid to the unique role of culture in leadership in the Chinese context. From the perspective of leadership development, leadership is a universal phenomenon that is not limited by country and region, but leadership style is influenced by culture (Fan & Zheng, 2000). The meaning, style and effect of leadership behavior must be influenced by culture, and is a culture-based phenomenon (Hofstede, 1980). The conclusion that leadership has a contradictory effect on performance should be explained in the cultural context. Williamson (2000) also emphasizes the critical roles of informal systems such as religion, culture, customs and other social norms in business decision-making and behavior. The four virtues (the class system, obedience, mediocrity, and human feelings) in Confucianism significantly influence Chinese entrepreneurs' leadership styles and business decisions (Fu & Tsui, 2003). The high degree of authoritarianism, benevolence to subordinates, and high ethical standards in paternalistic leadership (Farh & Cheng, 2000) are typical of Confucianism in leadership styles. Most leadership styles are generated in the context of Western culture, and there is no exploration of strategic leadership with Chinese culture as the origin.

Second, the second-generation succession in Chinese family firms provides a unique context for studying leadership succession. Unlike non-family firms, family firms have dual goals of economic and socio-emotional wealth (Gómez-Mejía et al., 2007). Family members in family firms may not be equivalent to professional managers within equity-diversified firms in strategic leadership studies (Li, 2021). As an important component of China's private economy, family firms were founded by the first generation of entrepreneurs after the reform and opening up. These family firms have been passed on to the second generation or are now facing their family succession (Li et al., 2015). In the second-generation inheritance of Chinese family firms, the second-generation successor is the legal heir of property power and has a legitimate status. However, due to the authority of family members and founding members in family firms, organizations may not recognize second-generation successors' personal and competence authority (Li et al., 2015). At this point, it is worth exploring how the second generation makes leadership decisions and constructs authority (Li et al., 2020). Li et al. (2015) argue that second-generation successors may establish personal authority and increase their legitimacy through portfolio entrepreneurship. However, portfolio entrepreneurship is only one way. Which leadership style is the most effective for second-generation successors to enhance their legitimacy in executing this strategic choice? This question needs to be further explored.

Research Review on Entrepreneurial Decision Logic

Origin of Causation

As a branch of modern logic, causation was coined by the philosopher and logician Arthur W. Burks in his book *Chance, Cause and Reason* in 1977. He defined causation as the logic of cause and effect, which can explain something and investigate the origin, development and ultimate destination of something. It is based on an important basic concept that life is a process of goal-directed action (Locke & Latham, 1990, 2002) and that goals are the outcomes individuals want to achieve. Causation emphasizes achieving goals and examines the forms of thinking, patterns, and applications of knowledge, focusing on causality.

Although causation was formally introduced as a philosophical theory, it is widely used in many fields of academic research, especially in management studies. Causation emphasizes forecasting, as do classical functional and strategic management management. Classical functional management and strategic management researchers believe that past experiences, patterns, and methods can contribute to the solution of future problems (Sarasvathy, 2001). Among the classical theories of managerial decision-making, the "means-ends" approach proposed by Simon, a famous American psychologist, highlights the main features of causation that are outcome-oriented and influence the outcome by using choices. The theory assumes that the actor chooses the most probable means to achieve the end among the available means to realize the expected end (Simon, 1973). Human resource managers hire the most suitable candidates using extensive knowledge of organizational behavior and psychometric scales and combining their past experiences. When developing a new product, managers must conduct market research, analyze the demand, and determine the price the market will afford through the shape of the demand function. Given this, the manager can help the company to make a more comprehensive decision about product development (Sarasvathy, 2001). Before the 1980s, when large and medium-sized enterprises faced relatively stable internal and external environments, the classical managerial decision-making theory with causation as the underlying logic was widely used by many managers in all aspects of enterprise management.

Furthermore, the theory helped managers to make correct decisions. The managerial decision-making theory is extensively used in real-life situations and thoroughly investigated by scholars. The research on managerial decision-making also extends the boundaries with the expansion of management science.

Entrepreneurship is an important area of management research. Since the Journal of Management officially launched the topic of entrepreneurship research in 1987, more and more scholars have been attracted to investigate entrepreneurship (Shane, 1997). It includes the study of decision logic behind entrepreneurial activities. Entrepreneurship involves deciding the way, the people, and the means to identify, evaluate, and develop entrepreneurial opportunities and produce goods and services (Shane & Venkataraman, 2000). In the entrepreneurial process, business actors should identify entrepreneurial opportunities and integrate entrepreneurial resources through a series of decision logic. Thus, decision logic plays an important role in the entrepreneurial process subtly. Although many scholars have studied decision logic in entrepreneurship, no researcher has systematically indicated the relationship between causation and entrepreneurial decision-making, an important manifestation of classical decision logic. It was not until 2001 that Sarasvathy formally introduced causation into entrepreneurship research based on the means-ends approach. He also defined causation in the context of entrepreneurial decision-making, making it a specialized term in entrepreneurship research. Causation in entrepreneurship research implies that actors carry out market research and other activities according to the predefined goals and screen out the optimal solution to realize the predefined goals. The entrepreneurial process is premised on goal determination, emphasizes competitive analysis, predicts the future, and selects a revenue maximization strategy (Sarasvathy, 2001, 2008; Chandler et al., 2011; Reymen et al., 2015; Yu et al., 2018). The causation model in the traditional entrepreneurial decision-making process emphasizes that it must rely on precise predictions and clear goals and select the means to produce these desired outcomes (Chandler et al., 2011; Yu et al., 2018).

Since causation has been given a specific meaning in entrepreneurial contexts, causation has been viewed as a traditional paradigm for entrepreneurial decision-making. Scholars re-examine the concept, context of the application, reasons for choice, and effectuation dimensions of this decision-making approach, similar to classical management theory, in conjunction with past entrepreneurship research. Generally, causation is combined with effectuation for research and discussion. Therefore, in this section, only some representative literature on causation is reviewed as an extension of causation. Regarding the definition of causation, researchers have found that past management concepts also apply to causation. They include the concepts of intentionality (Katz & Gartner, 1988), opportunity identification and assessment (Shane & Venkataraman, 2000), planning (Delmar & Shane, 2003), resource acquisition (Katz & Gartner, 1998), and deliberate exploitation of opportunities (Shane & Venkataraman, 2000). These concepts have helped to expand the boundaries of causation research and deepen the definition of causation. Causation generally applies in highly deterministic and predictable environments (Chandler et al., 2011; Welter et al., 2018). Numerous findings have shown that measures of causation are negatively correlated with measures of uncertainty (Chandler et al., 2011). Apart from examining the relationship between environment and causation, Dew et al. (2009) examine the relationship between individual choice and causation. They find that MBA candidates exposed to the classical paradigm of management in the classroom for a long time are more likely to adopt causation and the predictive framework for decision-making. By adopting causation for decision-making, firms demonstrate their role in performance, innovativeness and other dimensions, as causation positively correlates with employment size (Eyana et al., 2017).

Furthermore, the relationship between causation and firms' net profit margin is in an inverted U-shaped curve (Peng, 2020). Alzamora et al. (2021) found that causation can favor innovation through the dimensions of goals and contingencies. The above studies on the different dimensions of causation can expand the boundaries of the theory and help scholars explore more diversified decision-making styles in entrepreneurial contexts based on causation.

As entrepreneurial activities become increasingly active, scholars and entrepreneurs have found that traditional prediction-based decision-making in causation cannot fully explain entrepreneurs' decision-making behaviors and outcomes (Sarasvathy, 2001). Sarasvathy proposes a new entrepreneurial decision logic, effectuation, based on the assumption of bounded rationality and the criterion of satisfactory decision-making for entrepreneurial situations with high uncertainty and resource constraints. As entrepreneurial activities become increasingly active, scholars and entrepreneurs have found that traditional prediction-based decision-making in causation cannot fully explain entrepreneurs' decision-making behaviors and outcomes (Sarasvathy, 2001). Sarasvathy proposes a new entrepreneurial decision logic, effectuation, based on the assumption of bounded rationality and the criterion of satisfactory decision-making for entrepreneurial situations with high uncertainty and resource constraints.

Origin of Effectuation

With the in-depth research on entrepreneurial decision-making, scholars have found that the premise of environmental predictability limits the application of causation. However, entrepreneurial situations are highly uncertain and unpredictable, resulting in the limited effect of causation in entrepreneurial decision-making. Since the existing decision theories cannot provide a reliable decision logic for entrepreneurs in highly uncertain environments, many scholars have researched the relationship between environmental uncertainty and entrepreneurial decision logic and reached the following conclusions. Saravathy and Kotha (2001) argue that entrepreneurial decision-making under uncertainty involves three scenarios. First, suppose decision-makers perceive themselves as facing a relatively predictable future. In that case, they may adopt a decision-making model that involves systematic information gathering and analysis or the causation decision model. With this model, they can make predictions. Second, if the decision-maker believes the future is relatively unpredictable, they will use an approach similar to Bayesian estimation. They can collect as much information as possible through experimentation and iterative learning. Thus, they may transform a relatively unpredictable future into a relatively predictable one. Decision-makers can optimize their decisions by learning and accumulating experience. However, if decisions are to be made about future scenarios that are unknown or may not even occur, neither of these models can be used. Due to the high uncertainty of future scenarios, entrepreneurs cannot gather and analyze information to justify their decisions. In such situations, entrepreneurs rely on hunches and intuition to make decisions and usually act before analyzing (Shane & Venkataraman, 2000). Thus, this decision-making approach differs from causation, as decision-makers first conduct market research and SWOT (Strengths, Weaknesses, Opportunities and Threats) analysis, identify opportunities, and plan before taking action. The former emphasizes the entrepreneur's subjective initiative and is a paradigm of acting before knowing rather than the paradigm of knowing before acting advocated by causation.

To explain entrepreneurs' creation of new ventures in uncertain environments or the absence of markets, Prof. Sarasvathy thoroughly investigated decision logic in the entrepreneurial process in his doctoral dissertation (1998). In that dissertation, Sarasvathy invited 27 subjects from the most successful entrepreneurs in the U.S. from 1960 to 1985 and the Entrepreneur Of The Year National Award winners. He then conducted a 2-hour experiment and interview with each of these subjects. Subjects were asked to answer ten decision-making questions about the entrepreneurial process for a fictional business venture. The researcher audio-recorded the entire experiment and interviews and coded the recordings using oral report analysis. The results revealed that entrepreneurial experts exhibit particular behaviors and logic deviating from the standard patterns found in textbooks. They did not necessarily start with market research or have a clear vision of the new venture. With given resources, entrepreneurial experts usually use these resources to set action goals for entrepreneurial activities. The entrepreneurial goals are clarified through actual actions. Sarasvathy (2001) defines "effectuation" as the entrepreneurial action decision-making style of entrepreneurial experts, where a set of ends is taken as given, and the focus is on choosing between the possible effects of using this set of ends.

As an emerging theory that explains entrepreneurial behavior and guides entrepreneurial practice, effectuation has received much attention from scholars in entrepreneurship research in recent years. In entrepreneurial decision-making research, effectuation is generally considered the process by which entrepreneurs identify multiple potential markets under uncertainty, ignore predictive information, and invest in resources they can afford to lose. Moreover, entrepreneurs integrate more scarce resources by creating communities of interest in their interactions with external resource holders and capitalize on contingencies to create possible outcomes. In an uncertain and unpredictable environment, the goals of a specific task cannot be clearly defined. However, the resources or means available to entrepreneurs are known, and they can only create possible outcomes by combining the means available. As an alternative to causation, effectuation provides a series of principles that focus on means-oriented and control-oriented thinking. Effectuation is essentially a decision logic. It advocates that, in entrepreneurial environments with uncertain and unpredictable futures, entrepreneurs ignore predictive information, start with existing means, and invest resources within the limits of affordable losses. Based on this, entrepreneurs establish communities of interest with external resource holders and use contingencies to create possible outcomes. Effectuation emphasizes that strategies do not have to be formulated before entrepreneurship but can be shaped during entrepreneurial activities. Moreover, entrepreneurs can better cope with the high level of uncertainty in the environment and adjust to the available resources at any time (Sarasvathy, 2001).

Sarasvathy, in 2008, further describes effectuation as the professional logic of entrepreneurship, a dynamic and interactive process of producing new products or services. Moreover, he proposes five principles of effectuation to fully explain the theory (Bird-in-hand, Affordable Loss, Crazy Quilt, Lemonade, and Pilot-in-the-plane). The Bird-in-hand Principle emphasizes that the starting point for decision-making is the available resources and means; the Affordable Loss Principle emphasizes that actors should invest resources based on acceptable losses rather than expected returns; the Crazy Quilt Principle emphasizes that actors should focus more on creating entrepreneurial alliances or searching for resources than on competitive analysis. The Lemonade Principle emphasizes that actors should take advantage of the environment and situation to maximize their advantages, and the Pilot-in-the-plane Principle highlights the need for actors to identify and utilize opportunities with their initiative. The above five principles deepen the action guidelines of effectuation and help scholars and entrepreneurs better understand the theory.

In the twenty years since the introduction of effectuation, scholars have published more than 700 papers on its concept, dimensions, measurement, and process-performance relationships from 54 countries. These studies can be divided into five categories (Grégoire & Cherchem, 2020): the concept of effectuation, personal antecedents of choosing effectuation, effectuation and enterprise performance, effectuation and internationalization, and effectuation and innovation. These five articles provide insights into the concept, definition, and specific implications of effectuation from different perspectives. They extend the research boundary of effectuation and help scholars investigate it further. Although effectuation is one of the most popular topics in entrepreneurship research in recent years, many questions have been raised about the effectuation theory. There is a lively and ongoing debate about the future of effectuation research involving many prominent scholars. On one side of the debate are the proponents/advocates of the theory, including Prof. Sarasvathy, Prof. Read and Prof. Fisher. They advocate effectuation as an effective tool for entrepreneurial decision-making. The other side is represented by scholars Arend et al. (2015), who argue that it has an imperfect theoretical structure and lacks empirical testing and critical analysis.

Comparison of Two Types of Decision Logic

Causation and effectuation are two alternative approaches used by entrepreneurs in the development of new ventures (Sarasvathy, 2001). Causation refers to a decision-making approach that starts from a specific goal, develops a strategy and collects resources to achieve the goal. Its main decision-making criterion is the maximization of returns, characterized as goal-oriented and forecast-based. Effectuation is a decision-making process that starts from a limited set of entrepreneurial means, where decision-makers choose a path based on the expected losses and acceptable risks and continuously adjust the path according to short-term expectations (Sarasvathy, 2003).

The actor using causation needs to predict the future as accurately as possible and set a clear goal. Then, the actor may explore all the means to achieve that goal and calculate the best, fastest, most efficient, or most economical means. Finally, they can follow the steps to accomplish that goal. Effectuation thinking, on the other hand, proposes a decision-making model with an opposite process. Actors who adopt effectuation do not try to predict the future or have a clear goal. They use all the means based on their traits, preferences, abilities, knowledge, and acquaintances (their social network resources). At the same time, they create a variety of possible outcomes by utilizing contingent opportunities in the objective environment and various resources in their social networks.

To summarize, causation is to select an optimal means among a set of available means to achieve a desired outcome. It is a form of "many-to-one mapping." Effectuation is to utilize a given set of means to create a variety of possible outcomes and choose a satisfactory outcome. It is a form of "one-to-many or many-to-many mapping."

Causation and effectuation differ significantly in their thinking and principles of action. These differences inevitably lead to a distinct difference in explaining the entrepreneurial process, beginning with a different understanding of the source of entrepreneurial opportunities. The discovery school, represented by Shane, believes that reality is independent of human will and that exogenous shocks such as technological changes and consumer preference shifts create entrepreneurial opportunities. Entrepreneurs act as passive responders in opportunity development, must be alert, and search for existing market opportunities (Kirzner I, 1973). Entrepreneurship research prioritizes identifying and exploiting potentially valuable opportunities in complex market environments and creating new ventures (Shane, 2003). The creativity school of thought, represented by Sarasvathy and Venkataraman, holds that opportunities do not previously exist but are created by entrepreneurs in an uncertain environment (Venkataraman, 1997). Instead of recognizing an opportunity, entrepreneurs act on it first and then make adjustments based on feedback from the market. In this case, the opportunity creation process is a natural path-dependent process subject to contingencies.

In real-life decisions and actions, decision-makers may use different thinking logics, and the same decision-maker may use both thinking logics simultaneously. It depends on the specific situation of the entrepreneur. However, in the same space-time situation, each decision-maker has only one dominant thinking logic for a particular decision. Each thinking logic has its applications. Causation applies to start-ups in mature and stable industries. Entrepreneurs can learn about the industry's structure and competition rules by studying successful or benchmarked companies and gaining the necessary information to build and grow their businesses. They then collect reliable data to make accurate predictions. Effectuation applies to companies in a rapidly developing or unorganized industry. Currently, there is no universally accepted consensus in the marketplace, and the rules of the game for potential suppliers, customers, and competition in the industry are all being changed and shaped. In this way, entrepreneurs should create, influence and change the status quo through effectuation, and accumulate relevant experience and knowledge in their actions, thus turning opportunities into reality. Entrepreneurs should decide whether to use causation or effectuation as the leading decision-making logic, depending on the context so that the decisions can be better utilized.

There are distinct differences between causation and effectuation on many dimensions. Understanding the underlying and manifest differences can help scholars and managers better examine and apply the two decision-making approaches. Table 2-1 below illustrates the underlying differences between causation and effectuation:

Table 2-1 Comparison of Causation and Effectuation

Dimension	Causation	Effectuation
Prerequisite	Given outcomes	Given means
Decision-making model	What outcomes are possible given the means	What means to achieve the goal
Attitudes toward the future	Predicting the uncertain future	Creating an uncertain future

Dimension	Causation	Effectuation
Underlying logic	I can predict the future so that I can control it	I can control it, so I do not have to predict it
Capability	Specialize in the use of deterministic knowledge	Specialize in the exploitation of contingencies
Attitude toward risk	Expected return, maximizing return with manageable risk	Affordable losses, control the cost floor
Commitment base	It should be within reach	Having to do the best you can
Competitor attitude	Competing	Cooperating

Source: Organized by the author

Decision Logic and Enterprise Performance

As popular topics in entrepreneurship research in recent years, many scholars have studied causation and effectuation in depth. The studies are about the antecedents, consequences and measurements of causation and effectuation.

Research on the antecedents of causation and effectuation refers to studies investigating the antecedents of the effectuation of the decision-making styles that individuals select. These studies indicate a non-uniform personal style outcome (Grégoire & Cherchem, 2020). Some researchers have concluded that the more entrepreneurial experience an expert has, the more they use effectuation to make entrepreneurial decisions. Dew et al. suggest that entrepreneurial experts use effectuation more for decision-making and are more concerned with risky ventures than outcome prediction. MBA (Master of Business Administration) candidates may make decisions using the logic of causation and tend to support decision-making using a predictive framework (Dew et al., 2009). However, Baron (2009) points out that the traits of Dew's two groups of research subjects are not controlled, resulting in less credible findings. In addition to studying the practical experience of individuals, scholars also investigate the influence of entrepreneurs' personality tendencies on the choice of entrepreneurial decision-making styles. By examining the difference in decision-making between EENs (Entrepreneurial Educated Novices) and entrepreneurial experts, Batley (2014) concludes that entrepreneurial decision depends on the risk-taking of the user. The higher the risk-taking, the more likely it is to choose effectuation. By examining the use of effectuation and causation by emerging entrepreneurs, Store (2018) reveals that a combination of passion, entrepreneurial self-efficacy, and risk perception leads to the use of causation and effectuation.

Similarly, using a similar research model, Chen (2021) finds that entrepreneurs with high emotional complexity are likelier to adopt both types of entrepreneurial logic. Moreover, cognitive flexibility mediates the positive relationship. All three studies suggest that individual personality differences influence entrepreneurs' decision-making styles. Given these theoretical and methodological differences and the various empirical findings reported, it seems prudent to hypothesize that, at present, there remains inconclusive evidence on the possible relationship between individual characteristics and one's understanding/preference for effectuation (Grégoire & Cherchem, 2020). The empirical evidence explaining an individual's effective entrepreneurial decision-making styles remains inconclusive. However, the above findings also help to unravel some complex issues behind entrepreneurs' choice of decision logic. In addition, such studies are currently confined to individual actors. In the future, more in-depth research can be conducted on complex issues behind the choice of decision logic for entrepreneurial organizations.

The research on causation and effectuation analyzes the scenarios in which the two decision-making styles are applied. Since effectuation is based on environmental uncertainty (Sarasvathy, 1998), many scholars have verified the relationship between the choice of the two decision logics and environmental uncertainty through a series of tests. Chandler et al. show that causation is negatively correlated with environmental uncertainty, while one of the dimensions of effectuation, the experimental dimension, is positively correlated with environmental uncertainty (Chandler et al., 2011). Similarly, Yu et al. reach a similar conclusion through their research: in environments with high uncertainty, entrepreneurs tend to use a mixture of causation and effectuation, while in environments with less uncertainty, entrepreneurs prioritize causation as a decision-making approach (Yu et al., 2018). So, how can we quantify environmental uncertainty and determine the fit between environmental uncertainty and decision-making styles? Using an agent-based simulation model, Welter and Kim investigate the effectiveness of effectuation versus causation in uncertain and risky situations. They find that effectuation outperforms causation until entrepreneurs can correctly predict the future at a rate of more than 75% (Welter & Kim, 2018). The study shifts the relationship between environmental uncertainty and decision logic from qualitative to quantitative. In addition to studying the effect of environmental uncertainty on decision-making approaches, scholars have also investigated the effect of the institutional environment on the choice of the two decision-making approaches. Laine and Galkina (2017) examine the international activities of SMEs in the context of Russia's foreign trade sanctions and find that uncertainty in the institutional environment causes firms to shift their decision-making approaches from causation to effectuation. Besides the macro environment, scholars have also studied the impact of resources on choosing the two decision logics separately. Reymen et al. (2017) find that causation is less effective than effectuation in resource shortage. There are also studies on the market contexts in which the two decision-making styles are applicable. Zhang et al. (2021) show that the causation decision-making style is more effective for enterprise performance management in emerging markets. By studying the appropriate contexts for the two decision-making styles, scholars can better predict and explain the effects and impacts of the two decision-making styles in different environments, either separately or jointly.

Research on the consequences of causation and effectuation has generally investigated the effects of these two decision-making styles on firm performance, internationalization, and innovation. The effectiveness of causation and effectuation is measured by measuring both firms' outcomes on their performance, internationalization, and innovation. (1) Performance can best reflect an enterprise's competitive advantage and profitability. Therefore, studies have been conducted to examine how the choice of causation and effectuation affects enterprise performance. Eyana et al. (2017) investigate the impact of two decision-making styles, causation and effectuation, on the performance of Ethiopian tourism companies, respectively. They conclude that causation is positively related to employment size, and effectuation is positively related to financial indicators. Similarly, Mthanti (2014) surveys 94 top managers of South African technology firms and finds a positive correlation between the use of effectuation and the firm's operation, which is ultimately manifested in the firm's performance. Zhang et al. (2021) make the first innovative use of meta-analysis to investigate the relationship between two decision logics and enterprise performance. They also conclude that there is a positive correlation between the two decision styles and enterprise performance, and the productive decision style affects enterprise performance slightly more. Peng et al. (2020) examine the relationship between causation and effectuation and enterprise performance. They conclude that the relationship between effectuation and NVP (New Venture Performance) is a J-shaped curve, but the relationship between causation and NVP is an inverted U-shaped curve. It formally models the effects of both on performance. Entrepreneurship scholars investigate the effects of causation and effectuation on enterprise performance. In addition, they also study the effect of interaction between the two on enterprise performance. By studying 312 software companies, Yu et al. (2018) reveal that the interaction between the two positively affects enterprise performance when environmental uncertainty is high. However, when environmental uncertainty is low, the interaction can negatively affect the enterprise. Studying the effects of causation and effectuation on enterprise performance separately and jointly helps scholars further understand the mechanism and specific effects of the two on performance. The research results above show the relationship between the two decision-making styles and enterprise performance. (2) Under the background of rapid global integration, the internationalization ability of enterprises also represents their competitiveness. It is worth exploring how the two decision logics affect firms' internationalization capability and process. Using five international manufacturing firms in Italy, Nowinski and Rialp (2013) conclude that switching from causation to effectuation can help firms rapidly increase their commitment abroad. Sullivan et al. (2012) concluded that adopting an effectuation-based marketing program can help these international firms achieve superior performance by surveying nine globalized firms in Australia. Chetty (2015) has found that entrepreneurs with established relationships in foreign countries prefer to use effectuation for market selection and entry. The above studies found that adopting effectuation for decision-making is a more appropriate choice for firms' internationalization actions. The analysis of the characteristics of causation and effectuation shows that, due to the unpredictable international situation, the environment in which international enterprises are located is more uncertain, and effectuation will play a greater role. (3) In addition to the research on enterprise performance and internationalization, numerous studies have examined the potential impact of causation and effectuation on firm innovation. As early as the early 2010s, Coviello and Joseph (2012) observed that effectuation is associated with major innovations. Brettel Mauer et al. (2012) first validate the adaptation of a previous survey instrument to the specific context of firms' R&D programs through interviews and pilot studies. Using the validated instrument in a large survey, they discovered that effectuation positively influences R&D performance (efficiency and output), especially when innovation capacity is high. Blauth et al. (2014) used the same validation instrument and elaborated on these findings individually. At the same time, they survey employees in corporate R&D programs. These authors document the positive impact of using effective decision logic on practiced creativity and the negative impact of using causation on creativity. They show that these relationships are more influential under higher levels of uncertainty. Berends et al. (2014) investigate the product innovation process in SMEs and find that effectuation makes product innovation resource-driven, incremental, and open-ended. Causation is used especially in the later stages to set goals, plan activities, and invest resources to achieve the goals. Using technology-based SMEs as subjects, Alzamora et al. (2021) also find that effectuation promotes innovation by exploiting contingencies, while causation positively impacts innovation through goals and contingency elimination. That is, both can contribute to corporate innovation through different mechanisms of action. The above literature specifies the realistic impact of the two decision logics on entrepreneurship. Effectuation is more likely to lead to innovative performance for firms. Causation, on the other hand, facilitates firms' innovation in some dimensions but may also curb individual employees' innovations.

The study of the measurement of causation and effectuation analyzes the measurement of the two decision-making styles. The most recognized measures of causation and effectuation have been proposed and refined by Chandler et al. Chandler et al. (2011) suggest that because causation is a first-order construct, it is possible to measure causation directly from a seven-item Likert scale. Conversely, effectuation is a multidimensional formative construct and cannot be measured directly by a scale. Therefore, it is necessary to measure the four sub-dimensions of effectuation (experimentation, affordable loss, flexibility, pre-commitments and strategic alliances) through the four scales and effectuation. Based on the scales of effectuation mentioned above, Perry and Chandler et al. (2012) propose two specific formative measurement models for effectuation assessment (the mixed indicator measurement model and the composite indicator measurement model). Moreover, they guide the types of data collected in the model and the methods of data collection, construction and measurement, the objectives of data analysis, and the data analysis methods. They also support the two measurement models with methods and theories.

Review of Decision Logic Research

The previous section systematically reviews the contents and research on causation and effectuation and summarizes the relevant research results. Generally speaking, the two decision logics have gained much academic attention since they were proposed in 2001. Especially because of the great difference between effectuation and classical management decision theory in the starting point, process and logic, more and more scholars have been attracted to study the related topics. Through a comprehensive literature review, this paper will reveal the main notions, methodologies, and other dimensions underpinning the research on the two decision logic categories. Moreover, it summarizes the uniqueness of the existing studies and describes the contradictions reflected in the results of different studies and the shortcomings of the studies. Based on these observations and summaries, this paper proposes the future research direction on causation and effectuation to help advance its academic developments.

Causation is a summative overview of classical managerial decision-making theories. As a term exclusive to entrepreneurship research, causation succinctly summarizes the traditional approach to entrepreneurship. The entrepreneur decides on a predetermined goal and then chooses various means to achieve that goal (Sarasvathy, 2001). Causation inherits the central idea of the planning strategy approach and decision theory (Simon, 1959). It further specifies theoretical boundaries such as the objectivity of opportunities and the predictability of the future. Existing research has also found that causation embraces many of the classic management concepts of the past, such as intentionality, opportunity identification, assessment, and planning. Thus, it helps to extend the boundaries of causation research further. Effectuation is proposed to address the common real-life entrepreneurial situations, i.e., highly uncertain and unpredictable environments. Effectuation supports entrepreneurs in making decisions that facilitate favorable outcomes when they cannot grasp the patterns of new industries and opportunities. Effectuation overturns the logic of classical managerial decision-making theory, more realistically reconstructing entrepreneurial decision-making scenarios and increasing the legitimacy of entrepreneurship research as an independent discipline. The introduction of effectuation is an important milestone in advancing entrepreneurship theory, and it has even been evaluated as one of the most noticed theoretical constructs of entrepreneurship management in the last decade (Davidsson, 2006).

Research related to causation and effectuation can be specifically categorized into four groups: reasons for choice, conditions of use, outcomes of use, and measurement methods. Research on the reasons for individuals' choice of decision-making styles, taken together, points to an inconsistent outcome regarding personal style (Grégoire & Cherchem, 2020). Current research has not revealed a specific link between personal characteristics and decision-making preferences. The conditions of use of the two decision-making styles have likewise been of interest to numerous scholars. A widely recognized finding is that causation is negatively correlated with environmental uncertainty, while effectuation is positively correlated (Chandler et al., 2011). In addition, other scholars have studied the effects of institutional environment (Laine & Galkina, 2017), resource environment (Reymen et al., 2017), and local market environment (Zhang et al., 2021) on the two decision-making styles. Most scholars study the impact of two decision-making styles on firms. It focuses on performance (Eyana et al., 2017; Mthanti, 2014; Peng et al., 2020; Zhang et al., 2021), degree of internationalization (Nowinski & Rialp, 2013; Sullivan, 2012; Chetty, 2015), and innovation (Coviello & Joseph, 2012; Brettel et al. 2012; Berends, 2014; Alzamora et al. 2021). Theories should be quantified to link them to practice. The main well-recognized measures in research on the measurement of causation and effectuation are the scale of causation and effectuation and the scale of effectuation containing four sub-dimensions. They were proposed and refined by Chandler et al. (2011).

Many scholars recognize the theoretical legitimacy of causation and effectuation, but some argue that there are problems with the assumptions made in effectuation. In his 2015 publication, Arend explicitly identifies the overly omnipotent entrepreneur in the effectuation hypothesis, the failure to articulate the relationship between control and control outcomes, and the irrationality of the means-driven premise. At the same time, the option logic is used inappropriately, and the creation of new value is not explained. There is a lack of explanation for creating competitive advantage in the theory. Otherwise, the sustainability of entrepreneurial activity cannot be ensured (Arend et al., 2015). In response to the hypothetical problems of effectuation summarized above, Arend also proposes five future research areas. Hopefully, scholars can be motivated to thoroughly investigate the related issues, contributing to the development of effectuation as a solid decision theory.

As the emerging hot entrepreneurial topics, causation and effectuation are subject to theoretical and methodological challenges. Since effectuation substantially differs from the classical management decision-making process, it has been questioned even more. To validate the theory and promote its development, scholars in entrepreneurship research should conduct in-depth studies in the following areas: First, the motivation of individual entrepreneurs to apply causation and effectuation should be clarified. Second, it should clarify the significance of the restricted conditions for applying the two decision-making styles to the decision. Third, methods should be developed to measure entrepreneurs' psychological reasons for choosing causation/effectuation. Decision-making is vital in the entrepreneurial process, enabling entrepreneurs to identify, utilize and develop opportunities. Relevant scholars should follow the vigorous developments in entrepreneurship and study the two mechanisms of entrepreneurial decision-making: causation and effectuation. In addition to studying the impact of the mechanisms, they should recognize, question and refine the theory from its underlying logic. In the future, scholars may draw on the results of other disciplines, such as sociology and psychology, to broaden the scope of application of the two entrepreneurial decision logics through cross-disciplinary research. It can provide theoretical guidance for optimizing entrepreneurial decision-making behavior.

Vision Studies

Connotation of Vision in Ancient China

The word "vision" was often used in ancient China, mainly by fortune-tellers in fortune-telling. It refers to a special situation of five elements and the structure of generation and suppression of the Bazi (八字, eight characters). Generally, it is closely linked to Month Commander, forming a combination of strengths that dominate destiny. The structure of Bazi determines a person's character, career, marriage, study and life. If a person's structure is high, he/she has a strong Bazi. Structure determination is the key to the operation of Bazi reading, and the structure must be strictly delineated. If the structure is wrongly delineated, the good and bad fortune of one's destiny may be reversed. Therefore, determining the right structure is the most important lesson in the Bazi reading. There are a few principles for determining the structure of Bazi: based on the Month Commander's Ben Qi (本气, innate Qi), the Month Branch's innate Qi transits through Heavenly Stems, the Month Pillar, the Year Pillar, or the Hour Pillar. These are the standard direct structures.

Month Commander's innate Qi is impermeable, but Sheng Qi (生气, vibrant Qi), Yu Qi (余气, excess qi), Mu Ku Zhi Qi (墓库之气, tomb-vault Qi) are permeable to Month Pillar so that they can form structures. If the Qi of Month Commander is impermeable, but the innate Qi is pure, the structure can be determined using the innate Qi. The structure can be determined if the Qi of the Month Commander is complicated, but other earthly branches assist the innate Qi. If the Qi of Heavenly Stems does not access the Month Commander, but the year branch, day branch, and hour branch are very strong, and it is the suppression, relief, and consumption of the Day Pillar, the structure can also be determined. In the book on the four pillars of destiny by the ancients, the Bazi structures can be said to bear many names, totaling more than 200 items. However, in modern society, the Bazi structure is divided into eight structures (relatively strong structure, relatively weak structure, extremely strong structure, extremely weak structure, Qi-transforming structure, regulated structure, Qi-essence (象, Xiang) structure, flow-thru structure). The common structures are relatively strong, relatively weak, extremely strong, and extremely weak structures. The special structures are Qi-transforming, regulated, Qi-essence, and flow-thru structures. The classification of these eight structures is not all based on the Day Pillar. The four commonly used structures are based on the Day Pillar as the entity and are classified by preferences and constraints. The other four special structures are not divided by the Day Pillar. Qi transformation and preferences and taboos of Qi transformation define the Qi-transforming structure. The regulated structure is based on the cold, warmth, dryness and humidity, and the regulation and control of the climate. Qi-essence structure is based on Bazi Qi-essence to maintain the Qi and essence. Flow-thru structure is based on the flow in Four Pillars to maintain the flow in Four Pillars.

There are three major structures and five states in the Bazi prediction system. The three structures are balanced structure, extreme structure, and transforming structure. The five states are strong and weak energy in balanced structure, extremely strong and extremely weak in extreme structure, and only one state in transforming structure. The balanced structure is that the Daymaster (日柱, the Heavenly Stem that represents the day of their birth) is neither too weak nor too strong and is not transformed. In short, a weak Daymaster can be supported, and a strong Daymaster can be restrained. The balanced structure is about balance, which embodies the principles of the material dialectic "law of contradiction and unity, and the law of mass interchange." The balanced structure is divided into two states: strong and weak. Strong energy means that the Day Pillar is strong, while the body suppressor is harmless or powerful; weak energy means that the Day Pillar is weak, while the body helper is harmless or powerful. The balanced structure is one of the most common structures in the birth chart. It is characterized by the Day Pillar either being strong or weak, but never to an extreme level. In this case, a balanced destiny is preferred, where the strong Day Pillar is suppressed and the weak Day Pillar is supported. The extreme structure is that the Daymaster is extremely weak and cannot be helped, or the Daymaster is extremely strong and cannot be restrained. Extreme weak means that the Daymaster is too weak to help, and extreme strong means that the Daymaster is too strong to restrain.

The extreme structure is a one-sided situation, which embodies the principle of materialistic dialectics that things turn into their opposites when they reach the extreme. Extreme structure is divided into two states: extremely strong and weak. Extreme strong is when the Day Pillar is strong, and the body suppressor is injured or weak. Extreme weakness is when the Day Pillar is weak and the body helpers are injured or weak. Extreme weakness means surrendering, abandoning identity and obeying the God of Strength. Extreme strength is to feel that you are dominating the world. The luck feature of the extreme structure is that if it goes well, it will be a great fortune; if it goes bad, it will be a terrible fortune.

Transforming structure means the structure when the Daymaster merges successfully with the Month Pillar or Hour Pillar. Liu Qin (六亲, the six relationships with grandparents, parents, spouse, siblings, children, and grandchildren) attributes are still classified with the Day Pillar as the Tai Chi point. It can never be divided by the God of Transformation. The transforming structure is essentially a change, where one of the five elements transforms its properties and changes into another five elements to achieve its purpose. Therefore, it is a strategy to change and hide ourselves in a complex environment. In a competitive society, we should hide our ambitions and talents. No one wants to be surpassed, which is the weakness of human nature. Leaders want their employees to do many things, but only one thing is not desired: to exceed the leader.

Vision is rooted in the fertile soil of traditional Chinese culture. Traditional Chinese culture has a long history, and Confucianism, Taoism and Buddhism are the source of Chinese culture and the most beautiful flowers and the best fruits in the garden of culture. With different concepts, methods and levels, Confucianism, Buddhism and Taoism have spread their branches and leaves and blossomed in history, covering almost all corners of the spiritual culture of Chinese society. They can almost satisfy different classes' psychological needs and different groups' spiritual hopes.

A closer examination and study reveals two phenomena: First, big differences exist in the "visions" of Confucianism, Buddhism and Taoism. Second, Confucianism, Buddhism and Taoism greatly influence the "vision" of Chinese people, especially entrepreneurs. Confucianism, Buddhism and Taoism are three extraordinary and precious trees in the history of world culture. Buddhism originated in India, but it flourished and evolved in China. After Buddhism was introduced into China, it merged with the local Confucianism and Taoism. Briefly speaking, the differences in the thoughts, concepts, perspectives and visions of Confucianism, Buddhism and Taoism are reflected in the following aspects:

Confucianism: centered on indoctrination. It advocates Confucianism as a way of governing the world, where people should improve their character, manage their families, govern the country, and appease the people. Moreover, it advocates an enterprising spirit.

Taoism: centered on cultivating the moral character and ruled by Taoism. It advocates the unity of nature and man and the rule by doing nothing that goes against nature. It follows the laws of the universe.

Buddhism: Compassion at its core. Buddhism rules it. It advocates that all dharmas are empty and that there are cycles of cause and effect. It aspires to realize life.

Due to the different starting points and ultimate goals, the concepts, approaches, and methods of Confucianism, Buddhism, and Taoism, or their visions, are significantly different.

The story illustrates clearly and interestingly the "vision" of the common people and Confucianism, Buddhism, and Taoism. In Master Lü's Spring and Autumn Annals, School Sayings of Confucius, it is recorded that when the King of Chu lost his bow, his servant refused to return it. The servant said, "A man from the kingdom of Chu lost his bow, but another man from the kingdom of Chu found it. Why bother to look for it?" Confucius heard this and said, "It would be better to remove the word 'Chu' from his sentence." When Lao Tzu heard about it, he said, "It would be more appropriate to remove that word 'man.'" Finally, Buddha also learned about this. He commented: Chu Wang had a broad mind like the ocean, Confucius was tolerant of embracing the world, and Lao Tzu saw the world and its people as one. However, they have something in their eyes and someone in their heart.

The eyesight, bosom and vision of King Chu, Confucius, Laozi and Shakyamuni create a hierarchical structure. It can correspond to and satisfy different levels of spiritual needs. The word "vision" has grown in China's long history, and its connotation and extension have benefited from Confucianism, Buddhism and Taoism. As a result, various visions have been formed, and different cultures and histories have been reflected behind different visions.

Connotation of Vision in Modern China

Vision has three meanings in modern China. The first one is to designate the pattern. In Vol. 3 of *Tieweishan Congtan (Writings on Tiewei*

Mountain) by Cai Tao of the Song Dynasty, it wrote that "Later on, those who insisted on the idea of dealing with the world argued that the depth and breadth of a person's knowledge of things stemmed from his wealth and prestige." Chapter 29 of The Plum in the Golden Vase (Chin P'ing Mei, 金瓶梅) wrote that "by looking at a person's Bazi, we can tell whether or not he will have a life of honor and wealth. By looking at a person's face, we can tell whether or not he is lucky or bad in his life." Second, it The second refers to structure and format. In the first volume of *Waiting for the Dawn: A Plan for the Prince (Mingyi Daifang Lu 明夷待訪錄) - Eunuchs (yanhuan, 奄宦)*, Huang Zongxi wrote: "The eunuchs of the Han, Tang, and Song dynasties all came to power only when the monarchs were incompetent. In the Ming Dynasty, however, a pattern of checks and balances between eunuchs and officials was already in place, with eunuchs and officials restraining each other." In *Camel Xiangzi (Luotuo Xiangzi, 骆驼祥子),* Lao She depicted: "He was already big and tall. Though his limbs have not yet been shaped into a pattern by the years, he already looks like an adult." Third, it refers to the situation. In his poem "*Zaijingtang Ji - Jiangnan Jingshi Poems - To My Daughter and Son-in-Law (A Collection of Poems in Zaijingtang by Jiangnan Jingshi: To My Daughter and Son-in-law, 载敬堂集 •江南靖士诗稿 •示女与婿)*," Chen Zhiyu wrote: "My children, you must learn the four aspects of strategy that can help you to make success. I am getting old, and it pains me that I studied too late. You are more gifted than I am, and I hope you will open up new horizons."

The scope of perception of things varies from person to person, so that vision differs from person to person. Vision is interpreted as style or scale in *Cihai (辞海, a large-scale dictionary and encyclopedia of the Chinese language)*. In the 48th chapter of *A Dream of Red Mansions (Hong Lou Meng, 红楼梦)*, it wrote, "Because you do not know poetry, you love it when you see a simple one; once you are in this situation, you cannot learn it anymore." Lu Xun, in his novel *Call to Arms (呐喊, Na Han),* wrote in the story of *Kong Yi Ji (孔乙己)*: "The pattern of the hotels in Luzhen is different from that of other places." Vision is another worldview that cannot be described as big or small. It also has extremely abundant connotations and extensions. The wider, broader, higher, and farther the perception of the world, the clearer, sharper, finer, more detailed understanding of the development of something, and the closer the conclusion will be to the truth. Thus, it can guide people to take correct actions and achieve more ideal results.

On the contrary, the smaller, narrower and lesser the knowledge of the world is, the less people know the mechanism and trend of things. Then, people may focus only on the surface or a certain node, ignoring the background. However, everything must have its origin, cause and effect. On the other hand, the individual's heart, horizon, courage, wisdom, sense of mission, and insights all affect his or her vision.

Chapter 3

Entrepreneurial Vision Research Based on the Grounded Theory

Purpose

In recent years, with the acceleration of the construction of new infrastructure, digital industrialization has advanced further, and efforts have been made to speed up breakthroughs in key technologies. China's digital economy is booming, and the scale of the industry continues to grow rapidly. The digital economy has become one of the main engines of economic development. At the same time, the digital economy has also brought many new opportunities and challenges for business operations, with increasing complexity and uncertainty in management. In this process, Chinese enterprises are highly adapted to the uncertainties of the digital economy, seize the opportunities and avoid the shocks of the digital economy. We should learn more about the leadership traits of Chinese entrepreneurs and their contribution to firms' good performance under uncertainties. It offers important theoretical and practical implications for further exploring the secrets of Chinese firms to maintain their competitive advantage in the digitalization wave and for building management theories with Chinese features.

Entrepreneurial vision is a collection of personal traits and personality elements, such as an entrepreneurial mindset and height of thinking, that influence the effectiveness of entrepreneurial innovation, coordination and performance enhancement. Entrepreneurial vision is a concrete presentation of entrepreneurial leadership in China. Theories of entrepreneurial leadership have been grounded in the Western cultural context, and extensive explorations have been conducted on the relationship between leadership and micro-factors such as organizational behavior, team harmony, and conflict management (Li & Tang, 2022; Wang et al., 2022; Judge et al., 2002). However, these studies have seldom investigated the correlation between leadership and firm performance in uncertain environments from the perspective of the Chinese cultural context (Hitt et al., 2003; Zhang, 2021). Therefore, the conclusions of related studies cannot effectively explain the managerial advantages of Chinese firms in the wave of digitalization.

To summarize, this study will deal with the concept, characteristics and components of the entrepreneurial vision with Chinese features. Combined with the analysis of 13 typical Chinese entrepreneurs' cases with the grounded theory, it tries to construct a theoretical model of entrepreneurial vision.

Methodology

This study is based on entrepreneurial vision, a relatively new preface topic, with no mature theoretical framework for reference. In addition, this study deals with the concept of entrepreneurial vision. Therefore, selecting representative entrepreneurs as samples for case analysis and theoretical exploration is more suitable for research on such topics (Yin, 2014). In addition, compared with quantitative research, a case study allows for systematic analysis and understanding of the detailed textual information of the sample cases. As a result, the behavioral philosophies and activities of the sample subjects can be more deeply analyzed to obtain a complete and comprehensive view. Finally, multi-case studies can help us to establish more generalized entries if different entrepreneurs in the selected sample differ in personal backgrounds and upbringing. Therefore, we can understand the meaning of entrepreneurial vision more clearly. Given this, a multi-case method is adopted in this study.

There are three general approaches to cross-case study analysis: First, case categorization aims to reveal similarities or differences between case groups. Second, case matching aims to outline the corresponding characteristics of the cases. Third, case comparison is to arrange and compare the characteristics of all cases and decide which items are priorities (Eisenhardt and Graebner, 2007; Eisenhardt, 1989). In this paper, the third cross-case study analysis method is selected. The textual data are coded and analyzed based on the grounded theory. Inductive analysis is used, in which the concepts are gradually raised to the abstract level in a bottom-up spiral, and the interrelationships between the concepts are extracted. In the end, a theory of entrepreneurial vision is established.

Case Selection

(1) Selection of Typical Cases

This study aims to construct the concept of entrepreneurial vision. Therefore, it selects samples from typical cases to better present the key factors in entrepreneurial vision (Liu and Wu, 2012). The selected entrepreneurial samples must meet the following conditions: 1) the entrepreneur must be a successful entrepreneur, and the enterprise they founded must operate on a large scale. The enterprise must also have a good status and reputation in its industry. 2) There is sufficient information about the entrepreneurs in the case studies. We can sort out the key decision-making behaviors of the individual entrepreneurs in entrepreneurial and business activities because the entrepreneurs themselves permeate entrepreneurial vision in their daily entrepreneurial and business management activities. 3) The entrepreneurs should be excellent entrepreneurs with different personal backgrounds and growth experiences to fulfill the logical replication of the diverse cases. At the same time, the entrepreneurs' differences should be considered. Following the above three principles, this study finally identifies 13 outstanding entrepreneurs since the reform and opening up. Their basic information is summarized in Table 3-1, and the representative companies founded or operated by these entrepreneurs are summarized below.

Table 3-1 Basic Information of Outstanding Entrepreneurs Since the Reform and Opening-up of China

Name	Industry	Representative company	Time of entrepreneurial activity	Area of entrepreneurial activity	Achievements
Ren Zhengfei	ICT	Huawei	1987	Shenzhen, Guangdong	Multinational business leader and father of Huawei
Pony Ma	Internet	Tencent	1998	Shenzhen, Guangdong	Multinational business leader, iconic leader of the Internet industry
Lei Jun	Internet	Xiaomi	2010	Beijing	Founder of Xiaomi Technology
Li Shufu	Automotive	Geely	1986	Hangzhou, Zhejiang	Outstanding figure in the automobile industry, China's top ten philanthropists
Wang Chuanfu	Automotive	BYD	1995	Shenzhen, Guangdong	The first richest man in China's automobile industry
Dong Mingzhu	Home appliances manufacturing	Gree	1991	Zhuhai, Guangdong	Outstanding social entrepreneur, female business leader
Chu Shijian	Plantation agriculture	Chu's Orange	2002	Kunming, Yunnan	King of Tobacco of China, King of Orange of China
Yu Minhong	Education	EAST-BUY	1993	Beijing	Outstanding social entrepreneur
Duan Yongping	Computer, communication and electronic equipment manufacturing	BBK	1995	Dongguan, Guangdong	China's "Father of Investment"
Zhu Jianmin	Chemical raw materials and chemical products manufacturing	Oxiranchem	1992	Liaoyang, Liaoning	Meritorious Entrepreneur in the Private Chemical Engineering Industry in China
Luo Yun	Chemical raw materials and chemical products manufacturing	Tianyuan Group	1944	Yibin, Sichuan	Outstanding Entrepreneur of Sichuan Province
Feng Jiujing	Electrical machinery and equipment manufacturing	Rifeng Electric Cable	2009	Zhongshan, Guangdong	Benchmark enterprise in the segment of cabtyre cables
Qian Dawei	Household appliances manufacturing	Company M	1988	Foshan, Guangdong	Clean equipment enterprise in China

Source: Organized by the author

In this paper, twelve outstanding local entrepreneurs (Ren Zhengfei, Pony Ma, Lei Jun, Li Shufu, Wang Chuanfu, Dong Mingzhu, Chu Shijian, Yu Minhong, Duan Yongping, Zhu Jianmin, Luo Yun, and Feng Jiujing) are selected as success cases. At the same time, Qian Dawei, the founder of Company M, is selected as a failure case to compare the results summarized in the success cases.

On the one hand, in terms of success stories, the 12 successful entrepreneurs satisfy the three principles of the case selection mentioned above. First, these twelve entrepreneurs are excellent local entrepreneurs rooted in mainland China who started their businesses actively after the reform and opening up. They are highly representative and typical. Second, these twelve outstanding entrepreneurs have achieved some success in business management. Dong Mingzhu was entrusted with turning Gree around and leading Gree to the top. The rest of the outstanding entrepreneurs run iconic companies that they founded. The entrepreneurs' companies summarized above have all achieved remarkable success in their respective fields by adhering to their missions and visions. The reason for this is that the founders or core leaders of the companies actively put their inner thoughts into the companies' core organizational culture, which is translated into their strategic decisions. The entrepreneur is the heart and soul of the organization, and the entrepreneur and the company they found are constantly integrated and mutually reinforcing. Finally, the twelve entrepreneurs (Ren Zhengfei, Pony Ma, Lei Jun, Li Shufu, Wang Chuanfu, Dong Mingzhu, Chu Shijian, Yu Minhong, Duan Yongping, Zhu Jianmin, Luo Yun, and Feng Jiujing) vary greatly in their backgrounds and upbringing. Their resources, technology, experience and other reserves differ at the beginning of their ventures, fully demonstrating the entrepreneurial vision of local Chinese entrepreneurs. Thus, it is conducive to constructing, verifying and perfecting the theoretical framework of the entrepreneurial vision of local Chinese entrepreneurs.

On the other hand, in the negative case, Company M's Qian Dawei has a limited entrepreneurial vision, resulting in constrained business development. This failure case is a strong contrast to the previous success cases. First of all, Company M is a home appliance company founded in Shunde in 1988, which, like other companies, is an entrepreneurial company emerging after China's reform and opening up. It has more than 30 years of business history, with plenty of data to analyze. Second,

Company M's founder, Qian Dawei, was born in Shunde in 1958 and is one of the pioneers of clean equipment in China. He shared a similar upbringing with Midea's founder, He Xiangjian, and they ventured into manufacturing during the same period. They have grown stronger through independent development and M&As. They were converted from township enterprises at the same time. Both enterprises relied on their capital and management during their gradual development and underwent great changes in China's political, social and commercial culture. However, after more than 30 years of development, these two enterprises start from the same place, industry, and system. The entrepreneurs' education level is also basically the same. However, one has a revenue of up to 300 billion yuan, while the other has only about one billion yuan. One of the main reasons for the huge gap between their business development is the vision of the entrepreneurs. Thus, the gap between Company M's founder, Qian Dawei, and other successful entrepreneurs in terms of vision can be used as a negative case to verify the conclusions extracted from other cases.

(2) Completeness of Case Data

First, the cases are selected to ensure that the entrepreneurs or their core entrepreneurial teams can be interviewed. Second, the interviewees are willing to provide information about the enterprise and the entrepreneurial team. Thus, abundant primary data can be obtained for validation and saturation testing during the research process. The case samples in this study are Zhu Jianmin (founder of Oxiranchem), Luo Yun (chairman of Tianyuan Group), Feng Jiujing (founder of Rifeng Electric Cable), Ren Zhengfei (founder of Huawei), Pony Ma (founder of Tencent), Lei Jun (founder of Xiaomi), Li Shufu (founder of Geely), Wang Chuanfu (founder of BYD), Dong Mingzhu (chairman of Gree), Chu Shijian (founder of Chu's Orange), Yu Minhong (founder of EASTBUY), and Duan Yongping (founder of BBK). The research team can interview Zhu Jianmin (founder of Oxiranchem) and his TMT, Leary New Material Technology's core entrepreneurial TMT, who is in close contact with founder Wu Zhongqian, the TMT in close contact with Feng Jiujing (founder of Rifeng Electric Cable) and the TMT of Qian Dawei (founder of Company M). In this way, detailed and rich primary data can be obtained. In addition, the 13 selected sample companies are highly recognized by the public or the industry. The research team can obtain sufficient secondary data to fulfill the credibility and completeness of the data. This study strictly follows the sampling principle and the above criteria. Therefore, these 13 entrepreneurs are finally selected as the study cases.

Data Collection

After selecting the 13 case samples, the research team started collecting data using online platforms. In-depth interviews and academic papers are combined to collect interview data centered on entrepreneurial vision. At the same time, we collect published articles and biographies of entrepreneurs. Collecting textual data through multiple channels ensures the richness of the data. At the same time, different sources of textual information on entrepreneurial cases are complemented and corroborated with each other. Thus, it guarantees the credibility and completeness of the theoretical framework of entrepreneurial vision (Zhou et al., 2018).

The primary data for this study are acquired mainly through in-depth interviews with the entrepreneurs and their core TMTs. The research team conducts in-depth interviews with successful entrepreneurs or their core TMTs in two periods. Before conducting the in-depth interviews, the research team members outline the semi-structured interviews by combining the relevant literature and the collected interviews. They define the purpose and process of the entrepreneurial interviews to ensure that the interviews with entrepreneurs and TMT are closely centered on entrepreneurial vision. In addition, an interview team of 3-4 research members is organized for each in-depth interview. One team member is designated as the main interviewer, and another is a supplementary interviewer. The remaining members record the interviews and transcribe the text on the spot. After the end of the interview, the researchers organize the audio recordings promptly and discuss them with the interview team members. They record the ambiguous information and confirm and improve it in the later follow-up interviews. The research team follows the above interview process and in-depth interviews with the four entrepreneurs.

The secondary data of this study are obtained through public sources and literature searches. Specifically, public sources include the autobiographies of the 13 entrepreneurs, media reports, company websites, and thesis databases. Keywords include “Ren Zhengfei from Huawei," “Pony Ma from Tencent," “Lei Jun from Xiaomi," “Li Shufu from Geely," “Wang Chuanfu from BYD Auto," “Dong Mingzhu from Gree Electric," “Chu Shijian from Chu’s Orange," “Yu Minhong from EASTBUY," “Duan Yongping from BBK," “Zhu Jianmin from Oxiranchem," “Luo Yun from Tianyuan Group," “Feng Jiujing from Rifeng Electric Cable," “Qian Dawei from Company M. ” Based on these keywords, we search the Internet, read and screen the reports, articles and videos related to entrepreneurial vision. At the same time, the same keywords mentioned above are searched in the CNKI database. The 13 entrepreneurs mentioned above are selected as the objects of the study, and entrepreneurship, leadership style, entrepreneurial vision and other research categories with a high degree of relevance to the topic of this study are used as the selection criteria. Then, the related papers are filtered out. The specific data acquired are summarized in Table 3-2.

Table 3-2 Summary of Text Data Collection

Type	Entrepreneur	Type of data	Title	Summary
Primary data	Zhu Jianmin	In-depth interviews with entrepreneurs	Interview with Mr. Zhu, President of Oxiranchem	55 minutes, about 8,000 Chinese characters
	Feng Jiujing	In-depth interviews with entrepreneurs	Interview with Mr. Feng, Chairman of Rifeng Electric Cable	70 minutes, about 16,000 Chinese characters
	Luo Yun	In-depth interviews with entrepreneurs	Interview with Mr. Luo, Chairman of Tianyuan Group	40 minutes, about 7,000 Chinese characters
	Wu Zhongqian	Interviews with TMT	Interview with Mr. Wu, Mr. Zhou, Mr. Li, Leary New Material Technology	210 minutes, about 32,000 Chinese characters
	Qian Dawei	Interviews with TMT	Interview with Mr. Zhang, Mr. Li and Mr. Yang of Company M	70 minutes, about 15,000 Chinese characters
Secondary data	Ren Zhengfei	Biography	Ren Zhengfei: Huawei’s Winter, Creating Huawei - A Biography of Ren Zhengfei	About 400,000 Chinese characters
		Essays	Huawei’s Black and White	
		Paper	How Entrepreneurs Cope with Environmental Uncertainty: An Analysis Based on Ren Zhengfei’s Interview.	
	Pony Ma	Biography	A Biography of Tencent 1998-2016: The Evolution of China’s Internet Companies	About 210,000 Chinese characters
	Lei Jun	Biography	Lei Jun - Following the Trends, A	About 280,000

Type	Entrepreneur	Type of data	Title	Summary
			Biography of Lei Jun: Standing on the Cusp of the Wind	Chinese characters
		Paper	Research on the Growth Mechanism of Independent Intellectual Property Brands Driven by Entrepreneurship--A Case Study of Xiaomi Technology	
	Li Shufu	Biography	Li Shufu Again	About 190,000 Chinese characters
		Paper	"Authoritative but not Hegemonic" and Decoupled Identity Reconstruction: Li Shufu's Management Response to Geely's Acquisition of Proton	
	Wang Chuanfu	Biography	A Biography of Wang Chuanfu: The Myth of BYD	About 180,000 Chinese characters
		Paper	Wang Chuanfu's Innovative Entrepreneurial Thought System and BYD's Development	
	Dong Mingzhu	Biography	Dong Mingzhu: Behind the Unyielding Marketing, Dong Mingzhu: Hardness and Softness	About 280,000 Chinese characters
		Essays	Dong Mingzhu: The Iron Lady of Business	
		Paper	Characteristics of Female Entrepreneurial Leaders in Building Organizational Culture--An Example of Dong Mingzhu's Efforts for Innovative Organizational Culture Building,	
	Chu Shijian	Biography	A Biography of Chu Shijian, Chu Shijian's Management Style	About 400,000 Chinese characters
		Essays	Chu Shijian: Life has its ups and downs, but the spirit can be passed on	
	Yu Minhong	Biography	Never Say Die - Yu Minhong	About 100,000 Chinese characters
	Duan Yongping	Biography	A Biography of Duan Yongping	About 110,000 Chinese characters

Source: Organized by the author

Coding Strategies

This study strictly adheres to Corbin and Stauss' (2009) coding strategy and procedure of the grounded theory to summarize the relevant categories of entrepreneurial vision. Moreover, the theoretical modeling of the research topic is conducted to ensure the reliability of the study and the validity of the theoretical model (Glaser & Strauss, 2009). The following strategies are adopted to analyze the textual data in this study: First, a decoding team is established. It should avoid the influence of coders' misunderstanding on the coding results, reduce the case study errors and improve the theory's sensitivity. In this regard, two graduate supervisors and two master's degree students in business administration form a decoding team. The two graduate supervisors of the decoding team train the two graduate students on the theory and development experiences related to entrepreneurship and entrepreneurial vision. After that, each member of the decoding team is responsible for the initial decoding of one case. They discuss each member's decoding results to identify problems or doubts in the decoding process and provide solutions after deliberation. Then, the team members label some cases individually. The team members summarize the labels of each case. The four coders work together to translate the labels into concepts, classify them and identify core categories. Then, they perform axial coding and selective coding. If the group members have different opinions about the results during the procedure implementation, they will discuss the problems together until they reach a consensus. Second, a coding database is established. The team members create a form in Excel for each entrepreneur to record the results of open coding, axial coding and the modification process in detail. Finally, the coding process is comparatively analyzed. The final coding strategy is the core analysis strategy of the grounded theory, which is used throughout the entire coding process. The previous case's decoding results will guide the subsequent cases' decoding. At the same time, when new decoding results are found in subsequent cases, it is necessary to compare and analyze the results with those obtained from the previous analysis to ensure the correctness of the results or to revise the results of the previous analysis (Wu & Su, 2014).

Single-case Study

We follow the multi-case study method in the process of data analysis. A single-case study is conducted on the case the researchers are most familiar with or have the most reliable data. The scope and key points of data collection and analysis are further defined. Then, the data collection and analysis of the subsequent cases are carried out with emphasis. Finally, the structure of the study is iteratively revised and developed to reach theoretical saturation. Thus, selecting the starting point for analysis plays a key role in the research process. The data of Ren Zhengfei is chosen as the starting point for the study. The remaining 12 contemporary Chinese entrepreneurs are also analyzed in detail based on the single-case study.

Open Coding

Open coding is the process of decomposing, comparing, summarizing and integrating the collected raw data. Finally, it translates the raw data into concepts and classifies them. To avoid the influence of bias and stereotypes, we should break up the collected raw data before open coding. The working procedure of open coding is as follows: (1) Phenomena are defined. The primary data are divided into individual stories, thoughts, and events. They are given a name that can represent the phenomenon they reflect, which can be divided into two steps: "labeling" and "evidence invocation." (2) The concept is developed. The definition of the phenomenon is only designed to illustrate the basic connotation of the statement cited in evidence, not to form a relatively rigorous expression. Hence, they must be translated into concepts to develop complete concepts further. (3) The categories are explored. As a group of concepts, categories allow concepts seemingly related to the same phenomenon to be aggregated into conceptual clusters. At the same time, after the refinement of categories, it is also necessary to analyze the specific orientation of the categories. The categories with the same core concept are assembled into a primary category. Based on the open coding procedure mentioned above and the theme of this study, the researchers perform open coding on Ren Zhengfei's data, as shown in Table 3-3. The first step is labeling. We mark the relevant words or phrases in the source material that may express entrepreneurship or entrepreneurial vision. We label "(ax)" at the end to indicate the sentence. In the second step, the contents in the 'label' column in the 'Conceptualization' section are regrouped and summarized. After that, the concept of "Ay" represents the previous labels with similar core properties. The third step is "categorization." Concepts seemingly related to the same phenomenon are clustered into categories (Lin, 2004). After the above steps on the textual data, we finally get 113 labels, 69 concepts and 27 secondary categories describing Ren Zhengfei's entrepreneurial vision and spirituality since he founded Huawei.

Table 3-3 Summary of Open Coding on Ren Zhengfei

Category	Concept	Label	Single-case: Ren Zhengfei's information (evidence cited)
AA1 Thirst for Knowledge	A1 Willingness to learn	a1 Willing to learn	(a1) However, those who have worked with Ren Zhengfei often find Ren very willing to learn and correct his mistakes.
		a2 Encouraging employees to learn from their opponents	(a2) Ren Zhengfei encouraged Huawei's employees to learn from the world's strongest competitors, to compete with them face-to-face, and to allow for failure.
	A2 Inquiry	a3 Collaborative learning with universities	(a3) Ren Zhengfei thought that the second and third products should be launched immediately, but Huawei had no more technical strength then. So he approached professors to invite their students to visit Huawei, seeking the possibility of technical cooperation.
AA2 Perseverance	A3 Persistence	a4 Persistently developing the team	(a4) Only if we persistently demand our executives at all levels to self-discipline, integrity, a sense of responsibility, and a sense of mission can we foster a team of executives that support the long-term development of the company's business and embrace its bright future.
		a5 Persistence in studying hard	(a5) Because Ren Zhengfei did not abandon himself, he insisted on studying hard during the turmoil. He quickly demonstrated good scientific and technological literacy in the army and had several technical inventions and creations, twice filling the national gaps. For this, he was unanimously recognized by his leaders and staff.
	A4 Hard-working	a6 Studying hard amid turmoil	(a6) Back in Chongqing, it was already surrounded by "guns and bullets." However, Ren studied computers, digital technology, automatic control and other courses independently and also made friends with some teachers from Xi'an Jiaotong University. They also sent Ren some books.
			(a7) Because Ren Zhengfei did not abandon himself, he insisted on studying hard in turmoil. He quickly demonstrated good scientific and technological literacy in the army and had several technical inventions and creations, twice filling the national gaps. For this, he was unanimously recognized by his leaders and staff.
	A5 Keeping the faith	a7 Faith creates role models	(a8) "Rejecting opportunism" is my credo. With this belief, Huawei has achieved solid success in overseas markets by relying on its strength and perseverance. Huawei has undoubtedly become a role model for China's telecommunications companies.

Category	Concept	Label	Single-case: Ren Zhengfei's information (evidence cited)
		a8 Belief in independent R&D	(a9) In my opinion, I will never be able to get ahead in this way, and I do not want to go down this road, but I insist on my beliefs and try to find a way out for my personal development.
AA3 Brainstorming	A6 Collective wisdom and efforts	a9 Collective wisdom and efforts	(a10) In 1988, one of our products was in a life-and-death crisis, and the stability of the whole system was extremely poor. We re-adjusted our product line. Huawei gathered all the elites in Ningxia to solve the difficulties.
			(a11) We still remember the difficult days in the early 1990s. With the shortage of funds and technology, we relied on collective efforts and worked day and night to develop the first communication equipment we developed - a digital SPC exchange.
		a10 Collective efforts	(a12) Ren Zhengfei requires its employees to cooperate, to avoid one-person operation, and to avoid individual heroism. Employees should realize their value in the collective struggle.
		a11 Listening and learning from others	(a13) We should actively listen to the opinions of customers and colleagues. Huawei has always asked its R&D department to combine its R&D direction with the actual needs of customers in their regular work.
		a12 Adopting and learning from external advisors	(a14) Through the IMBA expert assessment, Huawei reorganized its supply chain and designed and established a customer-centered, lowest-cost integrated supply chain, laying a solid foundation for it to become a world-class enterprise as soon as possible.
	A7 Multiple access to information	a13 Abundant resources from many parties	(a15) The lawsuit between Huawei and Cisco tested the integration of resources and capabilities of the two companies in an all-around way. They are battling the entire media chain, customers, partners, government resources, technology, and legal weapons.
	A8 Sociable	a14 Many partners	(a16) This tactic made more and more customers recognize Huawei as a partner with long-term planning and development capabilities. For a time, competitors were frustrated by Huawei!
		a15 Collaboration with many friends	(a17) By 2005, Huawei had cooperated with Texas Instruments, IBM, Motorola, Lucent, Intel, SUN and other giant companies.
		a16 Friends around the world	(a18) Ren Zhengfei said in Walking Across the Eurasian Boundary: "China's diplomatic route is successful, and it has won more friends worldwide...... Huawei's transnational marketing follows China's diplomatic route,

Category	Concept	Label	Single-case: Ren Zhengfei's information (evidence cited)
			and is confident it will succeed. "
AA4 erudite	A9 Knowledgeable	a17 Knowledgeable	(a19) I also completed Fan Yingchuan's Advanced Mathematics Workbook from cover to cover twice and studied logic and philosophy. I also taught myself three foreign languages, and by that time, I had been able to read university textbooks.
		a18 Rich experience	(a20) Ren Zhengfei has been in a difficult environment since childhood. He had a rough life in school, in the army, and in the business world, which made him able to look at failures calmly and forgivingly.
		a19 Excellent learning ability	(a21) Ren Zhengfei has a strong ability to learn and correct mistakes.
	A10 Mastery	a20 Integrated understanding of international management and operation system	(a22) Huawei's reform requirements for introducing an international management and operation system were to accept it rigidly, optimize it, and then apply it solidly.
		a21 Reinventing concepts in practice	(a23) We have decided to train our current backbone into a professional team with advanced international standards. We hope that all members will strive to develop themselves. They can absorb advanced experiences and optimize themselves in practice only through serious self-criticism.
AA5 Strong Ambition	A11 Lofty ambition	a22 High ambition	(a24) If Huawei is content to produce ordinary communication products, it will always be led by the nose. It will never realize the great goal: "The Chinese have the power to achieve success."
		a23 Pursuing world-class technology and products	(a25) This lesson is also sufficient to show that if Huawei gives up pursuing world-class technological products and is only satisfied with the production of ordinary telecommunication products, then Huawei will always be led by the nose and will never realize the great goal of "The Chinese have the power to achieve success."
	A12 Ambitious goal	a24 Creating a world-class enterprise	(a26) Ren Zhengfei created "Huawei characteristics" with "negation" and negated "Huawei characteristics" to align with the world. In Ren's constant negations, Huawei continues approaching its goal of becoming a world-class enterprise.
		a25 Rooted in independent R&D	(a27) From the beginning, Ren Zhengfei set a clear goal for Huawei: to follow the world's leading technologies and build on its R&D efforts. The goal was to capture the Chinese market and open up overseas markets to compete with its foreign counterparts.
AA6 Pursuit	A13 Perfection	a26 Pursuing	(a28) We will shift from a technology-driven

Category	Concept	Label	Single-case: Ren Zhengfei's information (evidence cited)
of Excellence		top-notch technology	to a market-driven approach, emphasizing new technological means to meet customer needs. We should target the world's top technology and establish a first-class R&D team, not develop "the world's top technology that is unsellable."
		a27 Outstanding in independent R&D	(a29) By excelling in our R&D efforts, Huawei has become invincible in the fiercely competitive communications market and has grown rapidly.
	A14 Self-transcendence	a28 Be brave to transcend yourself, bold to self-criticize	(a30) To survive, we must transcend. To transcend, we must first transcend ourselves. The necessary condition for transcendence is to remove all mistakes in time; to remove all mistakes, we must first dare to criticize ourselves.
		a29 Self-denial, transformation and growth	(a31) Ren Zhengfei knows managers can only grow through continuous learning and self-denial. Like a snake shedding its skin, it grows once every time, even though it is painful and dangerous.
AA7 Indomitable Spirit	A15 Unwavering commitment	a30 Never give up	(a32) Huawei did not stop because of the tragic loss of its JK1000 development. In the most difficult moments, Ren did not give up on pursuing product technology but rather increased investment like a gamble. That is what makes him so extraordinary.
		a31 Never get discouraged	(a33) Ren Zhengfei hopes that every Huawei member will be like a spider when the storm comes, never giving up no matter how many setbacks and blows come their way. They should do their best to "mend the web" and wait for the crisis to end.
AA8 Strategic Positioning	A16 Systematic thinking	a32 Emphasizing the scientific research system	(a34) The only fundamental requirement is to be technically self-reliant. Without its scientific research support system, it is an empty talk about the status of the enterprise. Industrial independence is an empty word without its scientific and technological support system. Without an independent national industry, the nation cannot be independent.
	A17 Precise positioning	a33 Domestic and international layout	(a35) We started our internationalization plan from the beginning and invested a lot of money. We have formulated a two-front strategy: to maintain our leading position in the Chinese market while rapidly developing the international market.
AA9 Future Perspective	A18 Change and innovation	a34 Active breakthroughs and innovations	(a36) The biggest lesson is never to give up but to go forward. Moreover, we should take the initiative to keep innovating and making breakthroughs, going beyond our boundaries until we find a way forward.

Category	Concept	Label	Single-case: Ren Zhengfei's information (evidence cited)
	A19 Broadening horizons	a35 International competition vision	(a37) We should integrate the sense of crisis into our corporate culture so that employees can perceive a tense atmosphere at every moment. We have to be on par with our international competitors to curb the blind optimism of some employees and managers.
	A20 Future perceptions	a36 Accurately perceiving the future trend	(a38) For the future, we believe that the information economy can not return to the frenzied era. Therefore, the information industry can only return to the traditional industry, which will not be an emerging industry in the long run.
AA10 Overall Planning	A21 Big-picture thinking	a37 Global perspective to control organizational change	(a39) We must take a holistic view of the progress of the overall management structure and build an organically connected management system. Moreover, we should connect processes end-to-end to avoid the barriers that come with isolated reforms.
	A22 Insight into the essence	a38 Insight into the nature of corporate goals	(a40) Ren Zhengfei is a firm believer, to the point of paranoia. He believes that "survival is the real way out." He is convinced that survival is the most essential goal and is the unchanging natural law.
		a39 Insight into the main contradictions of organizational change	(a41) In the change, we have to grasp the main contradiction and aspect of the contradiction, control the direction, and plan before acting. At the same time, we must prioritize urgent matters, not seek perfection, work intensively and carefully, and avoid the blindness of seeking great achievements for ourselves.
	A23 Control of opportunities	a40 Sound rotation mechanism	(a42) Almost all Huawei's team members have had job rotations. This seemingly brutal training method has become one of the most effective ways for Huawei to cultivate future talents. Whether a promotion or demotion, it is an asset in life.
		a41 Sharp perception to grasp market opportunities	(a43) Huawei has succeeded in the Chinese market because it relies on the "wolf spirit," a keen sense of smell, to grasp the market demand and quickly launch products.
		a42 Seizing overseas market opportunities	(a44) After 2000, the political situation in Russia stabilized, and the economy continued to warm up. Furthermore, Huawei finally seized the opportunity by persisting in this market until today.
		a43 Rapidly seizing opportunities in rural emerging markets	(a45) Huawei quickly seized the opportunity to pick up the "leftover fruits" and started to enter the "rural areas." These emerging markets have low telephone penetration rates and barriers to entry, facilitating business development.
		a44 Capturing	(a46) We also should be able to react quickly

Category	Concept	Label	Single-case: Ren Zhengfei's information (evidence cited)
		fleeting opportunities	to capitalize on fleeting opportunities. In the operation of the market, new situations can arise at any time. Even the slightest development may affect the entire strategy.
AA11 Risk Perception	A24 Vigilance against crisis	a45 Strong sense of crisis	(a47) The article "Huawei's Winter" is a wake-up call to Huawei members with its deafening language. It warns about Huawei's future and conveys a strong sense of crisis to people.
	A25 Risk control	a46 Control of internal risks	(a48) We must always stay awake to strengthen executives' self-regulation and construct organizational regulatory mechanisms. Also, we must keep the executives honest and struggling. Only in this way will Huawei survive for a long time.
		a47 Powerful control and execution	(a49) In just over a decade, Huawei has made great achievements. It has not had the crisis of fuzzy execution and ambiguous management team on the road of high-speed development, largely attributed to the strong executive power.
AA12 Grey Thinking	A26 Wait-and-see approach	a48 Calm thinking	(a50) we should think calmly about the adaptive change of the entire back-end platform and move forward cautiously. Even a 1‰ increase in efficiency per year would be a welcome improvement. We must not go backward or create a bloated, bureaucratic organization.
	A27 Broad mind	a49 Tolerance	(a51) Ren Zhengfei has been in a difficult environment since childhood and has had a rough time studying, serving in the army, and venturing. Because of this, he could look at failures broadly and tolerantly.
		a20 Listening to criticism with an open mind	(a52) We communicate with our customers daily, and they are okay to criticize us. If they make suggestions, we can improve. For the media, we cannot be nice all the time. We cannot brag when making an achievement.
		a51 Broad-mindedness	(a53) As the Chinese saying goes, a gentleman is ready to die for his bosom frien ds. Ren Zhengfei's broad-mindedness made Li Yinan grateful. In June 1993, after graduating with a master's degree, Li Yinan firmly joined Huawei.
AA13 Free from arrogance and rashness	A28 Empty cup mentality	a52 Never getting complacent	(a54) Despite his world-renowned achievements, Ren Zhengfei remains conscious of crisis. He was treading on thin ice and was always vigilant against arrogance in himself and the Huawei people.
		a53 Never settling for the status quo	(a55) Regarding corporate development, Ren Zhengfei was always conscious. His concepts of crisis awareness, introspection, and

Category	Concept	Label	Single-case: Ren Zhengfei's information (evidence cited)
			forward-looking are the right choices to ensure the company's sustainability and prevent the company from being eliminated by the times.'
	A29 Humility	a54 Humility for people	(a56) No matter how powerful we become in the future, we should treat our customers, suppliers, competitors, and society, including ourselves, with humility. We should never change our humility.
AA14 Inclusiveness	A30 Talent absorption	a55 Providing a sound platform for talents	(a57)As a boss, Ren Zhengfei offers engineers a good development platform to create practical products.
		a56 Trust in talents	(a58) Ren Zhengfei trusts the talents and dares to let them go at critical moments. It is also important in Huawei's ability to always turn ill luck into good.
	A31 Failure tolerance	a57 Generosity and tolerance in the face of failure	(a59) In the face of failure, Huawei always has nine "life-saving hairs" like the Monkey King in the legend, helping Huawei to turn crisis into safety.
	A32 Acceptance of merit	a58 Reward according to merits	(a60) Employees work long hours with high loads, with weak strategic synergies. Employees were promoted and rewarded based on merit. Ren Zhengfei had high expectations for frontline staff, hoping they would always be passionate and energetic.
	A33 Listening to team advice	a59 Listening to middle management feedback	(a61) Later, I listened to the feedback from some middle-level managers that it is not true that the more platforms, the better; the bigger the platforms, the better; or the more comprehensive the platforms, the better. Therefore, we should reduce the number of platform departments, reduce the coordination, and streamline the platform staff, and naturally, the efficiency will be improved.
		a60 Listening to the advice of scientific and technological elite	(a62) In particular, Ren Zhengfei led Huawei to its peak. It has recruited talents on a larger and larger scale. In addition, many scientific and technological elites have offered their advice. Huawei's future development is far beyond that of ZTE and other companies.
	A34 Accepting external suggestions	a61 Listening to customer criticism and suggestions	(a63) We communicate daily with our customers, and they may criticize us more. If they give their opinions, we should improve them.
AA15 Innovation Orientation	A35 Technological innovation	a62 Customer-oriented technological innovation	(a64) Huawei has repeatedly emphasized that the product development path is customer demand-oriented. We adopt new technologies to meet customer needs. Technologies are just a tool.
	A36 Pattern innovation	a63 Customer demand system innovation	(a65) Ren Zhengfei has created a rapid response system for customer needs that is IT-supported, process-restructured, and combines

Category	Concept	Label	Single-case: Ren Zhengfei's information (evidence cited)
			centralized control and hierarchical management. It also laid the foundation for Huawei's entry into internationalization.
	A37 Cultural innovation	a64 Inclusive culture innovation	(a66) Cultural integration is the key to attracting overseas talents. Huawei's overseas institutes had difficulty recruiting foreign employees. Therefore, breaking down the narrow corporate and national cultures is necessary.
	A38 Management innovation	a65 Team management model innovation	(a67) Huawei began to move from the Ren Zhengfei-driven management model to the EMT management model. Huawei's new mission and strategy reflect the team's will and value aspirations. It has become more open and compatible with a global vision and international mindset.
AA16 Breaking Boundaries	A39 Open collaboration	a66 Open cooperation	(a68) We should closely follow the progress of the core network technology, grasp the key of the software and hardware in the core network, and form our original core technology. Based on open cooperation, we must continuously strengthen our leading capabilities in the core areas.
		a67 Reciprocal cooperation	(a69) However, during this period of cooperation, Huawei employees generally found that they were improved and were impressed by their partner's clockwork behavior. They had plans for everything they did and would execute them without fail.
	A40 Team integration	a68 "Wolf team" of collective wisdom and efforts	(a70) Ren Zhengfei's "wolf team" has a strong offensive force, also from strong teamwork. Teams need collective wisdom and effort. Everyone must be open-minded to build a good team so that the collective wisdom can be put to the best use.
		a69 Outstanding teamwork	(a71) Manfred Kickartz, Telefonica O2 Germany's Network Region South division vice president, praised Huawei: "Huawei has amazing teamwork. We thank the team for their extremely outstanding performance."
AA17 Prompt Decision	A41 Bold investment	a70 Daring to invest in areas like "chicken ribs."	(a72) The Board of Directors emphasized the change of vision in the winter and chose a chicken-rig strategy. It invested more in areas where others had reduced their investments and came up from the bottom. Without the courage to change, Huawei would not be what it is today.
		a71 Investment like gambling, even if R&D fails	(a73) Huawei did not stop because of the tragic loss of its JK1000 development. On the contrary, it put all the company's remaining funds and personnel into developing digital SPC exchange.

Category	Concept	Label	Single-case: Ren Zhengfei's information (evidence cited)
		a72 Determined to develop the international market	(a74) When we expand into the international market, western companies have already seized the fertile land we can see. It is only in those remote, turbulent areas with harsh natural environments that Western companies act slowly and invest little. In this way, we have a chance.
		a73 Resolutely capturing the emerging rural market	(a75) Huawei quickly seized this opportunity to pick up these "leftover fruits" and began to venture into the "countryside." These emerging markets had low telephone penetration rates and barriers to entry, facilitating its business development.
	A42 overriding all objections	a74 Eliminating the resistance to change processes	(a76) Any change may be resisted in various ways. To achieve the ultimate victory of change, leaders must correctly and tactfully cope with and withstand the pressures and obstacles from all sides. Moreover, they must develop appropriate change strategies for their organizations.
		a75 Facing the resistance to change firmly	(a77) To vigorously implement BPR (Business Process Reengineering), Mr. Ren granted Hu Hongwei the "imperial sword" to dismiss those who hindered the change!
AA18 Concerted Effort	A43 Consensus building	a76 Internal consensus	(a78) Huawei staff have formed a consensus that Huawei survives for the sake of its customers. The whole company should be centered around the customers, from executives to employees.
	A44 Clear division of labor	a77 Inter-company division of labor	(a79) In Shenzhen, hundreds of large and small subcontractors are dedicated to serving Huawei. In doing so, it utilizes the advantages of a specialized division of labor, reduces costs, diminishes management difficulties, and improves the competitiveness of Huawei's supply chain.
	A45 Responsibility	a78 Valuing results with accountability	(a80) We take responsibility and results as our value orientation and seek to establish a mechanism of self-motivation, self-management, and self-restraint. We can improve performance and employee competence through continuous goal-setting between managers and employees.
	A46 Setting an example	a79 Setting an example	(a81) Ren Zhengfei once told his employees: "For the company, I have diabetes, high blood pressure and cervical spondylosis. You are physically healthy. Why don't you work hard? "
AA19 Enabling	A47 Technical enablement	a80 Technical research	(a82) We work diligently and painstakingly and try to develop technical solutions day and night. We develop, validate, and test products and equipment without holidays or weekends, working all day. When someone feels tired,

Category	Concept	Label	Single-case: Ren Zhengfei's information (evidence cited)
			they sleep on a mat. It is the origin of Huawei's "mat culture."
	A48 Strategic enablement	a81 Breaking through industry barriers	(a83) Solution specialists should master many skills while specializing in one and should have access to channels for help in areas with which they are not familiar. Delivery specialists should be able to communicate clearly with customers about engineering and service solutions.
	A49 Resource integration	a82 Resource co-creation	(a84) We should liberalize the project team's management so that the team can be energetic based on sharing resources and creativity.
AA20 Outcome Sharing	A50 Willingness to share	a83 Sharing	(a85) Ren Zhengfei understands the respect and reward for knowledge and firmly believes that a high salary is the first driving force. Therefore, he proposes "not letting Lei Feng suffer" and is willing to share his earnings with everyone.
		a84 Benefit-sharing	(a86) I have been labeled as mysterious and great in the industry. I know that I am not what I claim to be. What is smart is the tolerance and traction of 130,000 employees and customers. I share the benefits of integrating their talents.
	A51 Mechanism fairness	a85 Fair compensation distribution mechanism	(a87) Equity in internal compensation means that people who contribute equally to the company should be paid equally. External competitiveness is mainly analyzed through the adjustment and payment of salaries.
		a86 Fair competition mechanism	(a88) "Collective resignation" allows everyone to start from nothing, reflecting the equalization of starting positions. The competition for jobs also reflects the equalization of competition opportunities. Behind this seemingly fierce approach it is actually "fairness."
	A52 No thought of gain	a87 No care about anything	(a89) Thousands of tiny fireflies light Huawei's glory. When there are no fireflies, they still glow, sustaining Huawei's light and brand in obscurity and without regard.
		a88 No thought of personal gain or loss	(a90) We should do everything seriously, whether big or small. We should be far-sighted, open-minded, conscientious, and not concerned with personal gain or loss. I am used to a quiet life where I do not deserve awards, which has trained me not to compete for honors today.
		a89 No regard for personal honor or disgrace	(a91) Ren Zhengfei has been reluctant to show up in public. He thinks about making Huawei a sustainable enterprise, not his honor or disgrace.
AA21 Family-	A53 Family	a90 Family	(a92) Ren Zhengfei was not an ordinary

Category	Concept	Label	Single-case: Ren Zhengfei's information (evidence cited)
country Integration	management	responsibilities	person, and he had no time for emotions. Family responsibilities and the urgency of his career led Ren to embark on a path of entrepreneurship and practical activities.
	A54 Respect for elders	a91 Caring for parents	(a93) I felt so much guilt and pain because I had not fulfilled my duty to care for my parents. I devoted all my efforts to my work and neglected the well-being of my parents. I was an unfit son.
AA22 Social Responsibility	A55 Economic responsibility	a92 Providing valuable inventions	(a94) Huawei has been the number one Chinese company in patent applications for six consecutive years. Most of the patents filed by Huawei are patents of invention, and Huawei has been the No. 1 patent applicant for invention in China for three consecutive years.
		a93 Providing valuable services	(a95) For this reason, Huawei has organized an assembly team with strong technical strength and conscientiousness. Facing the users directly, the team members should get along well with the users, train the users well, and provide advanced and high-quality after-sales service.
	A56 Legal liability	a94 Protecting by the law	(a96) Ren Zhengfei responded to the lawsuit from three aspects: First, methods and strategies of legal response; Second, following the American way of action; Third, the lawsuit involves two of the most well-known companies in China and the United States. The battle in the field of public opinion media is also in focus.
		a95 Compliance with the law	(a97) Ren Zhengfei, on the other hand, keeps a very low profile. Before Huawei was not listed, the company just needed to pay taxes, abide by the law, and be responsible for customers and employees, and he did not show his face. Huawei has never explained itself to the outside world.
	A57 Charitable activities	a96 Passionate about charity	(a98) In July 2007, Forbes China released the "2006 China Charity Ranking," and Huawei ranked sixth.
AA23 National Responsibility	A58 Awakening of consciousness	a97 Crisis awareness	(a99) Despite his world-class achievements, Ren Zhengfei has always maintained a sense of crisis and demanded himself with the standard that "there is no first place in my world." He inspired himself to lead Huawei people to march forward in the cruel environment.
		a98 Awareness of Danger	(a100) Ren Zhengfei's patriotism as an entrepreneur, his sense of concern, and his in-depth thinking about enterprise management demonstrate that Huawei has reached a high level of thinking beyond the reach of ordinary

Category	Concept	Label	Single-case: Ren Zhengfei's information (evidence cited)
			Chinese enterprises at this stage of its growth.
	A59 Mission	a99 National mission	(a101) Ren Zhengfei's remarkable feature is that he dares to show his strength and challenge the most powerful rivals. For the national industry's independence and a foothold in the market, he worked hard on R&D and was determined to build his brand to compete with foreign giants.
	A60 National Duty	a100 Responsibility of national revitalization	(a102) The main source of this kinetic energy is his sensitivity to the general trend of the times and his sense of mission to revitalize China.
		a101 Responsibility for the independence of national industry	(a103) Ren Zhengfei's remarkable feature is that he dares to show his strength and challenge the most powerful rivals. For the national industry's independence and a foothold in the market, he worked hard on R&D and was determined to build his brand to compete with foreign giants.
AA24 Valuing Friendship	A61 Sincerity	a102 Sincerity to customers	(a104) As early as in the early days of the company, Huawei was challenged by the question of whether it wanted immediate benefits or customers, and Ren Zhengfei made it clear that Huawei should touch its customers with sincerity.
	A62 Image building	a103 Setting up a positive image in the international arena	(a105) Huawei did not plan to exhibit at the event. However, Huawei needed to present a positive image and posture in an international event. Huawei decided to participate in the exhibition ad hoc to show all customers their determination for the international market.
AA25 Integrity	A63 Spirit of contract	a104 Contractual relationship	(a106) The relationship between an enterprise and its employees is contractual. The company has the right to hire and fire employees, and it should provide training and education for employees to expand their knowledge and skills. Because of this, employees can find a good job in another company at any time.
	A64 Integrity management	a105 Self-discipline and integrity	(a107) We emphasize self-discipline and integrity, a sense of responsibility, and a sense of mission for our executives, all of which embody the "virtue" of the executives in the company.
AA26 Calmness	A65 Strategic Focus	a106 Strong determination	(a108) I am sure you have all heard about the crisis we have been experiencing. It is not an exaggeration to say that such a crisis would have caused the closure of many other companies. However, I still run daily in such a crisis and work on my business.
			(a109) Ren Zhengfei warns us that only those lonely people with enough determination can become the lonely heroes of the Chinese

Category	Concept	Label	Single-case: Ren Zhengfei's information (evidence cited)
			business world. They are also likely to create a world-class business empire in China with a relatively long life.
	A66 Overall planning	a107 Balancing the overall situation	(a110) At the same time, he had to cut down his interests. Otherwise, he could not get the support of others for his resolutions. In this way, he balanced the overall interests of the department under his jurisdiction. The company's heights have been inadvertently leveled over the years.
	A67 Well-thought-out plan	a108 Promoting strengths and avoiding weaknesses	(a111) I do not think you must worry too much about your weaknesses but maximize your strengths. This way, we will be confident and solve our depression problem.
		a109 Strategic confidence	(a112) Ren Zhengfei said confidently: "Ten years later, the world's communications industry will be monopolized by a few giants, and Huawei will take a share."
AA27 Great Ease	A68 Flexible response	a110 Sensitive to resistance from all sides	(a113) Any change may be resisted in various ways. To win the ultimate victory of change, the leader must correctly and sensitively cope with and withstand the pressure and obstacles from all sides.
		a111 Responding to customer needs	(a114) Huawei's team responded positively to every request from customers. When the customer wanted a solution for the Spanish high-speed train, Huawei people built coverage along the magnetic levitation line in Shanghai within three months. They invited the customer to experience it on-site in Shanghai.
		a112 Technology iteration to respond to the market	(a115) I also know an important principle in Huawei's culture. We must act in the company's interest, constantly renewing ourselves and adapting to meet future developments.
	A69 active change	a113 Proactive breakthrough and innovation	(a116) I did not succeed; we are still a very small company. Nevertheless, the biggest lesson is not to give up but to go forward. Furthermore, we must take the initiative to keep innovating and breaking through, pushing ourselves until we find a way ahead.

Source: Organized by the author

Axial Coding

In the stages of conceptualization and categorization, the researchers decompose the textual materials and identify the relevant categories. The textual material is refined and abstracted to a certain extent in these two procedures. However, the final result is that the categories are almost always independent. The connections between the categories are not analyzed and explored in depth. At the same time, establishing relationships is a prerequisite for theoretical modeling entrepreneurial vision. Therefore, axial coding is designed to reexamine and reorganize the categories obtained from the above conceptualization and categorization stages. It should clarify the logical links between the categories and summarize the decoding process of the resulting primary categories. In this study, the 27 categories summarized in the previous open coding stage are sorted and summarized again. To this end, we derive nine primary categories (profound research, aspiration, perspective, modesty, courage and insight, win-win cooperation, patriotism, promise-keeping, and calmness), as shown in Table 3-4.

Profound research means the entrepreneur absorbs knowledge from the outside and examines and summarizes it during their entrepreneurial activities. Aspiration is the entrepreneur's ideal pursuit and self-realization; perspective indicates the entrepreneur's view of the environment and problems and his/her perception of risks; modesty represents the entrepreneur's tolerance in dealing with others. Courage and insight are how entrepreneurs show great courage when facing important business decisions. Win-win cooperation is a value proposition of entrepreneurs who share ideas and values internally and externally, unite the hearts and minds of employees, and assist external partners in their business process. Patriotism refers to the entrepreneur's thoughts and concepts of national rejuvenation and prosperity in business operations. Promise-keeping is the fundamental quality of valuing friendship and treating people with sincerity. Calmness is the entrepreneur's stable mentality of being calm and flexibly responding to crises and risks in a business start-up or operation.

Table 3-4 Axial Coding

Primary category	**Secondary category**	**Primary category**	**Secondary category**
Profound research	Thirst for knowledge	Courage and insight	Innovation orientation
	Perseverance		Breaking boundaries
	Brainstorming		Prompt decision
	Erudite	Win-win cooperation	Outcome sharing
Aspiration	Strong ambition		Concerted effort
	Pursuit of excellence		Enabling
	Indomitable spirit	Patriotism	Family-country integration
Perspective	Future perspective		Social responsibility
	Overall planning		National responsibility
	Risk perception	Promise-keeping	Valuing friendship
	Strategic positioning		Integrity
Modesty	Grey thinking	Calmness	Calmness
	Free from arrogance and rashness		Great ease
	Inclusiveness		

Source: Organized by the author

Selective Coding

Selective coding is to refine the core category within the categories after open and axial coding and to develop a storyline that describes the phenomenon or event. In turn, a novel theoretical model can be constructed. By analyzing and coding the textual data in the previous two phases, we have conducted an in-depth study on the logical relationship between the primary categories of entrepreneurial vision. The entrepreneur's profound research reflects their enthusiasm for knowledge and technology and rigorous attitudes toward entrepreneurship. The entrepreneur's patriotism shows he is always concerned about national rejuvenation and prosperity. Due to entrepreneurs' dedication to knowledge and technology and their strong sense of national responsibility, they develop great ambitions and pursue excellence in their hearts. It determines the entrepreneur's lofty aspirations or pursuit of ideals and requirements for self-realization. The entrepreneur's perception of self-worth determines the depth of thought. Entrepreneurs' mindset and understanding of the connection between things are determined by how much they tolerate other people and facts (modesty) and how much they want to work together for mutual benefit (win-win cooperation). Cognition and thinking greatly influence the entrepreneur's approach and specific business behaviors. It is reflected in whether entrepreneurs control decisions with great courage, handle crises calmly, and keep promises to others. At the same time, the realm of thought also affects whether the entrepreneur has a unique vision.

The nine dimensions of entrepreneurial quality, cognition, thinking, approach and action constitute the comprehensive quality of entrepreneurs' career pursuit. Furthermore, finally, "entrepreneurial vision" is found to summarize all the categories to describe and discuss entrepreneurs. Therefore, entrepreneurial vision is defined as the core category. The axial coding yields nine categories (profound research, aspiration, perspective, modesty, courage and insight, win-win cooperation, patriotism, promote-keeping, and calmness). The nine primary categories that constitute entrepreneurial vision are shown in Table 3-5. In this study, the primary and secondary categories, concepts and labels are correlated through selective coding. Based on this, it constructs a complete theoretical framework of entrepreneurial vision.

Table 3-5 Selective Coding

Core category	**Primary category**
Entrepreneurial vision	Profound research
	Aspiration
	Perspective
	Modesty
	Courage and insight
	Win-win cooperation
	Patriotism
	Promise-keeping
	Calmness

Source: Organized by the author

Multi-case Comparative Analysis

Based on the single-case study of entrepreneur Ren Zhengfei, this study summarizes and constructs a theoretical framework model for describing entrepreneurial vision in contemporary China. However, since the above conclusions are drawn from the single-case study, the theoretical model is far from theoretically saturated. First, the categories are only derived from Ren Zhengfei's case, insufficiently depicting contemporary Chinese entrepreneurs. Second, the relationship between the categories is only derived from Ren Zhengfei's case, with insufficient universality. Third, the categories are conceptually derived only from Ren Zhengfei's case but have not been saturated. Fourth, successful cases are usually conducive to generalizing categories as necessary conditions. The adequate requisites for these categories can be screened only through testing negative cases. Therefore, other contemporary entrepreneurs should be analyzed in detail.

The process and idea of analyzing the cases of the remaining 12 entrepreneurs are similar to Ren Zhengfei's case. That is to say, open coding, axial coding and selective coding are performed on the textual information of each case, and then the concepts and categories embedded in each entrepreneurial case are analyzed. Then, the logical relationships between the primary and secondary categories are analyzed to form a complete storyline.

The qualitative research and analysis of the textual data of the subsequent entrepreneurial cases are also conducted through an ongoing comparative analysis process. The preliminary concepts and primary and secondary categories summarized previously also guide decoding subsequent cases. In analyzing the subsequent cases, we identify some new concepts and primary and secondary categories that cannot be summarized in the original cases. These categories are then compared and analyzed with the previous decoding results, and even the concepts and categories in the previous cases are modified. The spiral comparative analysis across cases allows for a more precise formulation of concepts and categories and the inter-logical relationships between categories. The concepts and categories are almost saturated by the fourth entrepreneurial case (containing Ren Zhengfei's single case study), but new orientations (labels) are still emerging. By the sixth case, no new orientation emerges.

Meanwhile, Luo Yun, Zhu Jianmin, and Feng Jiujing case data are chosen to verify the saturation of concepts, categories, orientations, and relations. The results show that the model has good theoretical saturation and validity. In addition, the adequacy of the categories summarized in the successful cases is tested through the negative case of Qian Dawei. Table 3-6 shows the specific results of the new categories, concepts and orientations obtained from the comparative analysis of the remaining sample cases of entrepreneurs.

Table 3-6 New Categories and Orientations from Subsequent Case Studies

Case	New concept	New Orientation
Pony Ma	Bottom-line thinking, active change	Touching the sensitive point of the industrial economy, foreseeing the prospect of China's Internet, the first to propose "pan-entertainment" (perspective); the courage to appoint non-top talents to compete with strong rivals (modest); localized technological innovation, progressive technological innovation, the integration of the culture of engineers and product managers, and the cross-border pan-entertainment field (win-win cooperation); image change (promise-keeping);
Dong Mingzhu	Cross-border operation, moral responsibility	Pursuit of "Made in China" to the world (aspiration); proactive establishment of efficient and agile market mechanisms, future perceptions of smart home development (perspective); green technology innovation (courage and insight);
Yu Minhong	Teaching by precept and example	Parenting, proper teaching of children, moral education, sense of competition (patriotism);
Lei Jun	-	Commitment to building an integrated ecological chain, the pursuit of changing the social and industrial patterns (aspiration), rapid product iteration to respond to consumer demand (calmness);

Case	New concept	New Orientation
Chu Shijian	-	Revolutionary goals and the pursuit of fulfillment as the spiritual pillar (aspiration); investment layout of cigarette, planting a variety of crops to avoid risk (perspective); courage to invest in enterprises on the verge of bankruptcy (courage and insight);
Wang Chuanfu	-	-
Li Shufu	-	-
Duan Yongping	-	-
Positive case validation	Data from three cases, Zhu Jianmin, Feng Jiujing, and Luo Yun, are used to test the saturation of coding and modeling. No new categories are derived from the analysis of the three cases. Therefore, it is proved that the category coding meets the requirement of theoretical saturation.	
Negative case validation	The categories generalized from the positive cases are necessary for entrepreneurial vision. Negative cases can further test those categories to create necessary and sufficient conditions for entrepreneurial vision. Hence, Qian Dawei of Company M is added as a negative case of insufficient entrepreneurial vision, as a test of necessary and sufficient conditions for entrepreneurial vision. All the categories summarized in the previous section are necessary and sufficient conditions for entrepreneurial vision.	

Note: The content in parentheses in the Orientation column is the category.
Source: Organized by the author

Nine case entrepreneurs selected are analyzed for textual data and three cases for data validation. A theoretical model of entrepreneurial vision in contemporary China is described as follows.

The entrepreneur's profound research reflects his desire for technical knowledge when starting and running a business and his down-to-earth, relentless pursuit of industry knowledge. They brainstorm and quickly absorb knowledge from various sources and turn it into competence when encountering difficulties in knowledge. The patriotism of entrepreneurs stems from their strong national and social conscientiousness derived from their family-country integration and practical experience. Because of this, entrepreneurs are always concerned about the revitalization and prosperity of the nation in their business practices. Because of these two core qualities, entrepreneurs develop the spirit of pursuit of excellence and strong ambition. It determines entrepreneurs' cognition of high ambition, which is also the pursuit of their ideals and requirements for self-realization. Entrepreneurs' cognition of ambition determines the depth of their thoughts. It determines whether the entrepreneur's mind has the modest and open-minded thinking of accepting advice, accommodating the team and grey thinking.

Moreover, it determines whether the entrepreneur thinks of win-win cooperation in sharing values and ideas, concerted effort internally and enabling externally. The depth of such thinking also defines the entrepreneur's way of thinking and his/her understanding of how things are interrelated. Cognition and thinking greatly influence the entrepreneur's dealing with people and specific business behavior. It is reflected in entrepreneurs' courage in implementing important decisions such as innovation, organizational boundaries, and investment, their ability to remain calm in the face of crises, and their ability to keep their promises to customers and others. At the same time, the entrepreneur's state of mind also affects his/her evaluation of environmental changes and business development and determines whether the entrepreneur has a unique vision.

This study maps out the logic between the nine primary categories, deriving a theoretical model of entrepreneurial vision in contemporary China, as shown in Figure 3-1.

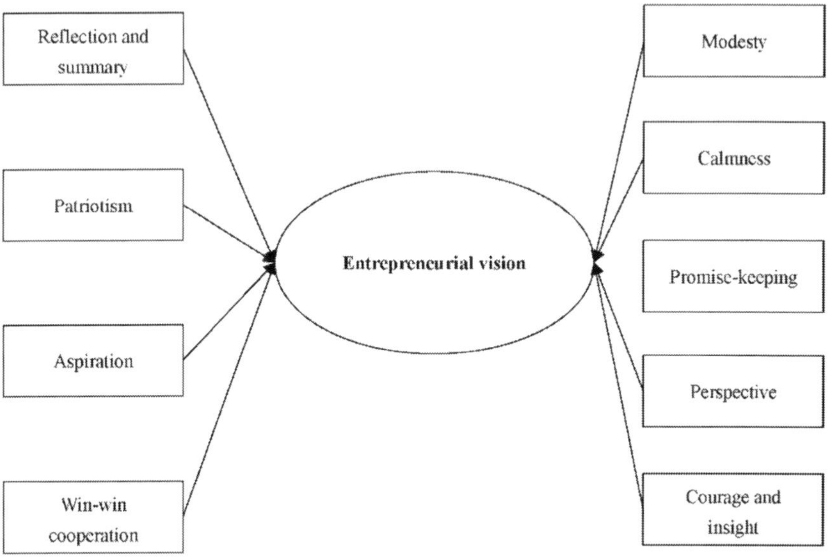

Figure 3-1 Theoretical Model of Entrepreneurial Vision in Contemporary China

Source: Organized by the author

Results of Data Analysis and Theoretical Construction

Entrepreneurial vision is the comprehensive embodiment of the entrepreneur's ambition, concept, courage, insight, composure, perspective, thinking, quality, breadth of mind and philosophy in entrepreneurial business and pursuing career achievement. Entrepreneurial vision is the entrepreneur's thinking, conception and control of the links between the country, society, enterprise and personal development. It synthesizes epistemology, methodology, leadership qualities, and behavior. Entrepreneurs' vision reflects their deep thinking about the country, society, enterprises and individuals. It directly affects the vision and mission of the enterprise led by the entrepreneur, which in turn determines the future of the enterprise and the height of its development. Entrepreneurs' realm and vision represent and determine an enterprise's future. Entrepreneurial vision is pivotal in whether an enterprise can be respected, internationally renowned, and sustainable. This paper summarizes the nine dimensions of entrepreneurial vision (aspiration, patriotism, courage and insight, calmness, perspective, profound research, promise-keeping, modesty, and win-win cooperation). The following is an analysis of the connotations and characteristics of each of these dimensions of entrepreneurial vision.

Aspiration

Aspiration refers to the business philosophy of an entrepreneur who, in pursuit of the peak of knowledge and technology and the growth and development of a business, strives to pursue career aspirations and excellence despite the difficulties encountered. Entrepreneurial aspiration is found in an entrepreneur's personal business philosophy. It is also permeated in the company's grand vision and deep corporate culture that the entrepreneur leads. Also, it constantly inspires the members of the company to make breakthroughs. Aspiration has three core dimensions: strong ambition, pursuit of excellence, and indomitable spirit.

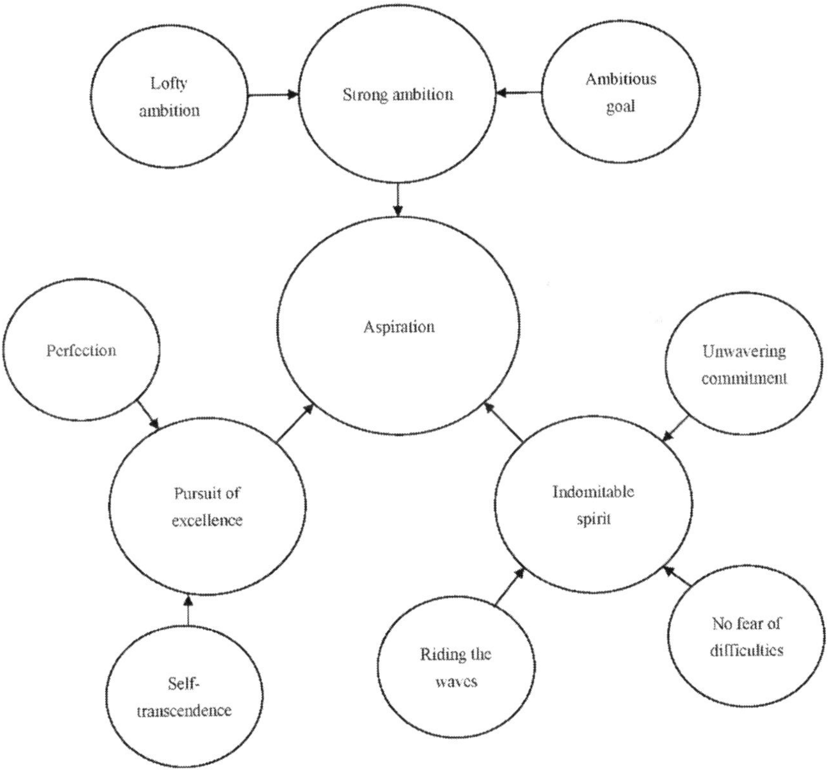

Figure 3-2 Dimensions of Aspiration

Source: Organized by the author

(1) Strong ambition

Strong ambition refers to the entrepreneur's extraordinary ambition and lofty ideals in his pursuit of changing the world and contributing to the country in entrepreneurial operations. It combines the entrepreneur's worldview, outlook on life and values, which are highly condensed and summarized from their management and operation of the enterprise and their personal experiences. Strong ambition contains two dimensions: lofty ambition and ambitious goal.

1) Lofty ambition refers to an entrepreneur's lofty intentions and determination to establish a business. Entrepreneurs with lofty ambitions are patriarchal and uphold the qualities of profound research. Because of this, they have lofty ambitions from the beginning of their businesses. Furthermore, they persistently and pragmatically apply their courage, calmness, insightfulness, and integrity to realize their ambitions. Ren Zhengfei set up Huawei with the lofty ambition of "making contributions to China." Moreover, he has continuously strived for world-class technology products on this path. Li Shufu dreamed of establishing a company that "manufactures affordable cars for the common people" when founding Geely Automobile. He has been struggling on this path. These cases reflect entrepreneurs' lofty ambition to lead their companies' development. In contrast, Company M's founder, Qian Dawei, had a shallow ambition, and his joy, prestige, and sense of purpose in life was to have the right to command others. So, founding a company and dominating its employees was his quest in life. The company is also destined to be extremely limited in its development height.

2) Ambitious goal is the goal that an entrepreneur pursues in his or her efforts to start and run a business against all odds. Entrepreneurs' lofty ambition reflects more the direction of their management efforts, while their ambitious goal reflects their commitment to leading their companies. Ren Zhengfei, the founder of Huawei, set the corporate goal of capturing the domestic market, developing overseas markets based on independent R&D, and following the world's advanced technology. Wang Chuanfu, the founder of BYD, set the ambitious goal of building a world-class automobile company when he led BYD to the automobile industry. It guided BYD's ground-breaking growth. On the other hand, Company M's founder, Qian Dawei, was the first to put his product into the local market

for sale from the time he developed his first product. However, he did not watch the foreign market until his followers built the same product. Subsequently, Company M was overtaken by its peers. Regarding specific targets, Company M released its sales performance targets for the next three years (RMB 1.5 billion in 2019, RMB 1.6 billion in 2020, and RMB 1.7 billion in 2021) at the "2019 Distributor Conference and New Product Launch." Midea's target in 2019 was over RMB 200 billion for exports alone.

(2) Pursuit of excellence

The pursuit of excellence means that when an enterprise is marching towards an ambitious goal under the lofty ambition of the entrepreneur, the strong ambition of the entrepreneur is broken down into specific targets for each stage of the enterprise's development. Furthermore, entrepreneurs utilize their capabilities and strengths to reach each goal while maximizing their resources. Thus, they strive to make their companies top-notch in the industry. Entrepreneurs adhering to the management concept of the pursuit of excellence play a pivotal role in promoting enterprises to break through technological barriers, enabling them to realize ground-breaking development, self-reliance and renewal. The pursuit of excellence has two core dimensions: perfection and self-transcendence.

1) Perfection. Entrepreneurs should lead their companies in pursuing knowledge and technology leadership, gaining market share, and controlling the supply chain and costs. They require their core team members to continuously research, develop, and keep pace with or surpass the top companies in the same industry. At the same time, entrepreneurs strive to efficiently configure the company's existing resources to produce the best results. Ren Zhengfei asked Huawei's R&D team to target the world's top technologies and to build a perfect R&D team. He emphasized the importance of meeting customer needs with top-notch technology. Wang Chuanfu has made great business profits from BYD's batteries and automobiles while maintaining a keen interest in batteries and automobiles. He knows all the technical details within BYD and has dominated the R&D of revolutionary technologies such as the blade battery for BYD cars. All the above cases show that the entrepreneurial vision of the pursuit of perfection plays a great role in leading enterprises' steady development.

2) Self-transcendence. Entrepreneurs are not satisfied with the current achievements of their enterprises but continue to explore management, operation, technology and other aspects to maximize their abilities and potentials. Compared with perfection, which involves catching up with the benchmarks and the best, self-transcendence is more about entrepreneurs' self-reflection on the development of the enterprises they lead. They strive to achieve perfection in all aspects of their business and even overcome their bottlenecks. Entrepreneurs' self-transcendence permeates the macro-vision and culture of their enterprises. Because of this, enterprise members are always vigilant, hungry, and constantly examining themselves to keep a humble learning attitude for enterprise development. Lei Jun chose to leave Kingsoft at its prime to go beyond himself and start a new business. He eventually led Xiaomi as a leading Internet company. In implementing Huawei's fundamental principles, Ren Zhengfei constantly emphasized the difficulty and importance of self-denial and transformation. Under his leadership, Huawei managed to overcome various crises with great ease.

(3) Indomitable spirit

Indomitable spirit. Although entrepreneurs may meet many difficulties, setbacks and challenges in realizing their strong ambitions and pursuing excellence in business management, their ambitions remain steadfast in their hearts and minds. They do not shrink from difficulties or succumb to failures and blows. Entrepreneurs with an indomitable spirit never give up easily or fear difficulties. Their perseverance brings the company together as a team with an iron will and guides the formation of an organizational culture of unity and solidarity. The indomitable spirit has three core dimensions: unwavering commitment, no fear of difficulties, and riding the waves.

1) Unwavering commitment. Entrepreneurs are strong-willed and never give up or change their lofty ambitions despite the many obstacles. Entrepreneurs' unwavering commitment and determination to never give up affects the entrepreneur-centered TMT to create a team with an iron will. When Huawei's independent R&D was frustrated in the early days of its establishment, Ren Zhengfei did not abandon his pursuit of products and technologies. Ultimately, they successfully developed the C&C08 digital SPC switch, which changed the direction of Huawei's development.

2) No fear of difficulties. Entrepreneurs are confident and motivated to overcome difficulties and obstacles and realize their ambitions when pursuing lofty ambitions and excellence. Entrepreneurs' spirit of no fear of difficulties will continuously motivate and inspire employees to face challenges and difficulties. In turn, it gradually forms an organizational atmosphere of no fear of difficulties and dangers and the courage to make breakthroughs, injecting strong psychological prophylaxis for the enterprise to meet the crisis and winter. Ren Zhengfei led Huawei through the stormy times without fearing the crisis. Furthermore, he did his best to fix the loopholes and develop new opportunities, eventually leading Huawei to survive the crisis. Wang Chuanfu met many obstacles in product development and design when he ventured into the automotive industry. However, he did not surrender but faced up to the problems and led the team to make a success. Ultimately, Wang Chuanfu transformed from a "battery expert" to an "automotive expert."

3) Riding the waves. In pursuing lofty ambition and excellence, the entrepreneur overcomes difficulties, learns lessons and experiences from them, and then moves forward. The unwavering commitment emphasizes the entrepreneur's firm will against difficulties; no fear of difficulties highlights the entrepreneur's confidence and motivation in the face of difficulties and crises. Riding the Waves focuses more on the entrepreneur's reflection and learning in meeting the challenges of overcoming obstacles and difficulties. Duan Yongping, after failing to invest in a foreign company at a low point in its history, constantly reminded and pushed himself to use his mistakes as a wake-up call. Eventually, he led his company to the top of the financial world step by step.

Patriotism

Patriotism refers to the quality of responsibility that entrepreneurs always care about the rejuvenation and prosperity of the nation in running their business. Nurtured by the excellent traditional Chinese culture, entrepreneurs highly identify with the Chinese nation and the value community of China. As a result, they are motivated to work for the people's well-being and the nation's rejuvenation in their lives and careers. Entrepreneurs who exhibit strong patriotism fulfill corporate social responsibility more vigorously, contributing to the growth of the company's social prestige and reputation within the supply chain. Patriotism has three core dimensions: family-country integration, social responsibility, and national responsibility.

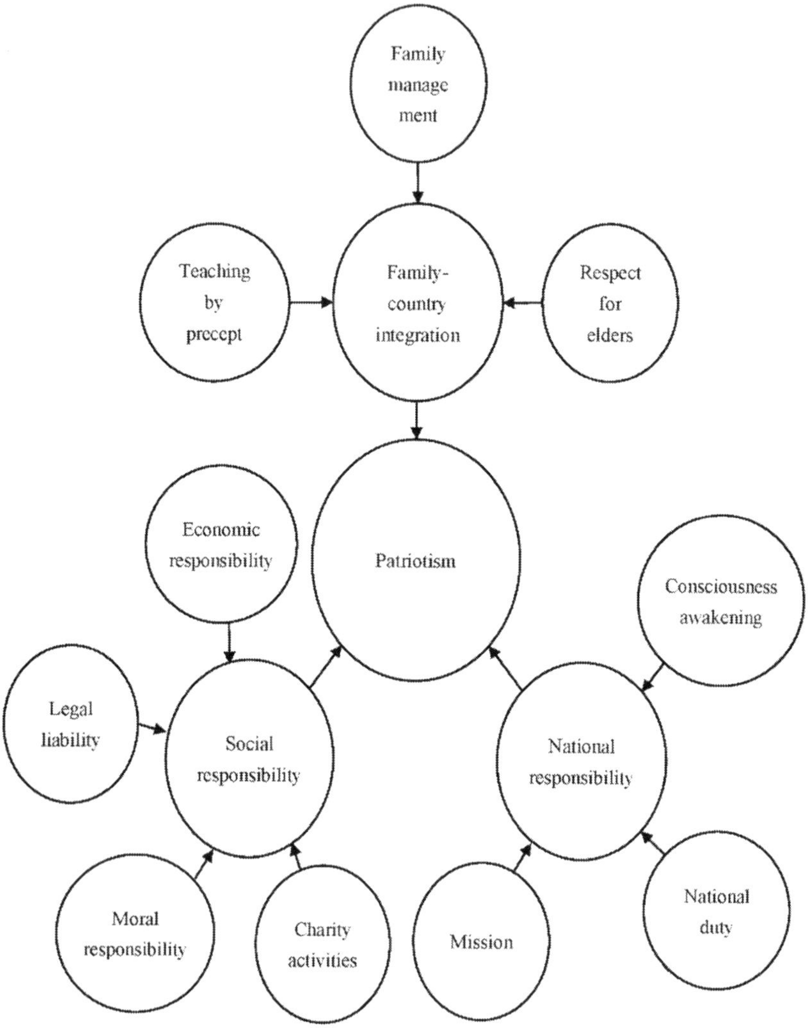

Figure 3-3 Dimensions of Patriotism

Source: Organized by the author

(1) Family-country integration

The concept of family is a key element in traditional Chinese culture, and the concept of linking the family with the country and analyzing the commonality of their organizational structures is called family-country integration. The family is a "small family," and "small families" constitute the country. The business organization serves as a link between families and the country. Entrepreneurs with excellent entrepreneurial vision pay great attention to family management, respect for elders, and setting a good example for their juniors in their "small family." These "small family" elements also affect the entrepreneur's thinking in managing the enterprise, handling the organization, and training the employees. Family-country integration contains family management, respect for elders, and teaching by precept and example.

1) Family management. Entrepreneurs have strong family concepts and family conscientiousness and pay great attention to the construction of family culture and family rules. Entrepreneurs who emphasize family management have a strong sense of family values and mission. They introduce these concepts and missions into their enterprises to form a strong organizational atmosphere of family consideration. Because of this, the employees in the organization are also cared for like a family, facilitating the formation of a cohesive organizational culture. Although Wang Chuanfu seldom talks about his family to his subordinates, the core team knows that he is hardworking and diligent, and highly attached and conscientious to his family. His strong family values and conscientiousness inspire and motivate the core team. Ren Zhengfei's responsibility to his family eventually led him to give up his job in the public institution and start his own business. Moreover, he formulated The Huawei Basic Law to create a wolf team with a collective concept.

2) Respect for elders. Entrepreneurs treat their elders with courtesy and respect and attach great importance to their words and deeds. Entrepreneurs' humility and respect for their parents and elders within the family will be embedded in how they treat their business partners and core team members. In turn, it facilitates building harmonious relationships and team trust and lays the conceptual foundation for building a harmonious and robust long-term internal and external environment. Although Ren Zhengfei has devoted all his energy to Huawei, he still cares about his parents during his busy work. His respect for elders has been practiced in his work, so he has built harmonious partnerships with many partners.

3) Teaching by precept and example. Entrepreneurs educate their juniors verbally and in action. They set an example by how they deal with

people, guiding the juniors to grow up quickly and on the right track. Entrepreneurs set a positive example for their families. They also act as role models for their subordinates in the workplace, guiding them on the desired path for the company's long-term development. Therefore, it is conducive to building the company's core competence with the entrepreneur's signature. Dong Mingzhu is a disciplined person in both life and work. At the same time, she takes herself as a role model for her son and hopes that he can also be strict in his studies and life. Dong also brings her education of her son to the growth of Gree, building an R&D team with a rigorous and meticulous attitude; Yu Minhong is concerned about his children's growth with patience and care. He teaches his children how to treat others and gives them corrections when necessary. Yu guides his children's correct growth into EASTBUY's education philosophy. He asks the teachers at EASTBUY to guide every one of their students through their schooling.

(2) Social responsibility

Social responsibility. The public expects enterprises to fulfill their economic, legal and ethical responsibilities at a certain stage of their development. Academic research on social responsibility has shown that enterprises actively fulfilling social responsibility can achieve good external benefits, such as improved consumer satisfaction. It also significantly affects the internal members of the organization, such as improving employees' sense of belonging to the organization and enhancing their work efficiency. Therefore, entrepreneurs' active fulfillment of social responsibility creates a favorable cultural atmosphere. It also reflects the patriotism of entrepreneurs who dedicate themselves to their country. Social responsibility comprises economic responsibility, legal liability, moral responsibility, and charity activities.

1) Economic responsibility. Entrepreneurs take the initiative to adapt to and lead the new normal of economic development. They implement the new development concept from their enterprises' reality, accelerate enterprises' transformation and upgrading, and intensify innovation's driving force. Moreover, they make new and greater contributions in supporting and cooperating with the Party and the government in properly solving tax issues, developing a mixed ownership economy, and boosting the sustained and healthy development of the economy. Ren Zhengfei

organizes an installation team with strong technical capabilities and a sense of responsibility in direct contact with customers to satisfy customers' needs. The team provides users with high-quality and advanced after-sales services. It promotes Huawei's technological innovation and upgrading in communication technology and leaves a good impression of Huawei on the customers. Li Shufu acquired Volvo Cars and absorbed foreign advanced technology to improve the quality and safety of automobile products. He also invested heavily in R&D within Geely Group for safety and quality improvements. Because of this, Geely Group's automobile technology has risen from being a follower to being at the forefront of the world in some of its technologies. Furthermore, it has pushed Geely to transform and upgrade from assembly and imitation to independent R&D.

2) Legal liability. Entrepreneurs must operate by the law and strictly abide by various laws and regulations in their production and business activities. Moreover, they should build a comprehensive corporate governance structure and provide employees with a healthy and safe working environment. Outside the organization, they should uphold the principle of fairness in competing with rivals in the same industry and not pollute the surrounding environment. After being sued by Cisco, Ren Zhengfei resolutely responded with the weapon of law and eventually resolved the infringement crisis. Although Huawei is not listed on the capital market, it pays taxes actively, abides by the law, and is responsible for its customers and employees. Luo Yun of Oxiranchem clarified from the beginning that the company's strategy and culture should align with national laws and regulations. He requested that the company's strategy be based on respecting the laws and regulations and tailored to the company's development orientation.

3) Moral responsibility. Entrepreneurs should lead their enterprises to conduct their activities orderly, conforming to the basic social ethics of fairness and justice. Enterprises should not violate business ethics and social morality in their operation and production. In fulfilling moral responsibility, entrepreneurs should actively protect the rights and interests of employees and consumers, create value for them, and provide consumers with high-quality services and products. They should strive to create a harmonious and healthy organizational culture and provide opportunities for employee development. Dong Mingzhu, who runs Gree

Group, has always been committed to creating a harmonious consumer environment, protecting consumers' legitimate rights and interests, and actively fulfilling moral responsibility. Gree eventually won consumers' trust with its honest and self-disciplined spirit and "Made in China." Wang Chuanfu has worked hard to build BYD's culture on fairness. Wang endeavored to improve BYD's internal rules and regulations, especially the fairness of the personnel promotion and evaluation system, which is open and transparent without any black-box operation.

4) Charity activities. Entrepreneurs actively lead enterprises to participate in public welfare activities and rescue disadvantaged groups. They contribute to social harmony and progress and improve people's living standards. Moreover, they are enthusiastic about charity activities and actively fulfill their social responsibility, facilitating the harmonious unity of corporate and social interests. The participation of entrepreneurs in charity activities is a mutually beneficial behavior that protects the long-term interests of their enterprises. It can effectively enhance the image and popularity of enterprises in social responsibility and foster the growth of enterprises into sustainable and renowned enterprises. Wang Chuanfu was awarded the "Charity Model with the Most Caring Behavior" title for his passion for philanthropy, raising BYD's visibility in social work. Duan Yongping donates when he recognizes the correct value of the recipient, and he once confessed that rational donation has become a way for him to enjoy life. The BBK Group, which he leads, is also highly regarded in the community.

(3) National Responsibility

National responsibility. Entrepreneurs take the initiative to undertake the historical mission, task and responsibility for the great rejuvenation of the Chinese nation. Most of today's outstanding Chinese entrepreneurs grew up when Chinese people struggled to build the PRC. While growing up in an era characterized by patriotism and the spirit of national rejuvenation, young people were deeply immersed in the atmosphere of "studying for the rise of China.". Therefore, entrepreneurs proactively shoulder the mission of national rejuvenation, actively fulfill the national duty in their respective fields, and are quite aware of it. They realize that they can only break the monopoly of foreign enterprises by their R&D investment in core technologies. Ultimately, they can strengthen the country and rejuvenate the nation.

1) Consciousness awakening. Entrepreneurs gradually recognize the gap between their enterprises, the industry, and the leading foreign giants during difficult business operations. They eventually developed their unique management philosophy by combining advanced experiences and lessons learned in China and abroad with their internal and external environments in China. In Huawei's operation process, Ren Zhengfei has always maintained an awareness of unexpected development and deep thinking about enterprise management. Such awareness and thinking have contributed to Huawei's endogenous drive for continuous growth and development, making Huawei sustainable and dynamic. Li Shufu was frustrated by the business practices during the early development of Geely. He gradually realized that if Geely wanted to grow and become a role model for national cars, it could not manufacture cars by purchasing the necessary components but should develop and learn to walk independently. It is the awakening of the consciousness of independent R&D that has created the national brand Geely today.

2) Mission. Entrepreneurs lead their companies to strive hard to improve their business. At the same time, entrepreneurs lead enterprises to find their positions and seriously operate the business. They should also shoulder their historical mission and lead the industry. Ren Zhengfei dares to challenge the strongest competitors in the industry. To strengthen the independence of the national industry and gain a foothold in the Chinese and international markets, he is determined to tackle the core technology and build a Chinese brand to compete with the foreign giants. Dong Mingzhu's vision of "making the world fall in love with Made in China" is accompanied by her mission to make the world fall in love with Chinese brands. In contrast, Company M's founder, Qian Dawei, was motivated by his desire to eliminate being looked down upon. He lacked a broader mission, and Company M was considered "private property" by the founder once it developed to a specific level.

3) National duty. Entrepreneurs actively fulfill their duties and obligations to the great rejuvenation of the Chinese nation while running their businesses. Compared with the mission, national duty emphasizes that entrepreneurs should take the initiative to undertake those duties that come from the commitment to the nation, society, and the enterprise. They

should also conform to the requirements of the industry and the ethical norms. A strong sense of national conscientiousness characterizes Chu Shijian's corporate values. Under his leadership, the Yuxi Cigarette Factory upgraded itself from importing to exporting. Having weathered the storm, the factory eventually became a national brand unique to China. Ren Zhengfei's leadership of Huawei in developing the global market is fueled by his strong sense of conscientiousness in rejuvenating China.

Courage and Insight

Courage and insight. Entrepreneurs dare to put their insights and judgments into action by making key decisions about the development of their businesses. Starting a business is like climbing to the top again and again. Entrepreneurial business requires extraordinary courage and insight. If an entrepreneur has no spirit of adventure, courage or determination, his or her enterprise may miss development opportunities. The enterprise led by an entrepreneur without great courage and insight may be excellent, but it will never become admired as an outstanding enterprise. Under the leadership of entrepreneurs who lack courage and insight, the enterprise acts prudently and steadily. It can only keep pace with or follow the top enterprises in the industry and can hardly dominate and lead the industry. The three core dimensions of courage and insight are innovation orientation, breaking boundaries, and prompt decision.

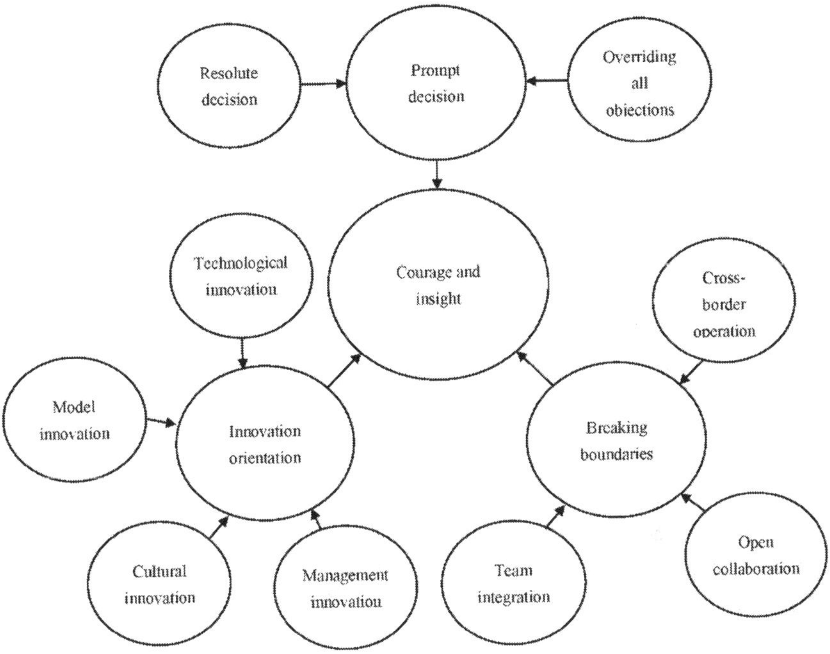

Figure 3-4 Dimensions of Courage and Insight

Source: Organized by the author

(1) Innovation orientation

In entrepreneurial practice, entrepreneurs strive to master core technologies and seek original breakthroughs in the industry. Moreover, they constantly lead the enterprise team to explore new areas in business practice and reflection. They stimulate new ideas by summarizing innovations with courage. The innovation of enterprise technology, model, culture and management examines whether entrepreneurs can think deeply and broadly and have great ambition and strong enterprise conscientiousness. It also examines whether entrepreneurs can uphold the realistic and pragmatic style in management and have profound knowledge of the industry. It also requires entrepreneurs to be highly courageous and adventurous, bold in exploring and daring to fail. Innovation orientation contains four aspects: technological innovation, model innovation, cultural innovation, and management innovation.

1) Technological innovation. Entrepreneurs are unsatisfied with their current technology level after learning and keeping up with the leading

technology of advanced enterprises in the same industry. On this basis, they dare to invest in R&D of production technology even if they are unsure whether they can overcome the bottleneck of technology, eventually making breakthroughs in original technology. The innovation of production technology is an important source of competitive advantage for enterprises and an essential guarantee for sustainable development. Entrepreneurs have superior courage and insight to lead enterprises' technological innovation. So they will not stand still and refuse to make progress. On the contrary, the enterprises forge ahead to reach the peak of the industry technology to maintain their core competitiveness, thereby dominating the competition with their competitors. Wang Chuanfu pursued the innovation of battery technology with great courage to dismantle the technological barriers of leading multinational enterprises. Under his leadership, BYD realized technological innovation in the core battery of new energy electric vehicles and became an industry leader in new energy batteries. Pony Ma has implemented progressive technological innovation in computer software with a strategy of trial and error and iterations. By listening to users' opinions and combining them with his thinking about products and services, his team has eventually developed many "national" software products. Under the leadership of Pony Ma, Tencent has transformed from being accused of simply copying and imitating its foreign counterparts to becoming a trend-setting giant in the Internet industry today. Pony Ma's insightful approach to technological innovation has been instrumental in the transformation of Tencent.

2) Model innovation. Entrepreneurs analyze previous enterprises, think about their business practices, and refine the basic logic to change the enterprise's value creation. In this way, they can enhance customer value and enterprise competitiveness. Business model innovation may include changes in the constituent elements of multiple business models or changes in the relationships between the elements or in the dynamics of the mechanism. Business model innovation helps companies to differentiate themselves from their competitors, and the products and services they provide are not homogenized. Business model innovation affects the organization internally by lowering management costs and improving resource allocation and productivity. Outside the organization, it can improve the ability to realize customer value and seek more

competitive edges and profits for the enterprise. However, business model innovation also means the organization must adjust and change its structure, strategy and size. In the process of change, many vested interests inside and outside the organization may persuade or even threaten entrepreneurs to give up innovation and change. Conservative forces may be reluctant to take the initiative to seek innovation or fear that a change may lead to many unfavorable situations. However, entrepreneurs with a great vision believe in their judgment and make bold decisions. When Ren Zhengfei reinvented Huawei's customer demand system, the future benefits were unclear. However, Ren resolutely decided to innovate Huawei's customer demand system, ultimately laying the foundation for Huawei's internationalization. Dong Mingzhu gradually developed a unique Gree business model in the long-term market practice. The model was promoted from top to bottom within the Gree Group. As a result, Gree has been ranked No. 1 in air conditioner sales worldwide for many years, paving the way for Gree to realize its vision of "making the world fall in love with Made in China."

3) Cultural innovation. To align the development of the enterprise with the internal and external environments, entrepreneurs learn from the experience of their predecessors and the market operation practice. According to the nature and characteristics of their enterprises, they form an enterprise culture that embodies the common values of the enterprise with the entrepreneur's business philosophy, followed by continuous innovation and development. Organizational cultural innovation is pivotal for a large enterprise, especially for an enterprise targeting the international market. However, it also places higher demands and requires more courage on entrepreneurs. Once the decision of cultural integration and innovation fails, it affects the operation and production efficiency of a department or a process of an enterprise. Also, it will negatively affect the atmosphere of the whole enterprise. While actively bringing in overseas talents to set up R&D centers worldwide, Ren Zhengfei has also been engaged in inclusive cultural innovation, striving to eliminate narrow corporate and national cultures. He eventually found a new cultural balance between national culture and internationalization. Pony Ma creatively integrated the engineer and product manager cultures in Tencent, complementing their strengths and weaknesses. Ultimately, Tencent's

corporate culture was formed with integrity, enterprise, collaboration, creativity, user focus, and technology for the good.

4) Management innovation. Combining changes in the internal and external environments and strategies, entrepreneurs use scientific knowledge and methods to link the development of the organization's members with its ambitious goal and vision. They improve the benefits of the entrepreneur's activities by adjusting and changing how the organization is managed. Entrepreneurs lead the development of organizational management innovation, facilitating the realization of corporate strategy and attracting key talents. Thus, it lays the organizational guarantee for the enterprise's technological innovation. It helps enterprises to solve the contradictions in product innovation and enhance their core competitiveness. Tencent, led by Pony Ma, was initially a small company founded by a few entrepreneurial members, but it gradually grew into an Internet giant in China. The company has gradually adopted the strategy of building an "Internet+" platform ecosystem by extending internally and externally. As a result, Tencent's organizational management style had to change accordingly. At this moment, Pony Ma innovatively proposed a flexible organization management model that fits the Internet industry. Li Shufu creatively developed more than ten HR management innovations, such as "meta-dynamic projects" and "new shift construction and management" in business practice. It has formed a human resource training system with Geely's features, attracting more and more Chinese and foreign automobile talents to join the Geely Group. Furthermore, it generates unique human resource advantages and promotes Geely to establish sustainable competitive advantages.

(2) Breaking boundaries

Entrepreneurs dare to break the existing organizational boundaries and break through past self-constraints to achieve new progress. Entrepreneurs boldly exceed their limits and break organizational boundaries. Based on this, the enterprise can eliminate the localism that is prone to occur in large enterprises, such as the fragmentation of the functions of organizational departments and the fragmentation of the psychological distance between members. It is more conducive to inspiring organizational vitality, coping with the fast-changing organizational environment, and sustaining its development. The boundary of an enterprise specifies its business scope, partners, team composition and other key elements. With its strong accumulation of resources and experienced members within the original boundary, the enterprise can easily handle business operation challenges. However, it does not positively impact the pursuit of ambitious goals but makes the business bureaucratic. Also, the entrepreneur's efforts to break boundaries may put the organization at risk. Thus, entrepreneurs need the courage and insight to overcome the difficulties and meet the unknown risks. Breaking boundaries contains cross-border operation, open collaboration, and team integration.

1) Cross-border operation. Entrepreneurs lead enterprises to conduct ground-breaking innovations and expand industrial boundaries to pursue lofty ambitions. Cross-border operation is briefly defined as developing and expanding an enterprise's business. It also meets the needs of entrepreneurs to lead enterprises to break the organizational life cycle and stimulate their vitality. Behind it is the entrepreneurs' profound understanding of how the industry develops and how to re-arrange and transform the enterprise strategy. When entrepreneurs operate in a completely unfamiliar field, they are less aware of the knowledge base of the industry, its development and competition. Because of this, they must have the courage to make relatively irrational decisions. With his visionary and courageous venture, Wang Chuanfu led BYD to cross the border from the battery industry to the new energy vehicle industry, which was not highly expected then. As Wang Chuanfu is deeply engaged in the battery industry, he has gained a deep understanding and thinking about the development of the battery industry and transformed the enterprise development strategy. Thus, it has driven BYD to develop into an outstanding enterprise. With his keen insight and courage, Pony Ma formally introduced his "pan-entertainment strategy" at Tencent's annual meeting, marking a cross-border move into the field of pan-entertainment. Tencent became the most important testing ground for Pony Ma's "platform + content" Internet concept. It laid a solid foundation for its later transformation from an instant messaging service provider to an Internet service provider.

2) Open collaboration. Entrepreneur-led enterprises and external partners work together to build a mutually beneficial innovation and collaboration platform based on projects and strategies. Open

collaboration between enterprises is a strategic choice for entrepreneurs to guide the development of their enterprises. Collaboration facilitates the rational integration of enterprise resources, the complementarity of advantages, and the development of new markets. It facilitates enterprises to improve the efficiency of resource allocation, concentrate resources to promote the innovation of the organization's core competence and achieve sustainable development. However, if the development of an enterprise's core competencies is held hostage by a partner, open collaboration poses a great risk to the survival and development of the enterprise. It requires entrepreneurs to evaluate and make bold decisions carefully. Ren Zhengfei knows it is not enough to develop independently, and Huawei needs to strengthen its leadership in core technologies based on open collaboration. Dong Mingzhu and JD have reached an open collaboration strategy that empowers both parties, bringing Internet traffic support to Gree Group and injecting physical economic support to JD.

3) Team integration. Entrepreneurs organize talented members with abilities and beliefs into specific teams to achieve the set goals. They support each other, cooperate to strive for the organization's common goal, and then integrate with team consciousness. In today's environment, entrepreneurs must lead their companies in a volatile and uncertain external environment. Their corporate strategies must change accordingly; because of this, organizations and teams should adapt to changes in strategy continuously. It is a key task for business leaders to accelerate team integration and form synergies in today's era. It is also a major challenge for business leaders. Team integration requires entrepreneurs to break down the organization's long-standing "departmental walls" and have the courage and boldness to meet the challenges of those with vested interests. Tencent realized that its existing business units no longer met the trend of Internet development. Pony Ma firmly established a new collaboration mechanism among Tencent's internal business units to break down the "departmental wall" flexibly. Despite the positive results, in the end, Pony Ma was tested for his courage and boldness in bringing together different members in the process. Against the risk of reduced production efficiency, Wang Chuanfu boldly set up a team to work with different departments for quality assurance of vehicles. The team was responsible for developing the quality assurance model, quality management

objectives, policies and programs. Ultimately, it provides institutional support for the good reputation of BYD's new energy vehicles.

(3) Prompt decision

Prompt decision. Entrepreneurs make bold decisions to seize fleeting opportunities at critical moments in the development of a business, emphasizing their control over the timing of business development. In leading a thriving business, entrepreneurs make resolute decisions without hesitation in the face of opportunity. Otherwise, they may squander their competitive advantage or give away opportunities to competitors. The timing of decision-making is crucial for entrepreneurs and businesses. Even if the decision is correct, but the opportunity is missed, the effect of the decision can be greatly reduced. The prompt decision contains a resolute decision and overriding all objections.

1) Resolute decision. Entrepreneurs dare to give up their immediate or local interests in favor of overall goals and long-term interests and prioritize the enterprise's overall development in their business practices. They base their determination and courage on practical business information, abundant industry knowledge and experience, and scientific and sharp thinking. Based on this, they can make resolute decisions rather than mindlessly making arbitrary decisions. With the wisdom of the industry, entrepreneurs make bold decisions to seize market opportunities. It helps mobilize employees, satisfy customers' urgent needs, and injects confidence into the company's internal development. When Huawei was on the verge of bankruptcy, and its employees had little confidence in the company, Ren Zhengfei boldly made a change and decisively invested in the "chicken ribs" area where others had cut back on their investments. Finally, Huawei has become what it is today. Li Shufu established the Geely Automobile Research Institute at the beginning of the development of the domestic automobile industry. He seized the opportunity to bring in a lot of elite automobile talents for Geely. He contributed greatly to Geely's breakthrough in developing vehicles, engines, automobile electronics and electrical appliances.

2) Overriding all objections. Entrepreneurs try their best to refute and exclude all opinions within the company by seizing the key points of decision-making based on their experience and scientific analysis. Given this, their decisions or opinions can be put into practice smoothly. Ren

Zhengfei, known for his boldness and "wolfishness," has led Huawei's process changes in crises. Even though he was forced to face pressure and difficulties from various parties within the organization, Ren's efforts against all objections drove Huawei to change its processes. Furthermore, ultimately, Huawei has achieved its later success.

Calmness

Enterprises face a variety of risks and challenges in the course of their development and growth. Excellent entrepreneurs remain calm and composed in various crises and are not frightened or panicked. They remain calm through careful thinking and flexible responses. It is also the connotation of entrepreneurial calmness. Entrepreneurs keep calm and think carefully in a crisis, enabling the enterprise to survive the crisis peacefully. More importantly, entrepreneurs' calmness enables enterprises to expand in an orderly manner rather than making blind decisions during their rapid expansion. It plays a key role in steadily improving a company's core competitiveness. Calmness has two core dimensions: rising to the occasion and great ease.

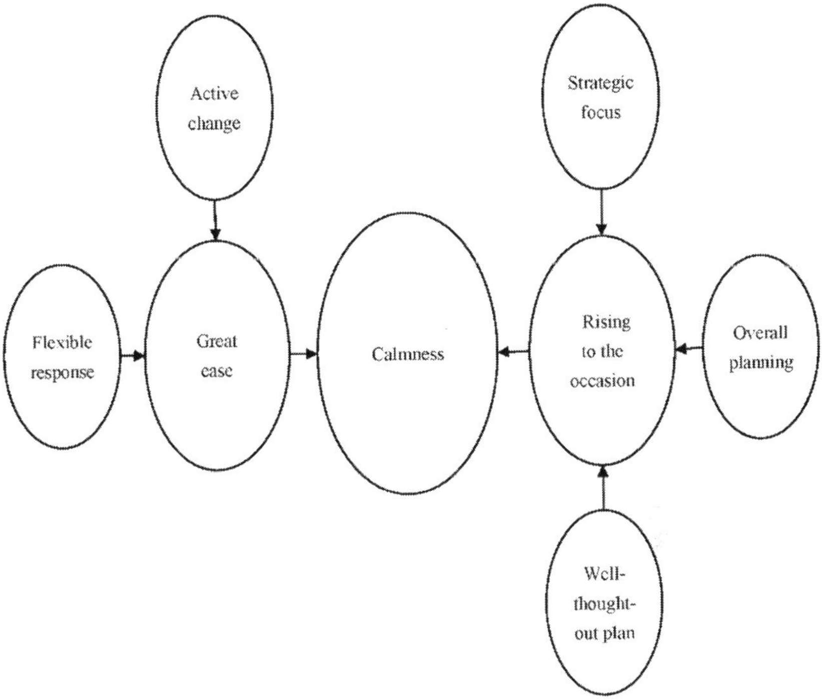

Figure 3-5 Dimensions of Calmness

Source: Organized by the author

(1) Rising to the occasion

Entrepreneurs can deal with the crisis and risk challenges of the enterprise by keeping calm and not panicking. Entrepreneurs may encounter various risks and challenges in leading the enterprise for production and management activities. They may affect the development and even the survival of the enterprise because of sudden changes in the internal and external environments. Entrepreneurs rising to the occasion can implement a comprehensive management plan for crisis outbreaks and take the initiative in crisis management. Entrepreneurs rising to the occasion attach great importance to the impact of crises and challenges on the company. They can always obtain effective information, gain industry experience and knowledge, and acquire scientific analysis capabilities. T to determine the extent of damage to the enterprise crisis to assess the effectiveness of the crisis plan. Based on this, they can make timely adjustments and revisions to the plan. Eventually, they can lead the enterprise to safely resolve the challenges of the crisis to the survival and development of the enterprise. Rising to the occasion includes strategic focus, overall planning, and a well-thought-out plan.

1) Strategic focus. Entrepreneurs have the strategic confidence, will and perseverance to realize their ambitions and grandiose strategic goals in an intricate and complex business environment. Entrepreneurs will make tactical adjustments in response to the risky challenges of the environment. However, they trust and adhere to the corporate strategy in the face of crisis and challenges. Therefore, they may not easily change the corporate strategy before the external situation has changed in a disruptive way. Rather, they may lead the enterprise to maintain its strategic direction and work towards its milestones. Entrepreneurs are confident and persistent in their strategies to form a strategic focus. It is conducive to the solid business and development of the enterprise to ensure that the enterprise can steadily progress to a sustainable business. Ren Zhengfei has maintained his composure during Huawei's unprecedented survival crisis and insists on exercising and working daily. Ren Zhengfei's ability to face the crisis so openly was due to his confidence in the strategic goals he set for Huawei at the company's beginning and his ability to control the company's business decisions from a holistic perspective. Yu Minhong maintained strategic focus even when EASTBUY was being sued and investigated in the U.S. Eventually, he successfully resolved the crisis with perseverance and persistence and paved the way for EASTBUY to be listed in the U.S. capital market in the future.

2) Overall planning. Entrepreneurs can think from the enterprise's overall situation and recognize the industry's development and changes. They can plan, integrate and coordinate the organization's work and think creatively to serve the overall development of the enterprise. In the face of crisis and challenges, entrepreneurs look at the interests of the enterprise as a whole and care for this and lose that. Nor do they lose the greater for the less. They take into account and coordinate the interests of all stakeholders within the enterprise and the enterprise as a whole and then lead the enterprise to resolve the crisis. Dong Mingzhu took over Gree Group at the time of the crisis. In response to Gree's weak product strength and poor market feedback, she coordinated the entire value chain from

R&D to sales to create quality products from a holistic perspective. Moreover, she insisted on grasping and satisfying the real needs of customers. Dong's holistic approach enabled Gree Group to rebuild itself against the wind and gradually grow into a business card for Chinese home appliances. Ren Zhengfei, when listening to the advice of a consulting firm to set up a management team, gave up his role as EMT chairman. Instead, he utilized a rotating chairmanship system that balanced the interests of all parties and enabled the company to grow in a balanced manner. He has also demonstrated his ability to make up for Huawei's shortcomings and to cope with the subsequent bottleneck.

3) Well-thought-out plan. Entrepreneurs who lead the development of their enterprises have a strong sense of confidence in their strategies, decisions and plans to deal with crises. Therefore, they always remain calm and confident in the face of crisis. Strategic focus emphasizes the entrepreneur's perseverance and persistence against difficulties, while overall planning emphasizes the entrepreneur's overall thinking and execution ability in response to crises or business development problems. A well-thought-out plan reflects an entrepreneur's calmness and comfort in knowing that the strategy, plan, or decision he or she is leading can successfully resolve a crisis. Ren Zhengfei scientifically recognizes Huawei's weaknesses.

For this reason, he used Huawei's strengths while trying to make up for its shortcomings when formulating his development strategy. It played a crucial role in Huawei's response to the existential crisis. Li Shufu made a plan to acquire Volvo Cars. At the time, the world was threatened by the economic crisis, and Geely was also affected, and its business efficiency declined. However, Li Shufu still had a good idea of the acquisition plan and believed that acquiring Volvo Cars would greatly improve Geely. The final development of Geely also confirms Li Shufu's thinking.

(2) Great ease

Great ease. Relying on extensive business experience, entrepreneurs draw on comprehensive and careful reasoning, calculations, analysis and generalizations to anticipate the risks and challenges before planning, formulating and executing a business decision or strategic goal. Moreover, entrepreneurs can summarize a well-developed plan of execution and response and adjust the plan in response to the environment. Ultimately, they can resolve crises calmly and skillfully. Entrepreneurs are always subject to the constraints of the business environment. If they persist in implementing the original plan, their enterprises may deviate from the expected trajectory or even suffer a business crisis. When the enterprise faces a crisis, flexible entrepreneurs may follow the trend and adjust the enterprise plan according to the environmental changes, bringing the enterprise out of the crisis. Great ease consists of flexible response and active change.

1) Flexible response: Entrepreneurs adjust their organizational strategies and plans to cope with the adversity of drastic changes. Focusing on their core resources, they cultivate their main business, consolidate the foundation of development, and enhance the competitive advantages of their enterprises. In a crisis, the entrepreneur's flexibility in responding to the market environment helps to minimize unnecessary losses compared to competitors. It is also conducive to maintaining the enterprise's scale and industry position, creating a competitive advantage for the enterprise. With the challenges of changing user demands in the mobile Internet era, Lei Jun broke the traditional order of brand building. They organized the rapid iteration of products for brand building to satisfy consumer demands. Under Lei Jun's flexible leadership, Xiaomi has gradually gained a unique competitive advantage. Ren Zhengfei has led Huawei to develop rapidly in the high-tech industry, where crisis and opportunity coexist. The core of this success is that Ren has always emphasized the need for Huawei to make timely adjustments to meet the rapidly changing market needs.

2) Active change. Entrepreneurs have been leading companies engaged in their main business for many years. Thus, they can anticipate and recognize potential risks and challenges based on their knowledge and experience in the industry. Then, they can take the initiative to change the status quo and actively explore greater benefits and competitive advantages for the enterprise. Entrepreneurs' flexible response to crises is more of a passive approach to challenges. Nevertheless, active change means that entrepreneurs, under their in-depth commitment to the industry and forward-looking vision, can proactively position themselves in the changing situation and develop a new path to cope with the crisis. Ren Zhengfei remained calm when Huawei was relatively small and threatened with a life-or-death crisis. Furthermore, he continued to seek technological

and business innovations and breakthroughs in the communications industry until he found a way forward.

Perspective

Good entrepreneurs can detect changes in the environment, emerging opportunities and hidden crises more accurately and sensitively than other leaders. The entrepreneur's sensitivity to environmental changes is mainly attributed to his or her future perspective. Entrepreneurs always seek new ideas and changes as they strive for self-transcendence, excellence, and dedication to research. They are constantly in touch with the sensitive frontiers of industry and society and develop a highly open international perspective. Moreover, they are keenly aware of and anticipate the future trends and prospects of the industry and the related changes in economic relations. Based on the future perspective, entrepreneurs accurately grasp opportunities and plan the overall layout and business mechanism using systematic thinking and the enterprise's strategic objectives. In growth and change, enterprises are exposed to many known and unknown crises. Entrepreneurs with unique perspectives have a keen sense of risk and adopt bottom-line thinking in decision-making and control. They emphasize crisis alertness and risk management and control. Perspective comprises three core dimensions: future perspective, strategic positioning, and risk perception.

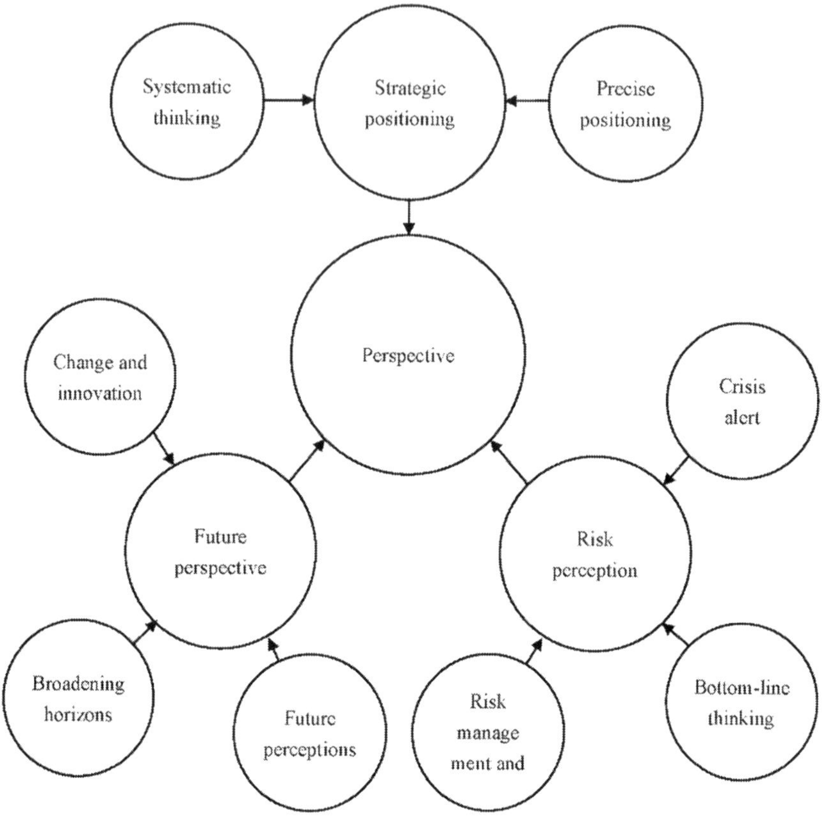

Figure 3-6 Dimensions of Perspective

Source: Organized by the author

(1) Future perspective

Future perspective. Entrepreneurs are deeply involved in the industry and have direct access to the sensitive needs of the industry and the market. As a result, they can observe, think and solve problems in a wider scope of the industry and the market. So, compared with their competitors, entrepreneurs can see further and have an economic, technological, and international perspective toward the industry's future. In the digital era, entrepreneurs are faced with the challenge of rapid changes in the market. They should see the changes and development trends of the international economy, industry and technology, grasping the general patterns. If an entrepreneur does not see the future of development, he or she will lead the enterprise forward as if he or she were a blind man feeling an elephant. How far an enterprise can go and whether it can become a century-old enterprise depends on how far the entrepreneur's perspective is. The future perspective contains change and innovation, broadening horizons, and future perceptions.

1) Change and innovation. Entrepreneurs take the initiative to grasp the international economic, industrial and technological changes and development trends, and even more should grasp this new trend to meet the demand for proactive breakthroughs and innovation. Innovation for development has become a necessary path for enterprise development. With the accelerated pace of economic development, enterprises would be abandoned by consumers and the market if they did not initiate innovations. Entrepreneurs rely on the future perspective to seek innovation and maintain the foundation of their business. It helps maintain and enhance an enterprise's core competitiveness, enabling it to gain a head start in dealing with the development of the digital era. Wang Chuanfu captured the trend of new energy electric vehicles with his keen future perspective. He proactively pursued innovations in battery technology to reduce costs and increase efficiency, laying a solid foundation for BYD's leadership in the new energy era. Pony Ma realized that the ecosystem of the Internet era is changing rapidly. Ma earlier recognized that initiating change and innovation is the key to being an agile enterprise and rapidly iterating products. Enterprises that anticipate problems earlier and take the initiative for change and innovation will not be rendered passive in the marketplace. Guided by Pony Ma's concept of seeking new ideas and changes, Tencent has achieved leapfrog development in the Internet era.

2) Broadening horizons. Entrepreneurs focus on business operation and management and are deeply rooted in the industry and market. They can increase cutting-edge knowledge through industry and market practice and broaden the industry and market insights. Entrepreneurs with broad horizons can better enhance their innovative R&D and organizational management capabilities. Entrepreneurs should combine the practice of traveling thousands of miles with the theory of reading thousands of books in the market context, and further corrections can only be made through market exchanges and tests. They must constantly communicate with insiders and outsiders in the industry, learn from each other, and improve their advanced technology and product experience. They should

constantly develop and produce products in the interest of their customers and gradually expand their horizons in the process. Chu Shijian actively learned from foreign tobacco companies about production, operation and management and introduced foreign advanced technology and equipment. He gradually developed an international vision during the exchange and learning process, laying a foundation for Yuxi Tobacco to go global. Wang Chuanfu met many international investment fund managers through fundraising in the financial market and broadened his horizons through mutual exchanges and discussions. In contrast, Company M's founder spent decades hanging out with several low-quality followers. Moreover, he was heavily nepotistic, ill-informed, and short-sighted. As a result, he lacked the entrepreneurial foresight and the ability to foresee future trends accurately, and his business lost the best opportunities for growth over and over again.

3) Future perceptions. Entrepreneurs can capture the industry's future development direction and opportunities more accurately and quickly from the subtle dynamic changes of the market under their dedication to the industry. Future perceptions emphasize entrepreneurs' sensitivity and accuracy in judging the future development trends of society, industry and enterprises. Broadening horizons describes the longer and broader observations of an entrepreneur with excellent vision compared to an ordinary leader. Entrepreneurs with excellent future perceptions can create unique value for customers. It plays a decisive role in whether a company can make proper decisions and strategies at a critical moment. Through the iterative upgrading of QQ and other instant messaging software and Internet infrastructure, Pony Ma identified the enormous value of entertainment to China's Internet economy. He also saw the later popular concepts of community and localization and the prospect of the Internet and smartphones. With his perceptions of China's Internet future, Tencent advanced the above business areas and eventually became one of China's Internet giants. Dong Mingzhu also noticed the wave of intelligence in the Internet era. With her keen sense of the market, she saw the huge potential of the smart home appliance market. In this regard, she led Gree to lay out the field of smart home appliances in advance. Gree won the battle against Xiaomi, Huawei and other challengers to maintain its dominance in home appliances.

(2) Strategic positioning

Strategic positioning. To realize lofty ambition and the ambitious goals of the enterprises, entrepreneurs define a clear image of their enterprise and products following the changes in the business environment. Thus, they can gain a favorable position among their customers. After determining the market and product positions, entrepreneurs actively explore the characteristics of the consumer segments and engage in precise positioning and in-depth marketing. They establish connections with consumers and eventually create brands efficiently and successfully spread the corporate image, laying the foundation for the enterprise to be recognized by customers and the industry. Strategic positioning consists of systematic thinking and precise positioning.

1) Systematic thinking. When sketching a clear image of the enterprise and determining its position in the industry, entrepreneurs start from the enterprise system, fully considering the different capabilities and potentials of the internal departments for holding and allocating resources. Based on this, they grasp the core key business to take a flexible and effective way to realize the enterprise's strategic objectives. An enterprise is an organic system, and entrepreneurs should establish the idea of subordination of parts to the whole to pursue strategic goals. Organizations should cooperate under systematic thinking, and entrepreneurs should accurately position each organic component of the system to optimize the enterprise. Finally, the strategic goal of the enterprise can be achieved. Ren Zhengfei emphasized the building of Huawei's independent and autonomous scientific research system to realize the strategic goal of industrial independence. To realize the ideal of "manufacturing quality cars affordable to the public," Li Shufu started to build Geely's supply system for globalized procurement of parts and components to reduce costs and increase the efficiency of automotive products. In contrast, Company M's founder, Qian Dawei, lacked systematic thinking and had no idea of organization, system and mechanism. As a result, Company M's management was disorganized, and the company stagnated.

2) Precise positioning. Entrepreneurs outline a clear image of the enterprise and determine the industry's position from the enterprise system, fully considering the different capabilities and potentials of the internal departments to grasp and allocate resources. Based on this, they grasp the

core key business and take flexible and effective ways to realize the enterprise's strategic goals. Compared with systematic thinking, which tests the entrepreneur's overall coordination of the division of labor and cooperation within the organization, precise positioning describes the entrepreneur's sensitivity to changes in the business environment and the accuracy of his or her judgment. Ren Zhengfei promoted Huawei's dual-line precise positioning layout in China and abroad, gaining Huawei a broad market. Pony Ma positioned Tencent as an Internet social service provider and expanded its business layout to related Internet sectors.

(3) Risk perception

Risk perception. Entrepreneurs have accumulated valuable wisdom and experience by fully understanding the market and industry specialization. Moreover, they accurately identify the characteristics and severity of specific risks or potential crises affecting the development prospects of the enterprise. Risks go hand in hand with business activities, and business risks will inevitably arise when a company develops. Excellent entrepreneurs have a keen sense of risk perception and can accurately judge the pitfalls and potential crises on the path forward. Thus, they can lead the enterprise to grow in the right direction. Risk perception includes crisis alert, management and control, and bottom-line thinking.

1) Crisis alert. Entrepreneurs keep a keen sense of possible danger or the wrong trends when they lead the production and management activities of the enterprise. The entrepreneur's sense of crisis keeps the whole organization sensitive to the stimuli of the external business environment. While boldly pursuing strategic goals and corporate visions, they maintain a state of vigilance and criticality so that the enterprise can remain competitive and dynamic. Regarding the sense of crisis, Ren Zhengfei said that he had been thinking about failure every day for more than ten years and was blind to success. Moreover, he did not have a sense of honor or pride in his heart but a sense of crisis. Ren Zhengfei's alertness to the crisis has made Huawei energetic even as it has grown larger and more complex. Pony Ma, who has led Tencent to grow and achieve a leading position in the industry, has often worried about the crisis of Tencent engaging in common malpractices among big companies. Pony Ma has been coordinating Tencent's internal businesses to integrate its advantageous resources. Thus, Tencent has become specialized and made cutting-edge

business innovations, boosting its strength. Comparatively speaking, Company M's alertness to the crisis was sobering. During the SARS outbreak in 2003, many purifier companies tried to raise prices and make huge profits. Company M issued a "Notice to Consumers" nationwide, maintaining the market's stability for some time. However, the company did not seize the opportunity to grow larger in scale, and peers finally surpassed Company M. Qian Dawei, founder of Company M, did not deeply realize the talent crisis and enterprise crisis when top management departed one after another. So far, he still lacks the foresight and risk awareness, so the enterprise has lost too many development opportunities.

2) Risk management and control. Entrepreneurs take various measures and methods to reduce the possibility of challenges and risk events when leading the development of enterprises or to reduce the losses caused by crises or risk events that occur in enterprises. They usually control risks by risk avoidance, loss control, risk transfer and risk retention. During BYD's imitation strategy in its early development, Wang Chuanfu sought to establish a perfect patent management team for risk management and control to avoid the risk of infringement. Pony Ma realized that instant messaging security in the mobile Internet era is a major crisis challenge for the enterprise and industry. For this reason, Pony Ma adopted an evasive strategy and worked with industry partners to develop security labels, improve Tencent's anti-risk and anti-virus capabilities, and manage and control communication security risks in advance.

3) Bottom-line thinking. Entrepreneurs predict the worst-case scenario for their business through industry expertise, business familiarity, and scientific analysis when running their business or pursuing corporate development. They accept this situation and take action. Entrepreneurs with bottom-line thinking strengthen the sense of bottom line, concern and responsibility in team building. To prevent the impact of the worst-case scenario on the enterprise, entrepreneurs enhance the checking of bottom-line management of subordinates, further prevent risks and investigate business problems. Dong Mingzhu is deeply aware that the independent core technologies are the important bottom line that determines the survival of an enterprise. Therefore, she proposes the slogan "Gree mastering core technology" and insists on independent innovation. Thus, Gree can be prevented from the tragedy of its decline due to the introduction of backward external technology. During the 2008 global

financial crisis, the export business suffered a severe blow, revealing Geely's weak resistance to the crisis in its vehicle trading model. Li Shufu reinvented Geely's development model by taking independent R&D of core components and addressing technological challenges as the bottom line. Thus, Geely stood out from many competitors and became an industry leader.

Profound Research

Profound research depicts entrepreneurs' dedication to exploring cutting-edge new technologies and knowledge in their field and their devotion to researching the leading knowledge and technologies closely related to their business's growth and development. Entrepreneurs focus on the industry's core business, constantly learn and absorb advanced experience and technology, and deepen their research in the industry. At the same time, they insist on independent innovation and transform it into a competitive advantage for the enterprise by combining the characteristics of their resources. Profound research has four core dimensions: thirst for knowledge, perseverance, brainstorming, and erudite.

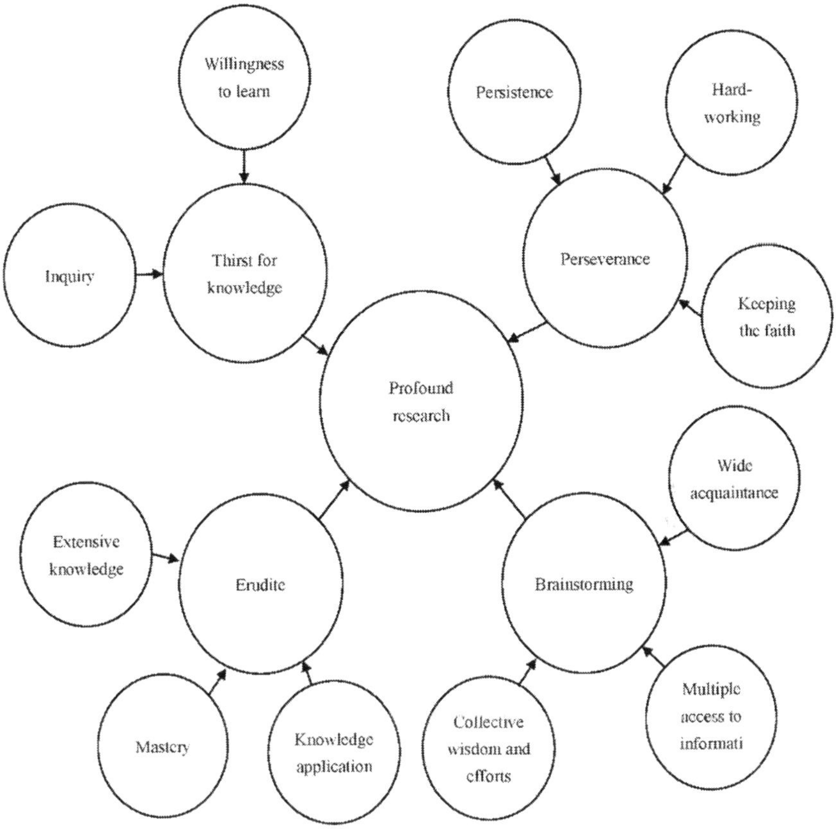

Figure 3-7 Dimensions of Profound Research

Source: Organized by the author

(1) Thirst for knowledge

Entrepreneurs are as eager to seek knowledge as they are thirsty for water, demonstrating their strong willingness to learn and their eagerness to pursue knowledge and technology. They have a strong curiosity about science and technology, a thirst for knowledge, and a dedication to thinking and challenging the status quo. It will inspire the employees to carry forward the spirit of inquiry in their work and create an organizational atmosphere of hard work and learning within the enterprise. Thirst for knowledge has two dimensions: willingness to learn and inquiry.

1) Willingness to learn. Entrepreneurs have a strong desire for knowledge and motivation to learn. They have been curious about the

unknown since they were young, wanting to explore unknown fields and acquire knowledge. Entrepreneurs with a strong willingness to learn are unsatisfied with the status quo, maintain a humble attitude toward the unknown, and endeavor to enhance their ability to learn and innovate. Leadership charisma with the spirit of exploration motivates subordinates or partners to work positively and innovatively. Because of this, organizations are willing to follow entrepreneurs and work according to their visions and aspirations, facilitating the growth of an enterprise into an outstanding enterprise with the entrepreneur's distinctive mark. Ren Zhengfei studied much more than required in college, even in an extremely harsh learning environment. His strong willingness to learn inspired Huawei's team to strive for excellence and innovation. Pony Ma, during his college years, devoted his energy to cutting-edge computer algorithms and novel knowledge, laying a solid knowledge foundation for later founding Tencent.

2) Inquiry. Entrepreneurs are humble and studious. When entrepreneurs realize they lack knowledge or ability in some aspects, they do not mind consulting with those who are inferior to them to compensate for the deficiency. Compared with the strong willingness to learn, inquiry highlights entrepreneurs' humble attitude when they are diligent in learning. A humble entrepreneur incorporates the idea of humility into his or her business philosophy. They are also more willing to listen to consumers and the market's business development and innovation desires. Lei Jun is willing to learn from other regions for the long-term development of his company. Ren Zhengfei leads his team in independent R&D while inviting college students in China to visit Huawei, communicate and seek technological cooperation.

(2) Perseverance

Perseverance. Entrepreneurs do not give up on learning and absorbing new knowledge, new technology, new methods and new ideas when meeting difficulties and setbacks, and embrace the learning challenges with perseverance. Entrepreneurs learn new knowledge and technologies and apply them to the production and operation of their enterprises to serve their customers. They may encounter many technological, personnel and system problems during this process. However, entrepreneurs with great vision will not give up lightly when encountering difficulties and challenges. Instead, they uphold a resilient character, keeping the faith. Perseverance is also embodied in the entrepreneur's long-term planning and operation of the enterprise. Perseverance consists of persistence, hard work, and keeping the faith.

1) Persistence. Entrepreneurs learn from business practice not overnight but for a long time, persistently and tirelessly. Enterprises achieve leapfrog development not through rapid learning and innovation. It requires the management team centered on the entrepreneur to work in the industry daily for years and persevere unceasingly. Ultimately, entrepreneurs can lead their enterprises to become the dominant players in the industry. Ren Zhengfei continued to learn under turbulent and difficult conditions and cultivated sound scientific and technological literacy, contributing significantly to Huawei's leapfrog development. Pony Ma insisted on learning from experience and lessons from practice and consistently revising and iterating on products. In the end, Tencent efficiently developed products well received by users and won market share and customer reputation for the company.

2) Hard-working. Entrepreneurs work hard and never give up on their efforts to study specialized knowledge and enhance their application skills. Persistence mainly depicts entrepreneurs' persistence and perseverance in learning and developing capabilities, while hard work emphasizes entrepreneurs' seriousness and diligence in learning and thinking, regardless of the environment. Entrepreneurs' hard-working spirit allows them to learn, think, and research diligently, regardless of their surroundings. The entrepreneurial example inspired the organization's members, creating a corporate culture where they work hard, think hard, and dare to innovate. Ren Zhengfei studied college courses hard by himself, even during the turbulent times. He carried forward the spirit of hard work within Huawei's R&D team, leading Huawei to achieve breakthroughs in technologies. Thus, Huawei led the industry in R&D. Pony Ma studied computer programming diligently, seriously and solidly in college. When he founded Tencent with his best friend, he integrated his diligence into Tencent's corporate culture.

3) Keeping the faith. Entrepreneurs who keep learning and researching can create a style and faith for their enterprises to sustain their competitive advantage. Entrepreneurs are bound to meet many difficulties and obstacles in their quest for technological innovation and

breakthroughs. Nevertheless, entrepreneurs with a grand vision do not give up easily. They uphold the character of tenacity, keeping the faith. Ren Zhengfei firmly believes that independent R&D is the only way to realize the independence of the national industry. He never gives up no matter how many obstacles and challenges he encounters during the R&D process.

(3) Brainstorming

Brainstorming. Entrepreneurs cannot satisfy the huge needs of their business by themselves on their way to explore cutting-edge technologies. Thus, entrepreneurs must draw on useful ideas, thoughts, or suggestions from various sources. Within the organization, entrepreneurs should mobilize the collective wisdom and efforts of the entire organization. Brainstorming embodies entrepreneurs' wide acquaintance, rich sources of information, and developed learning channels. Brainstorming encompasses three dimensions: collective wisdom and efforts, multiple access to information, and wide acquaintance.

1) Collective wisdom and efforts. While learning new knowledge and researching new technologies, entrepreneurs actively unite internal and external members of the organization to offer advice and suggestions and listen to their opinions extensively. They synthesize information resources from various sources to absorb knowledge and technology efficiently. Entrepreneurs build a corporate culture of collective wisdom and efforts, gradually enabling employees to develop a positive work attitude and enhancing operational efficiency. At the same time, through collective wisdom and efforts, employees can cultivate a sense of ownership and form a robust value chain with external partners. As a result, building, operating and managing a business as a whole is possible, giving full play to the entrepreneur's business philosophy and values. Ren Zhengfei learned from several partners and core management when studying and adapting the organization's management structure and model. He listened to their opinions and suggestions and eventually developed Huawei's operational management team system. In addition, Ren repeatedly emphasized avoiding one-person operations and personal influence in R&D and innovation. He has set an example by actively cooperating with employees in technological and management innovations.

2) Multiple access to information. Entrepreneurs can access information, opinions and resources from all directions. The richness of information resources directly determines the accuracy of the entrepreneur's access to industry trends and technology frontiers. It plays a key role in enterprises identifying the direction of growth and development. Lei Jun made many friends in the Internet industry when he was at Kingsoft. When he realized that the Internet era was coming and founded Xiaomi Technology, he fully mobilized all the available resources and gathered strength from all sides. He overcame the technical difficulties of designing and manufacturing cell phones and provided resources to support the construction of Xiaomi's ecological chain.

3) Wide acquaintance. Entrepreneurs rooted in the core business also make friends and learn advanced management experience and production technology from them. Compared with multiple access to information, wide acquaintance highlights how visionary entrepreneurs treat others with consideration and goodwill. They can learn from their friends and have good interpersonal relationships with them. Wang Chuanfu has been learning from his partners and competitors for many years of business experience. He has made more and more friends, widening his network and winning many friends worldwide. Ren Zhengfei has led Huawei to learn from and cooperate with world giants such as Texas Instruments, IBM, and Motorola. He has also gradually won respect and gained more partners in the process of a long-term partnership, broadening his circle of contacts within the industry.

(4) Erudite

Entrepreneurs have a strong personal capacity for absorbing new knowledge, technologies, methods and ideas. At the same time, they can quickly transform abstract knowledge into practical business skills by combining industry experience and their knowledge. They acquire knowledge through their efforts or by actively working with the organization's internal members or external partners. For the production and operation of a business, a key step missing is to transform abstract knowledge into a tangible ability. Individual entrepreneurs with a good vision should be able to internalize their knowledge. They should quickly turn the abstract knowledge they have acquired into the concrete ability to serve the development of the enterprise through operational thinking.

Erudite consists of extensive knowledge, mastery, and knowledge application.

1) Extensive knowledge. Entrepreneurs are knowledgeable and well-informed. They can only enrich their knowledge and learn from others by cultivating and studying the industry and cooperating with partners in extensive businesses. Only then can they think about integrating and assimilating the strengths of different parties and finally gather resources suitable for their enterprises' development needs. In the age of digitalization, knowledge must be rapidly integrated into the company to adapt to the changing environment. As the leader of a company or an industry, an entrepreneur must be knowledgeable and well-informed to identify the key information that makes a difference in the development of his or her business. Ren Zhengfei has a wealth of knowledge and insights. He has grown up in a difficult environment and has experienced many ups and downs, enabling him to remain calm in the face of Huawei's survival. He can access and learn the knowledge, techniques and methods crucial to Huawei's survival from the vast information resources.

2) Mastery. Through careful thinking and scientific analysis, entrepreneurs comprehensively understand the knowledge, theories and philosophical concepts of enterprise management and operation. They master the knowledge by systematically managing enterprise knowledge. Knowledge management helps entrepreneurs combine information processing and innovation capabilities, thus enhancing the adaptability and foresight of their enterprises. As a result, enterprises can better adapt to the fast-changing environment in today's digital era. Regarding Ren Zhengfei's theory of management reform, Huawei introduced the international management system and analyzed and summarized the system construction according to Huawei's characteristics. Pony Ma learned and extracted China's localized understanding of the Internet from users' big data. He created many novel and user-friendly application tools and programs based on this.

Entrepreneurs can translate the insights gained from knowledge management into the capabilities of practicing business after acquiring and developing their insights. Knowledge management is the management of the core competitiveness of enterprises in the era of the knowledge economy. To transform knowledge into the core competitiveness of enterprises, entrepreneurs must think about how to apply knowledge and transform it into flexibility and innovation. Pony Ma studied computer languages intensively during his college years. Furthermore, he knew how to translate computer knowledge applications into software products, demonstrating his strong knowledge application skills.

Promise-keeping

The entrepreneur honors the promises he makes to others. As an important personal character, integrity refers to the quality of being sincere and trustworthy to win the trust of others. The excellent traditional Chinese culture of business has always advocated integrity management. The promise-keeping means that entrepreneurs lead their enterprises to conduct a series of business activities with integrity as the code of conduct. In modern society, integrity is more than a moral code; it can generate important economic benefits for enterprises. The reputation and credibility of entrepreneurs and their enterprises is a rare and valuable resource comparable to material, human and financial resources to a certain extent. Promise-keeping has two core dimensions: valuing friendship and integrity.

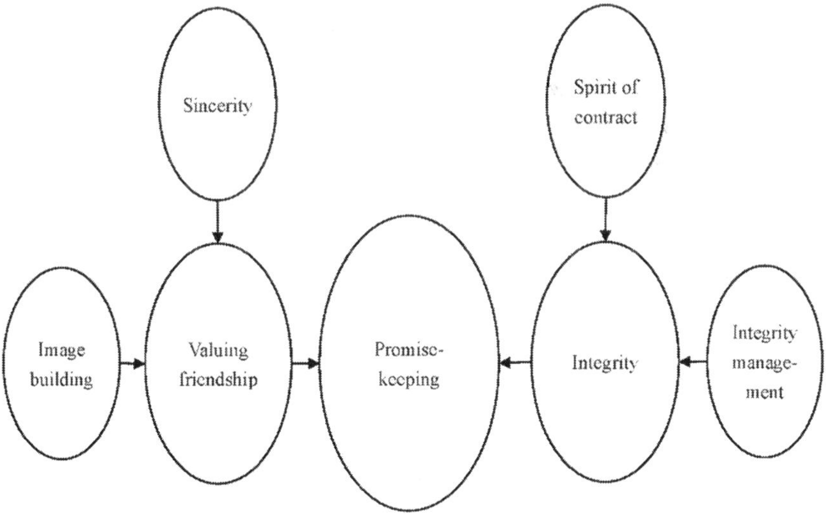

Figure 3-8 Dimensions of Promise-keeping

Source: Organized by the author

(1) Valuing friendship

Entrepreneurs treat their friends and partners seriously and their employees with righteousness. Valuing friendship embodies entrepreneurs practicing honesty, valuing credit and honoring the culture of trustworthiness. It reveals that entrepreneurs emphasize the people-oriented business values of establishing business with sincerity, prospering business with faith, and strengthening business with righteousness. It effectively improves the cohesion and fighting force of the staff team and plays a vital role in promoting enterprises' healthy, steady and sustainable development. Valuing friendship contains sincerity and image-building.

1) Sincerity. Entrepreneurs treat partners, employees and customers with sincerity and honesty and ultimately gain their trust. Entrepreneurs' sincerity in treating team members makes the organization's atmosphere more harmonious and solid. It is also conducive to enhancing employees' identity, sense of security, values and mission for the enterprise. It stabilizes the confidence of the workforce and creates a harmonious working environment and organizational atmosphere. As for external partners, entrepreneurs treat partners sincerely and build a symbiotic and win-win situation with them, continuously enhancing the enterprise's service and innovation capabilities. At the same time, it contributes to the company's reputation and status in the industry. In the company's early days, Ren Zhengfei clarified that Huawei should sincerely impress its customers. It has been proven that many customers in China and abroad are ultimately impressed by Huawei's customer-centered approach to running its business in the interests of its customers. Yu Minhong discusses learning and life with his students at EASTBUY in a frank and open manner when he teaches them. Through word-of-mouth, EASTBUY has eventually built a reputation for Yu Minhong in the education and training industry.

2) Image building. Entrepreneurs should build up a good image of themselves internally and externally through promise-keeping and integrity management. As entrepreneurs are at the core of enterprise management, their images are the external manifestation of enterprise culture. A charismatic entrepreneur directly influences the development direction of the enterprise and the relationship between the enterprise and

internal and external stakeholders. A good entrepreneurial image is the gold standard of an enterprise. Ren Zhengfei presents a positive image and posture in the international arena and always serves his customers with sincerity and truthfulness in his presentations to them. Ultimately, he is recognized internationally as an entrepreneur who treats customers sincerely and with courage. In addition to hardware, Lei Jun's Xiaomi sincerely considers user experience, listens to users' demands, and satisfies their needs through the Internet. Lei Jun establishes the image of an entrepreneur who sincerely treats Mi Fans as his family members.

(2) Integrity

Entrepreneurs uphold honesty and integrity in business practices, abide by their contracts, and match their words with deeds. Honesty reflects the entrepreneur's character. Faith is the sincere fulfillment of the agreement, reflecting entrepreneurs' norms of interpersonal communication in their activities. Integrity is a bottom line and basis for measuring whether an entrepreneur and the enterprise he leads have professional ethics. People cannot gain trust if they have no faith, and an enterprise can hardly establish its business if it has no faith. Integrity is a necessary condition for an excellent entrepreneur and an outstanding enterprise. Integrity consists of the spirit of contract and integrity management.

1) Spirit of contract. In the business society, entrepreneurs agree on the terms and conditions on behalf of enterprises and partners and actively fulfill the spirit of the contractual relationship of freedom, equality and trustworthiness. The spirit of a contract is essentially a form of respect and reverence for the contract, and its effect exceeds the binding effect of morality for both parties. The spirit of contract is one of the important rules of the business society. Entrepreneurs have the spirit of the contract of freedom, equality and trustworthiness, demonstrating their commitment to responsibility. It also reflects the business reputation of the entrepreneur and his or her company. Ren Zhengfei attaches great importance to contractual relationships. Even when Huawei was challenged to survive, he still actively fulfilled the contractual relationship with customers and employees, earning high trust from both employees and customers.

2) Integrity management. In production, operation and management activities, entrepreneurs emphasize honesty and trustworthiness and do their best to obey the law, be honest and trustworthy, treat people sincerely,

and gain their trust. Entrepreneurial integrity is a bridge that promotes effective communication within and outside the enterprise and is the cornerstone for the survival and development of the enterprise. Integrity management is the spiritual impetus to boost the productivity of the enterprise. By shaping corporate integrity as a core value, entrepreneurs attach great importance to human resources, which is the most active element of productivity. Through spiritual appeal, entrepreneurs create sincerity within the organization. It can fully mobilize the organization members' enthusiasm, initiative and creativity. Moreover, employees highly identify with and support the entrepreneur's strategic goals and vision so that the enterprise's productivity can be released and improved. Dong Mingzhu, who leads Gree Group, has always adhered to the entrepreneurial spirit of integrity management and is responsible to the customers and society. She rallied the hearts and minds of Gree's employees and captured its customers, laying the spiritual foundation for Gree's longstanding position as a leader in China's home appliances industry. Ren Zhengfei has always set a good example of honesty and integrity and consistently stressed self-discipline, honesty, a sense of responsibility, and a sense of mission to executives. Ultimately, Huawei has established itself as an enduring and united company committed to excellence. In contrast, Company M tried to bring in an R&D team for technological innovation. The originally planned R&D expenditure was RMB 1 million per year, and Qian Dawei agreed to bring in the R&D team at that time. However, when it came to the cost of bringing in the R&D team, Qian Dawei abruptly changed his mind and reduced the R&D funding from the original RMB 1 million to RMB 200,000 per year. Ultimately, the R&D project failed, and the R&D team did not want to work with Company M anymore.

Modesty

A visionary entrepreneur has a deep commitment to his or her country and is deeply involved in his or her industry, with high aspirations. In pursuing the entrepreneur's aspirations and self-realization, the higher the entrepreneur's awareness of his/her aspirations, the more he/she realizes that he/she cannot achieve the ambitious goals by his/her alone. Therefore, entrepreneurs must be very humble to accommodate all kinds of opinions, both inside and outside the team. They must be open-minded and receptive to the opinions and perspectives of others. Modesty has three core dimensions: grey thinking, free from arrogance and rashness, and inclusiveness.

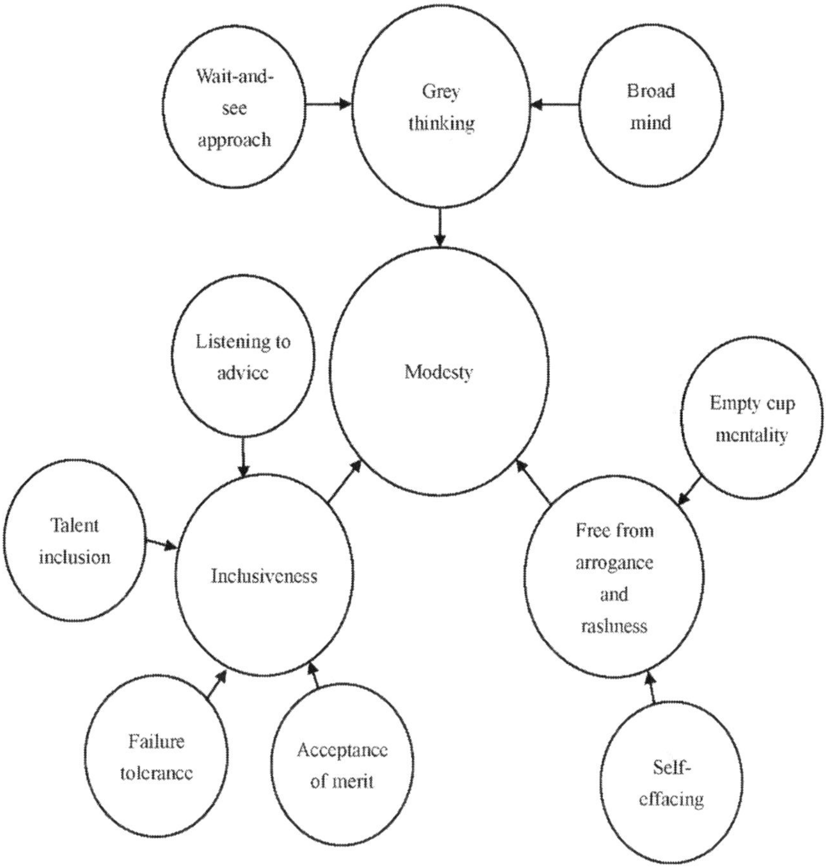

Figure 3-9 Dimensions of Modesty

Source: Organized by the author

(1) Grey thinking

Grey thinking is a non-absolute way of thinking. Entrepreneurs can balance all kinds of contradictions and conflicts inside and outside the organization through their wisdom and ability. The grey scale was originally a photography term, but managers introduced the grey scale into enterprise management. They suggest that managing an enterprise should not be done with all-or-none thinking. Instead, managers should be able to master the appropriate gray scale between black and white. Grey thinking is the manager's professional and calm thinking when dealing with difficult problems in the enterprise. Entrepreneurs manage their businesses without bothering about small matters; wait and see what happens when challenged. They are open-minded and tolerant of criticisms and accusations. It embodies entrepreneurs' grey thinking. Grey thinking contains two connotations: a wait-and-see approach and a broad mind.

1) Wait-and-see approach. The entrepreneur first observes all stakeholders' attitudes and views, then takes different measures depending on different situations and their experiences and analysis. Ren Zhengfei, after soberly considering Huawei's adaptive changes, prudently pushed for a step-by-step change in Huawei's organizational structure. The Geely M&A team, led by Li Shufu, repeatedly researched the situation, hoping to find out the vulnerabilities of the M&A counterparty and especially its strengths. After a sober analysis, he concluded that Geely's strategy aligned with Ford's quest for a responsible seller.

2) Broad mind. Entrepreneurs are broad-minded, generous, and tolerant of others. Entrepreneurs' broad mind embodies their great wisdom. Entrepreneurs should do everything properly in business operations and management. As the Chinese saying goes, a great person's mind should be broad enough for poling a boat. Entrepreneurs with lofty ambitions and aspirations should have a broad mind to accommodate elite talents as they stand tall and see far. They should create an atmosphere of mutual achievement within the company, where all people contribute to one another. Ren Zhengfei has always been willing to accept and correct criticisms of his activities from inside and outside the organization. Pony Ma personally led more than a dozen "Diagnosing Tencent" expert talks after the battle between Tencent and Qihoo 360. He listened with an open mind to the views and criticisms of all sides. Ma faced up to the sharp critics and was open-minded in listening to them. Afterward, Tencent carefully analyzed and responded to all the views expressed at the meeting, removing many obstacles to Tencent's leapfrogging into the world of mobile Internet. In contrast, Company M's founder, Qian Dawei, treated the company as his personal property and had to personally approve the recruitment of a cleaner for RMB 1,000. As a result, it could not retain talented people, and Company M could not grow. Qian Dawei is now 70 years old but still controls the company firmly. The company has lost hope, but it is still struggling to survive.

(2) Free from arrogance and rashness

Entrepreneurs should always maintain a modest and cautious attitude. They should neither be proud of their temporary successes nor be impatient because of immediate difficulties. Entrepreneurs can achieve countless milestones of success and significant outcomes from the start-up to the growth and development of the business. Nevertheless, they always maintain an empty-cup mentality. They are not satisfied with their achievements or arrogant or complacent. Nevertheless, they are willing to remain humble all the time. Free from arrogance and rashness contains two dimensions: empty cup mentality and self-effacing.

1) Empty cup mentality. Entrepreneurs are always challenging themselves and never satisfied in whatever situation they are facing in practice. They readily reorganize the knowledge they possess, empty out the outdated ones, and leave space for the entry of new knowledge to ensure that their knowledge is always up-to-date. They are never complacent but never stop learning, and they are forever refreshed and energized. Ren Zhengfei maintains a sober mindset and always considers himself an empty cup. He is unsatisfied with the status quo and always looks forward to ensuring that Huawei can develop sustainably and not be eliminated by the times. Lei Jun became the general manager of Kingsoft before the age of 30. Nevertheless, he was not content with the success of Kingsoft and wanted to start up again to meet the challenges.

2) Self-effacing. Entrepreneurs humbly treat talent and success and choose to tolerate and compromise to value talents. A humble entrepreneur can build up positive interpersonal relationships within the enterprise. The workforce also feels respected and valued by the enterprise and has a sense of belonging and mission, providing stronger support for the development and growth of the enterprise. To convince Zhang Xiaolong, the founder of WeChat, who did not want to work in Shenzhen, to join Tencent, Pony Ma gave in and set up an R&D center in Guangzhou for Zhang. Lei Jun shocked the industry by creating a miracle with Xiaomi's mobile phones. He modestly says that there is no magic formula for his miracle but that he worked hard with Xiaomi's employees, Mi Fans, and himself to create a satisfactory result. In contrast, Company M's Qian Dawei took things personally. He did not trust anyone except for a few sidekicks. He treats his subordinates as his rivals and often argues over trivial matters. The whole company lacks a culture of trust, tolerance, understanding, mutual

help and friendship. Naturally, the company has lost the power and momentum of development.

(3) Inclusiveness

Entrepreneurs can embrace and accommodate talents of diverse styles and abilities. Broad-minded entrepreneurs practice grey thinking and are open to advice. In addition, they must tolerate the talents and teams within the organization. Entrepreneurs encourage talents and team members to rise to the challenge without fear of failure. They recognize and reward their achievements and encourage their researchers to continue their efforts to make breakthroughs in the field. Especially for high-tech companies, their core R&D team is the lifeblood of their development and survival. In this regard, entrepreneurs should create an inclusive team to promote efficient research. Inclusiveness consists of talent inclusion, failure tolerance, acceptance of merit, and listening to advice.

1) Talent inclusion. For sustainable enterprise development, entrepreneurs tolerate and accept the shortcomings and shortcomings of talents with an open mind and can do it with modesty. Pony Ma, who has always been reluctant to face the media, is tolerant of Zhang Xiaolong's unwillingness to accept interviews. In the final debugging stage of developing a 10,000-gate switch, Ren Zhengfei learned that many engineers were football fans who had just graduated from school. As the World Cup was just around the corner, he listened to his engineers and adjusted their working hours. In this way, the engineers could work and relax simultaneously, providing them with a good platform for development. Ultimately, the team achieved their goal and developed a practical product. In contrast, the former vice president commented on the development of Company M: "Due to Qian Dawei's narrow-mindedness, the company is staffed by locals, aged and poorly educated. There are no talents in the company, only lackeys."

2) Failure tolerance. Entrepreneurs do not blame their subordinates for mistakes or failures but rather tolerate them and encourage them to continue challenging themselves for success. Wang Chuanfu is patient with BYD's technical staff and allows them to make mistakes. Pony Ma encourages internal competition and internal trial and error. He believes that there is no success if there is no failed attempt. Even if some teams fail in the competition, it is still a source of inspiration for the successful ones, which can be interpreted as "internal trial and error."

3) Acceptance of merit. Entrepreneurs have a broad mind to tolerate and accept the merit and achievements created by members of the enterprise and do not feel threatened and challenged because of subordinates' achievements. The entrepreneur's acceptance of team members' merits builds a more solid corporate atmosphere. It also enhances the enthusiasm and sense of mission of the employees. Dong Mingzhu has established a dual-channel development path for management and professional development in Gree. She advocates that "those who are competent are promoted, and those who are mediocre are dismissed" when selecting talents, offering a platform for all kinds of talents to show their strengths. Ren Zhengfei has been rewarding and promoting employees based on their merits and expects this to keep the frontline employees passionate and energetic forever.

4) Listening to advice. Entrepreneurs listen carefully to internal and external advice and make decisions based on that advice after careful consideration and analysis. Management and innovation depend on the feedback of frontline employees, partners and customers. Entrepreneurs with a broad vision realize that advice from all sources is a gold mine. Listening to advice is also a way of communicating with stakeholders. It enables the acquisition of information from stakeholders and strengthens the construction of a harmonious culture within and outside the organization. In the face of Huawei's management structure reform, Ren Zhengfei listened carefully to the feedback of middle management and incorporated the middle management team's suggestions into the organizational process. Dong Mingzhu's morning elevator conversations are the perfect platform for grassroots employees to voice their opinions and express themselves. During the elevator ride, Dong Mingzhu can receive input from frontline employees on the company's development, helping her to identify talented employees.

Win-win Cooperation

Entrepreneurs work together with internal members or external partners of the organization. The two or more parties involved in a transaction or a shared task are mutually beneficial and can accomplish mutual gains. A broad entrepreneurial vision is reflected in an entrepreneur's open-mindedness to accept the opinions of others. Furthermore, entrepreneurs can realize value creation and benefit sharing with internal members and external partners. Win-win cooperation has three core dimensions: concerted effort, enabling, and outcome sharing.

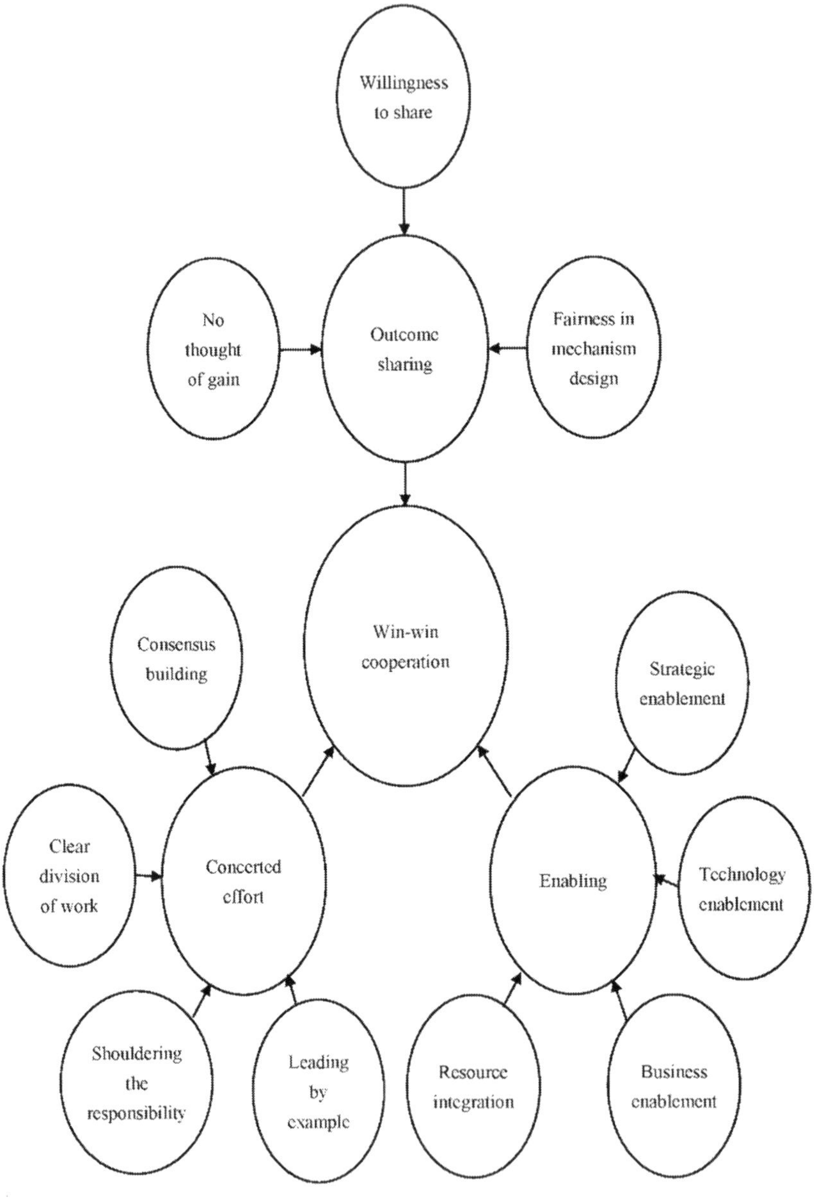

Figure 3-10: Dimensions of Win-win Cooperation

Source: Organized by the author

(1) Concerted effort

A concerted effort is the most important aspect in translating the entrepreneur's thinking of win-win cooperation to each organization member. That is, the entrepreneur brings together the ideas, thoughts, and strengths of the organization's stakeholders around the entrepreneur, or the soul leader, in a concerted effort to achieve the goals of the enterprise. For entrepreneurs to bring members together, they should delegate and share the authority under a precise and clear division of labor. Moreover, they should lead by example when the enterprise encounters risks and challenges. The concerted effort consists of four aspects: consensus building, clear division of work, shouldering responsibility, and leading by example.

1) Consensus building. Entrepreneurs gather different viewpoints, respect differences, tolerate diversity, and form a common understanding of the key aspects of the future destiny of the enterprise. Consensus-building between entrepreneurs and employees clarifies the enterprise's goals and visions and enhances the organization's cohesion. Cohesion is the driving force for the development and growth of an organization and is also an important factor in promoting its survival and development. Under Ren Zhengfei's leadership, Huawei people have reached a consensus that the reason for survival is the customer. From top to bottom, the entire company is focused on the customer, which ultimately enables Huawei to survive and achieve leapfrog development. To this end, employees and Huawei realize win-win cooperation.

2) Clear division of work. Entrepreneurs focus on business, divide the business process into several relatively independent positions as finely as possible, and assign different positions, especially incompatible positions, to different departments for execution. Moreover, the organizational structure or positions are relatively stable and fixed, forming an interrelated and mutually restraining mechanism. Chu Shijian established a perfect quality management system for Yuxi Tobacco Factory. It involves the quality inspection section, TQC office, three-level quality supervision and testing station, and other product quality supervision organizations divided into work and cooperative.

3) Shouldering the responsibility. Entrepreneurs dare to undertake and shoulder the responsibility for the whole organization, contribute to

the enterprise, and realize their lofty ambition and the ambitious goal of the enterprise. Lei Jun consciously undertook his responsibility against counterfeit and substandard pirated software. He coordinated and organized the fight against software piracy and finally eliminated the counterfeits with the cooperation of the whole company.

4) Leading by example. Entrepreneurs set an example for the organization's members through their practical actions. Entrepreneurs leading by example can inspire employees invisibly, achieving an effect beyond preaching subtly. Every move of the business leader affects employees' work, leaving a deep impression on them. In this way, they can better unite members, increase employees' satisfaction and sense of belonging, and improve the company's R&D and production efficiency. Wang Chuanfu started with battery technology but did not abandon his pursuit of technology because of his commercial success. Instead, he spends half his working hours in the research center, leading his team in technological research. In this regard, he emphasizes the importance of BYD's engineering culture. Furthermore, Dong Mingzhu is the role model most often cited by Gree people, as she has seldom taken a vacation but has traveled a lot on business for more than 20 years at Gree.

(2) Enabling

During their cooperation, entrepreneurs and their partners enable each other in business, technology, resources, and strategy. The shared thinking of entrepreneurs for win-win cooperation should be realized by enabling partners outside the organization. Enabling contains four aspects: business enablement, technology enablement, strategic enablement, and resource integration.

1) Business enablement. Entrepreneurs' needs for enablement are met in business development so that the partner's ability for new business can grow from nothing and develop from weak to strong. When facing new needs in cooperation with partners, entrepreneurs take the initiative to negotiate and coordinate with partners to satisfy the needs by reshaping and broadening the business. When Yu Minhong sought out EASTBUY partners, he realized that many of his colleagues and close friends shared thoughts with him and better understood his philosophy. Therefore, he expanded his business and trained his partners in the competencies needed for the new business.

2) Technology enablement. Entrepreneurs work with their partners to help them develop their technological capabilities from scratch, from weak to strong. Technology enablement allows partner companies to be more dynamic in their innovations. With the vitality of innovation, enterprises can gain a foothold in the diversified and individualized market, thus realizing the goal of win-win cooperation. Tencent Cloud, built by Pony Ma, uses information technology such as the Internet of Things, cloud computing, and big data to help Tencent's SME partners build an open and win-win industrial ecosystem.

3) Strategic enablement. Entrepreneurs provide and integrate various important resources inside and outside the enterprise to achieve the partners' mission from the global strategy. Wang Chuanfu joined the automobile industry and decided to focus on electric vehicles, winning the competition in the automobile field with his advantages in batteries. Furthermore, he has helped his upstream and downstream partners in the industry transition to new energy vehicles through strategic integration.

4) Resource integration. Entrepreneurs gather business resources into an organic whole. The integration is not a simple superposition of resources but an organic organization with improved quality of business resources. That is to say, resources are grouped and structured according to the rules of resource integration of the enterprise to enhance the resource utilization capabilities of the partner enterprises. Li Shufu has laid the foundation for the rapid development of Geely Automobile by integrating global automobile resources. On this basis, Geely cooperates with foreign manufacturers to provide them with integrated resources for mutual benefit and win-win results.

(3) Outcome sharing

Entrepreneurs allow members of the organization to share the fruits of the enterprise's growth and development. Entrepreneurs' sharing thinking is not limited to ideas but manifests in sharing value in practice. For the organization's internal stakeholders, the entrepreneur first gathers all the scarce and important resources of the organization and undertakes to consolidate them into clusters. Afterward, they open access to the resource clusters to all project teams or business units, retaining only ownership and oversight of the clusters. Ultimately, it realizes resource integration and sharing. Project teams produce outcomes using the shared resource clusters and transform the outcomes into products or services required by different internal processes or functional units. Based on this, the outcome can be shared within the enterprise, thus realizing the co-production of outcomes. After that, entrepreneurs should create a mechanism for the fair distribution of shared benefits to the organization's members. Finally, the internal cycle of value sharing is constructed. As for the external stakeholders, entrepreneurs emphasize cooperation and sharing with them. Outcome sharing encompasses the willingness to share, fairness in mechanism design, and no thought of gain.

1) Willingness to share. Entrepreneurs are willing to share the fruits and benefits of business development with members or external partners of the organization. Ren Zhengfei knows how to respect and reward knowledge. He introduced the slogan "not letting Lei Feng suffer" in Huawei. When Huawei has made a profit, Ren Zhengfei is happy to share it with everyone. Dong Mingzhu is glad to share the dividends of the company’s development with Gree’s employees and has formulated several incentives for them. She has proposed to help the senior employees handle their household registration problems and provide loans for Gree employees to subscribe to Gree shares. So they can share the profit dividends of the enterprise after holding the shares. On the contrary, Company M has no culture of sharing. Qian Dawei decides on all major and minor matters of the company. Qian wants to put every penny the company earns into his pocket. As a result, the company is short of talent. Those who are capable choose to leave, and those who stay cannot find a suitable job elsewhere.

2) Fairness in mechanism design. Entrepreneurs establish sound, perfect, reasonable, fair and just distribution mechanisms, employee compensation, and promotion mechanisms. Employees are evaluated using a systematic and standardized approach by performance appraisal indicators. Entrepreneurs establish fair competition, promotion, and compensation allocation mechanisms to find and screen out excellent managers and employees for the enterprise, thereby enhancing the ability of enterprise management and innovation and development. Dong Mingzhu has established a promotion process, selection, public announcement, and hiring process for different positions in Gree. Moreover, the employee promotion mechanism is operated fairly, just and openly. Ren Zhengfei has developed a fair internal compensation system

that requires equal pay for equal contributions within the company. The specific evaluation criteria of compensation are, firstly, whether it can help to realize the corporate strategy, secondly, whether it can help to improve the corporate strategy, and finally, whether it can facilitate the organization's growth. In short, Huawei's salary distribution standard evaluates performance objectives fairly and justly.

3) No thought of gain. In sharing the fruits and benefits of enterprise development with members or partners of the organization, entrepreneurs are neither mean nor worry about personal gains and losses. They do not suffer from immediate gains and losses. Entrepreneurs with excellent entrepreneurial vision have lofty aspirations and ambitions and have a longer-term vision than ordinary leaders. Hence, entrepreneurs should consider the enterprise's long-term interests rather than merely focusing on immediate ones. Ren Zhengfei is reluctant to show his face to gain honor and is most concerned with making Huawei a sustainable company rather than personal gain or loss. As a role model for Gree, Dong Mingzhu has often emphasized that she is not personally concerned with gains and losses. Instead, she cares more about whether she can do her job to the best of her ability and lead Gree to grow into an admired and great company.

Summary

Over the past 40 years of reform and opening up, China's economy has been growing at a rate that has attracted global attention. Even uncertainties such as the financial tsunami, the US-China trade war, and the COVID-19 pandemic have not shaken the momentum of China's sustained economic development. Behind such resilience is the entrepreneurial vision shown by countless Chinese entrepreneurs. The entrepreneurial vision with Chinese features can help companies identify, grasp and sustain various opportunities, helping them avoid risks and grow significantly.

After a case study based on the grounded theory, this paper summarizes the nine core dimensions of the entrepreneurial vision with Chinese features (aspiration, patriotism, profound research, vision, modesty, courage and insight, win-win cooperation, promote-keeping and calmness). First, the dimensions of aspiration, profound research and vision facilitate identifying opportunities. Second, the dimensions of modesty, win-win cooperation, courage, and insight facilitate the organization's ability to grasp opportunities. Finally, patriotism, calmness and promise-keeping are conducive to maintaining opportunities. Uncertainty is both a potential risk and an opportunity for greater growth. Entrepreneurs can avoid risks in uncertainty and control the identification, utilization and maintenance of opportunities. It is an important foundation for Chinese enterprises to maintain sustainable performance in an uncertain environment (Figure 3-2). Furthermore, the entrepreneurial vision with Chinese features is the "central pillar" that enables Chinese enterprises to seize uncertain opportunities.

On the one hand, identifying and exploring the above core dimensions and influencing mechanisms facilitate our further understanding of the internal logic of how Chinese companies achieve sustainable development despite the great uncertainty of the digitalization wave. On the other hand, it also facilitates our comparison with Western leadership theories. Thus, we can better interpret the differences between entrepreneurial leadership traits under the influence of Chinese culture and Western leadership, laying a foundation for developing leadership theories with Chinese features.

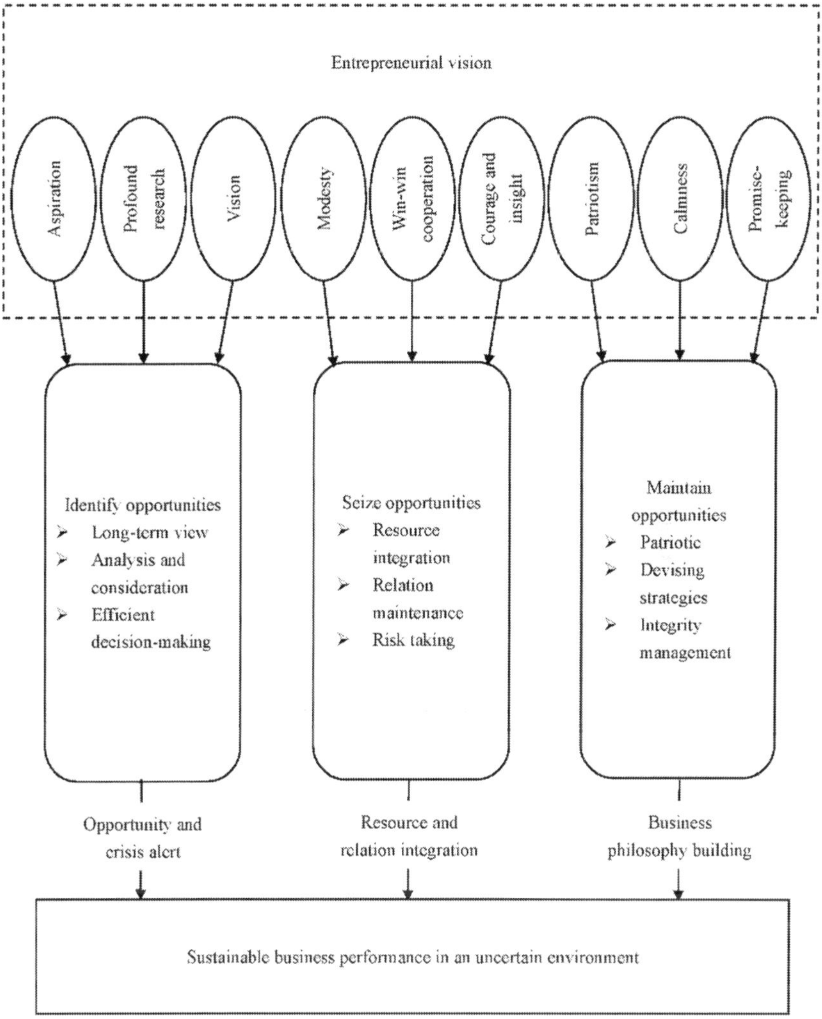

Figure 3-11 A Model of Entrepreneurial Vision Influencing Enterprise Performance in Uncertain Environments

Source: Organized by the author

Chapter 4
Scale Development and Verification of Entrepreneurial Vision

Scale Development

Principles and Steps of Scale Development

Stevens (1971) defines construct measurement as using quantitative methods to describe the degree to which a subject possesses certain behaviors or characteristics according to some rules. The measurement of a variable is the basis for theory testing, and its accuracy determines the reliability of the overall research conclusions. The instruments used in the measurement of variables are called scales. The most basic requirement for a scale is that the data obtained accurately reflect the characteristics of the research subject (Chen et al., 2012). The validity of a scale refers to the consistency between the theoretical construct and the measurement of the scale, indicating the extent to which the scale captures the theoretical content intended to be measured. Scale reliability refers to the consistency between multiple scale measurements and reflects the extent to which a scale can be reused. Reliability and validity are the basic criteria to ensure the quality of the scale. Some principles must be followed in developing entrepreneurial vision measurement scales to develop scales with good reliability and validity (Chen et al., 2012).

First, the target construct should be defined in detail so that the scale developer knows what needs to be measured. Moreover, the scale should be developed to maximize the inclusion of the components of the construct. Second, measurement items should be developed with precise wording and clear meanings. The similarity between the items of this scale and those of other related constructs can be minimized. Finally, efforts should be made to eliminate the influence of random factors in the scale on the measurement results, such as biased expressions in the scale items and the induction of the results due to the layout of the measurement items.

It aims to develop a scale with items highly consistent with the theoretical constructs and good construct validity. For this purpose, the researcher needs to develop and validate the scale step by step through the standardized scale development procedures. In these steps, the more supporting evidence obtained, the better the quality of the scale can be ensured.

In the first step, the researcher must define the construct to be measured clearly. In this process, the scale developer should define the nature of the construct and clarify the difference between the target construct and other similar constructs. They should determine the level of the target construct (individual/team/group) and identify its internal components.

In the second step, initial measurement items should be generated. Scale developers can obtain initial measurement items in two ways and generate initial items by combining the two methods. The deductive approach integrates the existing literature and develops measurement questions corresponding to the scope of the indicators. The inductive approach involves researching the respondents to collect a wide range of measurement items that match the content of the variable and then filtering and categorizing the items. It should be noted that, in generating the database of initial items, the measurement questions should have wider connotations than the target construct. With insufficient certainty, the measurement questions may even contain what eventually turns out irrelevant.

The third step is the evaluation of content validity. Content validity refers to the consistency between the content of the scale and the construct that the researcher wants to measure. Scale developers should evaluate the validity of the measurement questions in the database of initial measurement items and delete those that are easily misinterpreted and do not reflect the content of the construct. Most of the existing studies use qualitative methods to assess content validity. Experts make subjective judgments about whether the target construct is consistent with their knowledge. Some studies have also used quantitative methods to assess content validity. For example, some directly evaluate how well the measure of the construct matches the definition (Schriesheim & Hinkin, 1990). If the quantitative score exceeds 60%, it indicates good validity.

The fourth step is the construct validity test. Scale developers should conduct both exploratory factor analysis and confirmatory factor analysis. Exploratory factor analysis is conducted when there are no clear theoretical expectations for the target construct dimensions applicable in the early stages of development. Confirmatory factor analysis is used when the construct has clear theoretical expectations, and the scale's construct validity is determined by checking the fit between the measurement items and the hypothesized model.

The fifth step is internal consistency and stability evaluation, a reliability test. In addition to structurally conforming to expectations, the scale needs to measure the target construct consistently, stably, and reliably. a Likert scale is usually tested using Cronbach`s alpha coefficient. The reliability is acceptable when the coefficient is greater than 0.7 (Nunnally, 1978). In addition, retesting is performed on the same set of subjects in two periods using the same measurement instrument. The correlation coefficients of the two measurements are examined to determine the reliability of the retest.

The sixth step is the evaluation of constant validity and discriminant validity. Since the latent variables are not directly observed, we do not know whether the scale items measure the target construct or some other related construct. Thus, we should evaluate the scale's constant validity and discriminant validity. Convergent validity means the same construct is measured differently, and the scores should be highly correlated. Discriminant validity tests the difference between a scale and other relevant constructs. The Multitrait-Multimethod Matrix (MTMM, Campbell & Fiske, 1959) is usually used for judgment.

Finally, a logical network of relationships is established. The validity of the scale is further verified through causal inference between variables. If the developed scale yields inter-variable correlations consistent with theoretical expectations, we can infer that the scale has good validity.

Pre-test Scale Development

Following a standardized scale development procedure (Cardon et al., 2013), this paper develops and validates the entrepreneurial vision scale through a three-stage process. First, based on a research paradigm of case study and theoretical inquiry (Nunnally, 1994), an initial item base is developed to measure entrepreneurial vision consistent with the theoretical construct, with nine dimensions coded. Cumulatively, 56 initial items are composed, with more than five items in each dimension. Second, under the guidance of the expert panel, the research team screens the 56 initial items one by one. The specific principles are as follows: Semantically repetitive items are merged. In the dimension of promise-keeping, two items ("I value credit in my business dealings with my partners" and "I fulfill my promises to my employees") are merged into one ("I act on what I say"). Second, items with controversial expressions are removed. In the feedback survey, a controversial expression is found. "It is normal for colleagues and subordinates to be negligent by accident, and they should be given more chances to redeem themselves." Negligence can be interpreted as either general organizational misconduct or illegal behavior with criminal tendencies. Therefore, the subject of this item is controversial and should be deleted. Third, items with incomplete descriptions are deleted. After that, using the Likert 5-point scale, human resource managers of 15 enterprises are invited to evaluate the questions of the pretest questionnaire. They are asked to check whether the items are clearly described, free of ambiguity, and in line with the management practices of their enterprises. The feedback results show that the mean value of 3 items is less than 2.5. After discussion by the expert panel, these three items are revised, and feedback is given to the human resource managers until there are no objections. A 30-item pre-test scale of entrepreneurial vision is finally developed, as shown in Table 4-1. At last, based on the preliminary evidence, a sample group of SMEs in the Greater Bay Area is selected to test further the structure of the developed scale and the criterion-related validity evidence.

Table 4-1 Preliminary Scale of Entrepreneurial Vision

Dimension	Code	Item
Aspiration	ZC_inv1	I want to make the world a better place through my business
	ZC_inv2	I believe that there is always scope for improving the quality of our business
	ZC_inv3	I always reflect on my shortcomings and stay alert to complacency
Vision	YG_inv1	I keep abreast of the latest and most up-to-date industry trends
	YG_inv2	I have a keen insight into market opportunities
	YG_inv3	I can grasp the potential opportunities in the market
Modesty	XH_inv1	I am very tolerant of my friends, family, colleagues and subordinates
	XH_inv2	I am receptive to criticism and do not resent it
	XH_inv3	I am genuinely delighted by the success of my colleagues and subordinates, and I never worry about them surpassing me
Courage and insight	DS_inv1	If there is an innovative project with high risk but high potential returns, I prefer to take a risk rather than miss the opportunity
	DS_inv2	I am not afraid to step out of my comfort zone and develop new business when a good opportunity arises
	DS_inv3	I am willing to make prompt decisions when less informed so I do not miss a critical moment.
Win-win cooperation	GC_inv1	I never care about personal gain or loss
	GC_inv2	I can bring most of the team members together to work towards a set goal
	GC_inv3	I do not mind assisting a colleague or subordinate if they can contribute to a critical task
	GC_inv4	I am pleased to share the results of my cooperation with my colleagues and subordinates
	GC_inv5	I believe in "one for all, all for one"
Promise-keeping	XS_inv1	I act on what I say
	XS_inv2	I believe that reputation is the foundation of an enterprise, and an enterprise that loses its reputation will never have a bright future
	XS_inv3	I would rather lose money than keep my credit when cooperating with other companies

Dimension	Code	Item
Calmness	CB_inv1	I have confidence in my professionalism
	CB_inv2	I am confident in my ability to cope with unexpected situations
	CB_inv3	I adapt to change flexibly
Profound research	YZ_inv1	I am interested in all kinds of cutting-edge knowledge and study whenever I have time
	YZ_inv2	I think we must be humble in learning and not pretend to know what we do not know
	YZ_inv3	I often study and think day and night to figure out a new point
	YZ_inv4	I can quickly put what I have learned from books into practice
Patriotism	JG_inv1	I hope my company can go global as an influential Chinese brand.
	JG_inv2	In my opinion, entrepreneurs must take on more social responsibility after achieving personal enrichment
	JG_inv3	I consider entrepreneurs' moral integrity more important than their ability to make money

Source: Organized by the author

Scale Measurement and Testing

Sample and Pretest Scale Purification

After the initial 30 items for entrepreneurial vision measurement are determined, the scale should be pretested following the basic steps of the scale (Cardon et al., 2013; Scheaf et al., 2018). Three hundred ninety entrepreneurs were randomly selected in Guangzhou based on the Guangzhou Federation of Industry and Commerce and Tianhe District Hi-Tech Management Committee. The questionnaire was distributed to the respondents via email. After two reminders, 93 entrepreneurs did not reply to the email, and 24 said they did not want to participate in the survey. With the exclusion of questionnaires with incomplete and contradictory answers, 169 complete questionnaires were received, with a valid recovery rate of 43.33%. Among the 169 valid samples, 138 of them were male. For age, 13.62% were aged 35 and below, 38.09% were aged 36-45, 31.06% were aged 46-55, and 17.23% were aged 56 and above. By education level,

64.68% had a bachelor's degree or below, and 35.32% had a master's degree or above. By industry, 15.32% worked in finance and insurance, 9.15% worked in construction and real estate, 22.55% worked in machinery manufacturing, 20.64% worked in energy and chemical industry, 21.28% worked in consumer services, 7.87% worked in high technology, and 3.19% worked in water and electricity supply.

This study purified the pretest items against the Corrected Item-Total Correlation (CITC value) criterion. The results (Table 4-2) showed that the CITC values of 30 items were greater than 0.4. In other words, eliminating any item could not improve the internal consistency coefficient of entrepreneurial vision. In addition, the 30 items were divided into high-score groups (top 20% in scoring) and low-score groups (bottom 20% in scoring) using the item discrimination analysis method. The results show significant differences between the high-score and low-score groups ($p<0.001$), indicating good discrimination between the entrepreneurial vision pretest scale items.

Table 4-2 Results of Internal Consistency Test for Initial Scale

Item No.	CICT	Cronbach's Alpha if the item deleted	Item No.	CICT	Cronbach's Alpha if the item deleted	Item No.	CICT	Cronbach's Alpha if the item deleted
ZC_inv1	0.389	0.963	DS_inv2	0.723	0.961	CB_inv1	0.849	0.960
ZC_inv2	0.772	0.960	DS_inv3	0.821	0.960	CB_inv2	0.449	0.963
ZC_inv3	0.365	0.964	GC_inv1	0.364	0.964	CB_inv3	0.861	0.960
YG_inv1	0.779	0.960	GC_inv2	0.818	0.960	YZ_inv1	0.328	0.964
YG_inv2	0.810	0.960	GC_inv3	0.781	0.960	YZ_inv2	0.817	0.960
YG_inv3	0.827	0.960	GC_inv4	0.814	0.960	YZ_inv3	0.818	0.960
XH_inv1	0.768	0.961	GC_inv5	0.829	0.961	YZ_inv4	0.451	0.963
XH_inv2	0.803	0.961	XS_inv1	0.822	0.960	JG_inv1	0.415	0.963
XH_inv3	0.448	0.963	XS_inv2	0.473	0.963	JG_inv2	0.495	0.962
DS_inv1	0.746	0.961	XS_inv3	0.836	0.960	JG_inv3	0.764	0.961

Exploratory Factor Analysis

First, the means and standard deviations of the items were examined to ensure that the responses to each item were normally distributed. Extremely high abnormal distribution may affect the matrix of correlation coefficients with other variables (Nunnally, 1994), affecting the subsequent regression results. The sample was found to be normally distributed through the sample test. The KMO value and Bartlett's test of sphericity are important indicators to judge the adequacy of the sampling and the suitability of the sample data for exploratory factor analysis. According to the rule of thumb, the larger the KMO value of sampling, the more common factors among variables. The common discriminatory criterion is that the exploratory factor analysis is effective if the KMO value is greater than 0.9; it is acceptable if the KMO value is above 0.7; it is not effective if it is above 0.6; and when the KMO value is less than 0.5, the sample data are not suitable for factor analysis (Lu, 2004; Wu, 2010). The chi-square of Bartlett's test of sphericity reaches a significant level, indicating that there is a common factor between the original correlation matrices, and exploratory factor analysis can be performed. The KMO test (KMO = 0.828) and Bartlett's test of sphericity were performed on the 30 items. The results show that the KMO value is greater than 0.7, the chi-square of Bartlett's test of sphericity is significant, and the samples are considered suitable for factor analysis.

With the help of SPSS 23.0 and based on principal component analysis and varimax-rotation method, exploratory factor analysis was conducted following the principle of factor extraction with the characteristic root value greater than 1. Those items whose factor loadings are less than 0.5 or cross-factor loadings are more than 0.4 with a difference of less than 0.2 were eliminated. Finally, six factors and 18 items were developed, as shown in Table 4-3. The factor loadings of these 18 items are all above 0.75, and the cumulative proportion of variance explained reaches 81.27%. Therefore, their factor loading structure aligns with the expectation of coding based on the grounded theory.

Table 4-3 Results of Exploratory Factor Analysis on Entrepreneurial Vision Scale

Item	**Factor structure**					
	F1	**F2**	**F3**	**F4**	**F5**	**F6**
I want to make the world a better place through my business	0.854					
I believe that there is always scope for improving the quality of our business	0.857					
I always reflect on my shortcomings and stay alert to complacency	0.793					
I am very tolerant of my friends, family, colleagues and subordinates.		0.861				
I am receptive to criticism and do not resent it		0.832				
I am genuinely delighted by the success of my colleagues and subordinates, and I never worry about them surpassing me		0.853				
I can bring most of the team members together to work towards a set goal			0.892			

Item	**Factor structure**					
	F1	**F2**	**F3**	**F4**	**F5**	**F6**
I am pleased to share the results of my cooperation with my colleagues and subordinates			0.857			
I believe in "one for all, all for one"			0.901			
I act on what I say				0.833		
I believe that reputation is the foundation of an enterprise, and an enterprise that loses its reputation will never have a bright future				0.825		
I would rather lose money than keep my credit when cooperating with other companies				0.826		
I have confidence in my professionalism					0.820	
I am confident in my ability to cope with unexpected situations					0.835	
I adapt to change flexibly					0.827	
I hope my company can go global as an influential Chinese brand.						0.806

Item	Factor structure					
	F1	F2	F3	F4	F5	F6
In my opinion, entrepreneurs must take on more social responsibility after achieving personal enrichment						0.758
I consider entrepreneurs' moral integrity more important than their ability to make money						0.796
Dimension title	Aspiration	Modesty	Win-win cooperation	Promise-keeping	Calmness	Patriotism
Cronbach's α by dimension	0.835	0.844	0.817	0.839	0.827	0.836
Cronbach's α	0.857					
Cumulative proportion of variance explained	81.27%					

Confirmatory Factor Analysis

The confirmatory factor analysis was conducted using 18 items from the six dimensions of entrepreneurial vision in the above study. The sample is mainly based on the Administration Committee of Songshan Lake Hi-Tech Industrial Development Zone in Dongguan. As a national key development zone, Songshan Lake Hi-Tech Industrial Development Zone gathers many biotechnology enterprises (Huawei Device, Huabei Electronic Technology, Shengyi Technology, TP-Link Technologies, Goertek Intelligence Technology, Hongshanhu Pharmaceutical, Fapon Biotech, Zhongsheng Pharmaceutical, Boao Muhua). The development zone has gathered over 300 biotechnology enterprises and 23 new material enterprises above the designated size. At present, there are 11,389 enterprises registered in the zone. In this survey, 320 questionnaires were distributed by email using questionnaire links generated by Wenjuanxing and Credamo. Finally, 145 complete questionnaires were received, with an effective recovery rate of 45.31%. Among the 145 valid samples by gender, 122 were male. By age, 38.17% were 35 years old and below, 28.44% were 36-45, 14.06% were 46-55, and 19.33% were 56 years old and above. Regarding education level, 56.42% had a bachelor's degree or below, and 43.58% had a master's degree or above. Regarding industry categories, 22.78% worked in biomedicine, 31.09% in electronic information, 17.64% in machinery manufacturing, 11.15% in new energy and materials, and 17.34% in consumer services.

The confirmatory factor analysis is mainly used to determine the measurement model and test the construct validity. This method emphasizes the theoretical significance of the model. We will first test the entrepreneurial vision scale's reliability and then conduct a confirmatory factor analysis of the entrepreneurial vision construct using AMOS. Finally, we will conduct correlation analysis using SPSS to test further the entrepreneurial vision scale's convergent and discriminant validity. The reliability of the entrepreneurial vision scale is first analyzed to ensure the reliability and consistency of the measurement. For Likert scales, the Cronbach alpha coefficient is often used for internal consistency analysis (Wu, 2003). Generally speaking, in scale development studies, the coefficients of the subscale dimensions should be above 0.7, and the coefficients of the total scale should be above 0.8. According to the above criteria, the coefficient of the total scale of entrepreneurial vision is 0.873, and the coefficients of other dimensions are all above 0.830. As a result, the sub-dimension and total scale of the entrepreneurial vision scale have satisfactory reliability.

Next, AMOS is used for factor structure assessment and confirmatory factor analysis using fixed loadings and the maximum likelihood method. Four common metrics are used for the overall fit of the confirmatory factors (the ratio of chi-square to degrees of freedom (χ^2/df), Normed Fit Index (NFI), comparative fit index (CFI), and Root Mean Square Error of Approximation (RMSEA)). Generally, χ^2/df tests the model's fit to the sample data, which should be less than 2. NFI indicates how the model explains the variance of the overall sample data. CFI is a conditioning of the sample size to avoid the interference of sample size. The closer these two values are to 1, the better. Generally, values greater than 0.9 indicate a good model fit. The closer the RMSEA value is to 0, the better. Generally, RMSEA<0.1 is adopted as the criterion. Based on the above criteria, the fit of the six-factor model of entrepreneurial vision is shown in Table 4-4. χ^2/df was 1.055, NFI and CFI were greater than 0.9, and the RMSEA value was less than 0.1, which indicated a good fit. It suggests that the entrepreneurial vision scale has good construct validity.

Table 4-4 Confirmatory Factor Analysis Results of Entrepreneurial Vision Scale

Model	χ^2	df	NFI	TLI	CFI	RMSEA	SRMR
Six-factor model (A, B, C, D, E, F)	126.659	120	0.930	0.995	0.996	0.015	0.041
Five-factor model (A+C, B, D, E, F)	289.215	125	0.839	0.878	0.900	0.075	0.064
Four-factor model (A+B+C, D, E, F)	444.333	129	0.753	0.773	0.808	0.102	0.076
Three-factor model (A+B+C+D, E, F)	601.783	132	0.665	0.669	0.714	0.123	0.090
Two-factor model (A+B+C+D+E, F)	766.232	134	0.574	0.561	0.615	0.142	0.103
One-factor model (A+B+C+D+E+F)	871.690	135	0.515	0.492	0.552	0.153	0.111
Reference standard	$\chi^2/df<2$		>0.9	>0.9	>0.9	<0.08	<0.05

Note: A denotes aspiration; B denotes modernity; C denotes win-win cooperation; D denotes promise-keeping; E denotes calmness; F denotes patriotism. The factor merging strategy is adopted based on the similarity and correlation coefficients.

Figure 4-1 shows the measurement model's factor loadings. The standardized coefficients of the factor loadings of the latent variables all meet the standard value of greater than 0.6, all reaching the 0.001 level of significance. It initially reflects that the convergent validity of the factors is relatively satisfactory (Revelle & Zinbarg, 2009).

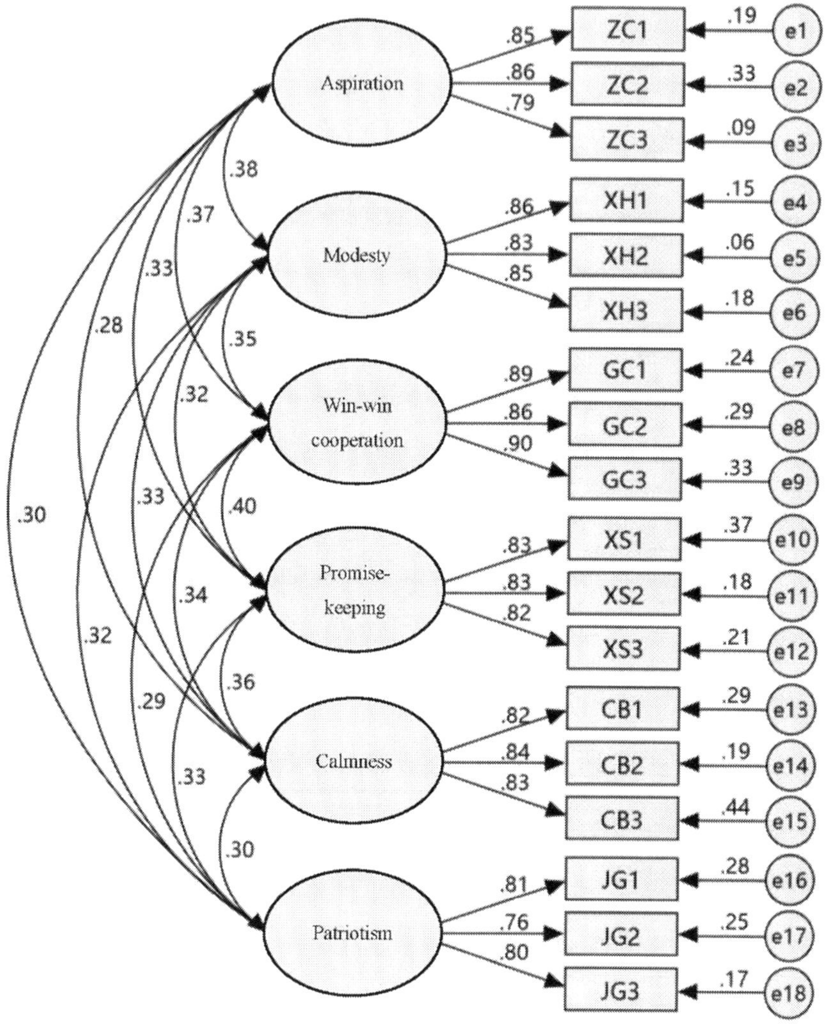

Figure 4-1 Factor Loadings of the Measurement Model of Entrepreneurial Vision

Source: Organized by the author

This study also focused on the discriminant and convergent validity of entrepreneurial vision. The test of discriminant validity consists of testing two hypotheses. One tests the correlation with similar concepts of international entrepreneurial alertness, and the other tests the irrelevance or weak correlation with the concepts differentiated from international entrepreneurial alertness. The correlation coefficients between the factors, the CR (combined reliability) and the AVE (average variance extracted), were examined. It can be found that the CR of the factors is distributed between 0.770 and 0.840, significantly greater than 0.6. The AVE of the factors is distributed between 0.519 and 0.619, significantly greater than 0.5, and the arithmetic square root of the AVE is greater than the correlation coefficient of the factor with the other factors. The results are shown in Tables 4-5. Thus, the six entrepreneurial vision dimensions have good convergent and discriminant validity.

Table 4-5 Correlation Coefficients, CRs, and AVEs for Factors of the Entrepreneurial Vision Scale

Dimension	**1**	**2**	**3**	**4**	**5**	**6**	**Cronbach Alpha**
1. Aspiration	(0.758)						0.801
2. Modesty	0.382**	(0.787)					0.825
3. Win-win cooperation	0.368**	0.353**	(0.761)				0.819
4. Promise-keeping	0.330**	0.323**	0.396**	(0.782)			0.834
5. Calmness	0.279**	0.328**	0.337**	0.361**	(0.780)		0.836
6. Patriotism	0.298**	0.324**	0.297**	0.326**	0.293**	(0.723)	0.825
AVE	0.574	0.619	0.605	0.613	0.610	0.533	
CR	0.801	0.830	0.821	0.824	0.824	0.760	

Note: * * represents p<0.01; diagonal brackets indicate the arithmetic square root of the AVE value.

Summary

Based on the case studies, this study developed a scale of entrepreneurial vision in the Chinese context and conducted various tests. Through theoretical clarification and case studies, this study identified six dimensions of entrepreneurial vision in the Chinese context (aspiration, modesty, win-win cooperation, promote-keeping, calmness and patriotism). The measurement indicators under each dimension were theoretically reorganized, and it was found that the literature well supported each dimension. It re-validated the rationality of qualitative data coding in the previous chapter.

To examine the reliability and validity of the newly developed scale, this study first conducted an exploratory factor analysis of the newly developed scale with a sample of 169 entrepreneurs. Twelve items were excluded based on the results of the exploratory factor analysis. The final scale with 18 items in six dimensions was developed. Confirmatory factor analysis was conducted on the final scale with a sample of 145 entrepreneurs to test the goodness of fit, convergent and discriminant validity with the International Entrepreneurial Alertness Scale. The test results concluded that the entrepreneurial vision scale is reliable and valid.

This study, on the one hand, examines and improves the results of identifying the important and unique concept of entrepreneurial vision in China in an exploratory study. It accomplishes the development and testing of the entrepreneurial vision scale. On the other hand, it lays the foundation for the subsequent empirical research on the relationship between entrepreneurial vision and enterprise performance. It provides a valid scale that has been tested for theoretical validity and reliability.

Chapter 5
Theoretical Analysis and Hypotheses

The previous chapter provides a systematic literature review of the theoretical perspectives and related research topics. In this section, based on the existing literature, multiple theoretical perspectives are adopted to analyze the relevant issues and formulate research hypotheses.

Entrepreneurial Vision and Enterprise Performance

Firm growth and development are the micro-foundations of an economy's competitiveness (Acemoglu et al., 2015; Yang, 2011). Economics and management studies have been conducted on enterprise growth. They mainly investigate the influencing factors of enterprise performance, including financing constraints, legal environment, government regulation, market competition (Li et al., 2016; Du & Guo, 2012), firm size (Zhang et al., 2005), corporate governance (Yang, 2013), entrepreneurship (He & Li, 2005), and social capital (Jiang & Zhao, 2006). Entrepreneurial ability is the key to determining enterprise performance among the many influencing factors. Much evidence shows that entrepreneurial ability and leadership behavior have far-reaching and important effects on enterprise performance (Waldman et al., 2001). Entrepreneurial vision, an important organizational component of entrepreneurial strategic leadership, is particularly critical to the growth of firms in traditional Chinese culture.

Studying how entrepreneurial strategic leadership affects organizational performance began with the debate over "what role managers play in organizational operations" (Katz & Kahn, 1978). Critics continued the analytical framework of industrial organization theory, emphasizing that enterprise performance is external to the institutional environment and that technology, markets, and industrial policies influence organizational performance much more than managers. However, this study neglects decision-makers' influence on organizational construction and information processing (Poter, 1980). Based on the upper echelon theory, it is suggested that managers' strategic leadership is crucial to enterprise performance, especially for the organization's survival in a highly uncertain environment. Based on the logic of the upper echelon theory, entrepreneurial vision as a key element of strategic leadership has a critical impact on enterprise performance.

On the one hand, entrepreneurs with high vision are good at tapping and stimulating the creativity of their employees. The resource-based view recognizes that scarce, valuable, and hard-to-imitate resources and capabilities are fundamental for an enterprise to gain a sustainable competitive advantage. Creativity, as a novel and useful source of ideas, is the basis and premise of employee innovation and is crucial in enhancing enterprise performance. The componential theory of creativity identifies domain-relevant skills, creativity-relevant processes, and task motivation as the core triangular theory of creativity. Both creativity-relevant processes and task motivation are closely related to leadership vision. For high-vision leaders, their trust and understanding of employees affect individual skill learning and intrinsic motivation. It even affects individuals' likelihood of seeking and utilizing feedback to improve relevant skills. High-vision leaders' trust and understanding of their employees results in a cognitive style consistently matching their employees. When the cognitive style of leaders is consistent with that of employees, it means that leaders and employees have similar behavioral preferences and outcome expectations. At this time, the employee's behavioral choices better meet the leader's expectations of the employee's role, and the leader's behavioral style better meets the employee's cognitive preferences. A high level of reciprocity develops between the leader and the employee. The high level of reciprocity stimulates the intrinsic motivation to innovate, facilitating employees' creativity. At the same time, a high level of reciprocity enhances the ability of employees to learn skills and increases their receptivity to feedback from the leader. In turn, it promotes creativity. It can also be explained by the similarity matching theory in the person-environment fit theory. Similarity matching refers to individuals sharing similar characteristics with other organization members, which can facilitate individual cooperation and enhance individual performance. Jansen et al. (2006) showed that shared goals and outcome expectations make it easier for individuals to gain support from superiors, which is more conducive to individual goal achievement. When the leader-employee cognitive styles are differentially fit, the leader and the employee will have different behavioral preferences and role expectations. This difference leads to an uncertain work environment, which may distract the individual from his/her role and consume huge individual resources to adapt to the environment. All of this reduces individuals' time and energy on learning relevant skills, weakens their intrinsic motivation to innovate, and thus hinders the generation and development of their creativity.

On the other hand, entrepreneurs with high visions have a stronger ability to acquire and integrate resources. The ability to acquire and integrate organizational resources determines the organization's survival. The relationship between the organization and the environment and the organization's operation determines the status of the organization's resource acquisition. Chester I. Barnard's Inducement-Contribution Theory explains the resource acquisition ability of the conventional organization. He pointed out that the resource acquisition ability of conventional organizations is based on their contribution. Entrepreneurial ability is crucial (He & Li, 2005). Resource acquisition is a series of resource-seeking and acquisition behaviors carried out by enterprises. The resources can come from a variety of sources. It may come from external purchase or attraction of resources, or the enterprise can internally accumulate it. Resource integration is one of resource development's most important and difficult steps. Sirmon et al. (2007) pointed out that only those valuable and scarce resources that are efficiently integrated can create value. Therefore, enterprises should integrate resources through certain processes. Only through the integration of resources can the enterprise enhance its various dynamic capabilities (Wang & Ahmed, 2007) to ensure the improvement of enterprise performance and promote the growth of the enterprise (Nason & Wiklund, 2018). It can be seen that the process of resource integration in enterprises is extremely important. Sirmon et al. (2007) proposed a specific approach to resource integration: stabilization, enrichment and refinement, exploration and creation. Stabilization refers to small and gradual adjustments to the existing resource portfolios and allocations; enrichment and refinement means integrating, expanding, and extending resources in depth; and exploration and creation involves creating new resources and capabilities through an exploratory process. For high-vision entrepreneurs, their strong relational social networks built on their reputations deepen, and trust and reciprocity gradually deepen. Full learning, exchange, joint analysis and problem-solving among network partners can facilitate cognitive enhancement and improve the ability to access and integrate resources. At the same time, the rapid learning ability of high-vision entrepreneurs enables them to patch together resources, creatively utilize the portfolio of resources at hand, break the constraints of resource use, and improvise. As a result, they can promote the rapid and efficient coordination and allocation of internal resources to strengthen the organization's resource acquisition capability, thereby enhancing organizational performance (Sonenshein, 2014; Yu et al., 2017). Based on this, the following hypothesis is proposed in this study:

H1: For an enterprise, the higher the entrepreneurial vision, the better the enterprise performance.

Mediating Effect of Decision Logic

How does entrepreneurial strategic leadership affect enterprise performance? A major consensus is that it depends on the entrepreneur's information search and decision-making. The attention-based view (ABV) suggests that enterprise behavior results from how enterprises direct and allocate the attention of their decision-makers (Ocasio, 2011). The theory interprets how attention at the individual, socio-cognitive, and organizational levels interact to shape enterprise behavior, thus providing new integrated perspectives for understanding enterprise cognition, organizational structure, and strategy formulation (Ocasio, 1997). For entrepreneurs, different decision logics (causation vs. effectuation) play a key role in how they process information and make decisions (Bromiley & Rau, 2016). It enables them to see complex situations from different perspectives, think about alternatives, and notice and react to stimuli. Subsequently, it may lead to more informed decisions and potentially better outcomes (Bartunek et al., 1983). However, the effects may vary among different decision logics.

An important theoretical and practical issue that has long been debated between the planning and learning schools of strategic management research is what strategies enterprises should adopt to better cope with environmental change. The planning school, represented by Ansoff (1991), believes formal plans are necessary for stable and unstable environments. They should work on better rational forecasting to develop effective plans to enhance performance (Brews & Hunt, 1999). The learning school of thought, represented by Mintzberg (1994), argues that under uncertainty, enterprises should learn from the marketplace and practice to foster flexibility and adaptability, thus responding quickly to unanticipated new opportunities. Planning-based strategic decision-making introduces causation to organizational strategies, emphasizing rational predictive analysis and planning to gain competitive advantage (Reymen et al., 2015). Learning-based strategic decision-making, on the other hand, perpetuates effectuation (Alveraz & Barney, 2007; Mintzberg & Water, 1985), which emphasizes developing new markets through flexibility and trial and error.

For decision-makers, the two types of decision logic are reflected in the differences in the types of strategic choices, and the underlying analytical frameworks differ substantially. The core of causation emphasizes forecasting, believing sufficient information can be searched to predict the market effectively and gain a competitive advantage. Hence, it is preferred to comprehensively and systematically collect all information needed to predict the future. Also, it should devote efforts to analyzing the information's rationality to control uncertainty (Sarasvathy, 2001; Fisher, 2012). The core of effectuation stresses control, arguing that the future does not should be predicted if the change is effectively controlled. Hence, it is preferred to control the unpredictable future through iterative learning and pre-commitments (Chandler et al., 2011). The two decision logics represent differences in information gathering and acquisition in decision-making. They also represent the differences in entrepreneurs' integration of different resources.

Goal orientation highlights explicit strategic objectives and comprehensive market forecasts. It provides significant guidelines for enterprises to select appropriate resources for integration (Sarasvathy & Dew, 2005; Sarasvathy et al., 2008). To achieve the established strategic objectives, enterprises adopting goal orientation can design a complete strategic plan through comprehensive competitive analysis. Because of this, enterprises can purposefully supplement the insufficient resources at a low cost, thus enhancing the efficiency of resource integration (Chandler et al., 2011; Dutta et al., 2015). Goal orientation embodies the logic of "utilization" and emphasizes the full integration of available resources and capabilities. It will accelerate the integration of resources within the enterprise (Wiltbank et al., 2006; Reymen et al., 2015). In addition, as goal orientation pursues the maximization of expected returns, it motivates enterprises to expand and optimize their resource portfolios to enhance the quality of resource integration (Fisher, 2012; Sarasvathy, 2001; Guo et al., 2016). It can be seen that goal orientation facilitates the resource integration of enterprises. Market competition is becoming increasingly fierce and complex in the transition economy. Goal orientation is particularly crucial for enterprises to formulate an effective competitive strategy to drive the efficient operation of resource integration activities.

Under the logic of means orientation, the starting point for strategic entrepreneurial decisions is not the opportunity but the resources. Enterprises adopting means orientation identify and capture the value of resources in integrating the resources at hand (Dutta et al., 2015; Welter et al., 2016; Sarasvathy, 2001). Establishing strategic alliances means orientation motivates enterprises to acquire insufficient resources in their interactions with external partners to build an advantageous resource portfolio (Chandler et al., 2011; Deligianni et al., 2015). By applying means orientation, enterprises can flexibly integrate diversified resources according to changes in the external environment to pursue the fit between their internal resources and capabilities and the environment. In addition, means orientation facilitates enterprises to explore the value of different resource portfolios in experimenting with business models, thereby creatively integrating resources (Guo et al., 2016). As Alvarez and Busenitz (2001) point out, enterprises' market opportunities arise from identifying undiscovered resource portfolios. In resource consolidation, enterprises can identify new resource values, thus creating new opportunities. However, it should be noted that such new opportunities may not imply improved enterprise performance but rather higher risks and failures (Baker & Nelson, 2005). For different entrepreneurs, differences in entrepreneurial vision can lead to differences in decision logic. However, decision logic is crucial in the relationship between entrepreneurial vision and enterprise performance. Based on this, the following hypotheses are proposed:

H2: Causation mediates the relationship between entrepreneurial vision and enterprise performance.

H3: Effectuation mediates the relationship between entrepreneurial vision and enterprise performance.

Moderating Effects of Industrial Complexity and Dynamics

Industrial complexity is associated with increased heterogeneity in the number and types of competitors, suppliers, and consumers interacting with enterprises (Aldrich, 1979; Dess & Beard, 1984). These conditions contrast with simpler environments characterized by stable and limited competitive pressures, such as in monopolistic and duopolistic industries (Luciano et al., 2020; Snowden & Boone, 2007). Given this distinction, Dess and Beard (1984) argued that managers need more information-processing capabilities to cope with complex environments, and they should systematically search for information and develop response plans to reduce organizational uncertainty in complex environments. Following this logic, we believe that causation and effectuation affect enterprise performance in complex environments more than in simple environments.

Consistent with planning-based strategies, causation emphasizes responding to environmental changes by better anticipating the future. It motivates enterprises to purposefully collect and analyze market, technological, or policy information under established strategic objectives to capture and anticipate trends in changing customer needs (Reymen et al., 2015; Parida et al., 2016). As Drucker (1998) points out, the purposeful search helps identify market opportunities and reduce uncertainty. External information search based on causation enhances enterprises' understanding of unmet market needs and their value, thereby identifying potential opportunities available in the market. Moreover, it accelerates the effective integration of resources to avoid uncertainty and gain a competitive advantage in the marketplace.

Entrepreneurs who adopt causation tend to conduct comprehensive searches and consider multiple complementary perspectives (Graf-Vlachy et al., 2020; Wong et al., 2011). In this case, they become more capable of gathering and interpreting large amounts of multivariate information in complex environments (Snowden & Boone, 2007). They will better understand the impact of the environment, such as the product market space occupied by different competitors, the emergence of niche opportunities, the bargaining power of different suppliers, and the possibilities for cooperation with different competitors and suppliers. They should recognize the interdependencies between industry participants rather than considering them individually, as their relationships are more complex in complicated environments. The direct information processing capabilities of entrepreneurs who adopt causation allow them to understand better and participate in the actions of competitors and other industry participants (McNamara et al., 2002). It enhances strategic adaptability and enables optimal strategic choices that lead to superior corporate performance in these environments (Nadkarni & Narayanan, 2007; Snowden & Boone, 2007). Research has shown that at higher levels of industrial complexity, industry knowledge and the variety and depth of more complex information processing processes are essential for gaining competitive advantage (Ferrier, 2001; Luciano et al., 2020).

In contrast, entrepreneurs with causation do not have an advantage in organizational decision-making when faced with simpler environments. As Snowden and Boone (2007: 2) explain, simple situations are characterized by stability and clear causation, requiring direct management and monitoring, such as adherence to best practices. However, entrepreneurs with causation may be more likely to resist such practices. Even in simpler environments, they may over-complicate the decision-making process and get trapped by too many choices. Decisions may be delayed and organizational agility reduced (Nadkarni & Narayanan, 2007).

Furthermore, they may lead to unnecessarily complex solutions, thus increasing coordination costs. There may be irrelevant information or structures that are not easily integrated into the organization. Entrepreneurs with causation may tend to overcomplicate supply relationships or engage in diversification strategies that are less important to the core business, diminishing operational efficiency or increasing the risk of project failure (Palich et al., 2000; Sternberg et al., 2021). Causation and effectuation may be more favorable to enterprise performance under increased environmental complexity. However, the mismatch between entrepreneurs' capacity to bear information search and uncertainty and the structure of simple environments leads to weaker effects of entrepreneurs' causation and effectuation on enterprise performance in simple environments (Calori et al., 1994; Curseu & Rus, 2005). Based on this, the following hypotheses are proposed:

H4: Industrial complexity reinforces the positive correlation between causation and enterprise performance.

H5: Industrial complexity reinforces the negative correlation between effectuation and enterprise performance.

Dynamics reflects the instability of an industry (Dess & Beard, 1984), characterized by rapid technological change or frequent product introductions, market breakthroughs, or regulatory changes. Under these conditions, entrepreneurs are bound to make quick decisions to compete (Baum & Wally, 2003; Judge & Miller, 1991). Competitors and technologies are constantly changing, the window for strategy closes quickly, and information rapidly becomes outdated (Eisenhardt & Bourgeois, 1988). These conditions contrast with more stable environments. In stable environments, change does not occur as quickly or is easily predictable, and enterprises have more time to search for and evaluate information (Dean & Sharfman, 1996; Fredrickson, 1984). Given these differences, entrepreneurs' causation and effectuation have a greater impact on enterprise performance under more stable conditions. That is, the facilitating effect of causation on enterprise performance is strengthened, and the inhibiting effect of effectuation on enterprise performance is magnified. However, under dynamic conditions, the impact of entrepreneurs' causation and effectuation on enterprise performance diminishes. That is, the facilitating effect of causation on enterprise performance is weakened, and the inhibiting effect of effectuation on enterprise performance is decreased.

In high-uncertainty environments, effectuation leads to forming strategic alliances between enterprises and external stakeholders (usually investors, partners, and customers) to share valid information. Thus, they progressively deepen their search and grasp of market opportunities (Alvarez & Barney, 2014; Fisher, 2012). Effectuation involves exploring potential strategic options and business models, facilitating enterprises to obtain market feedback from the trial-and-error and learning process. Thus, they can develop and explore new businesses (Guo et al., 2014). Effectuation emphasizes the importance of maintaining flexibility, as it enables enterprises to quickly adjust their organizational processes and capabilities to capture potential opportunities embedded in environmental changes (Wiltbank et al., 2006; Bock et al., 2012; Sarasvathy, 2001). Entrepreneurs with causation tend to engage in more integrated search and evaluation than effectuation. They are likely more effective in stable conditions because these environments give CEOs greater flexibility to consider alternative perspectives and make optimal decisions. Research has shown that exhaustiveness in making and integrating strategic decisions in stable environments improves corporate performance but is negatively associated with corporate performance in more dynamic environments (Fredrickson, 1984; Fredrickson & Iaquinto, 1989). As Dean and Sharfman (1996: p. 376) explain, in a dynamic environment, the exhaustiveness of strategic decision-making is problematic because it slows decision-making and forces consistency in decisions made at different times and in different situations. In this way, gathering and processing all relevant information would be futile, as industry trends are unpredictable and information becomes outdated quickly (Baum & Wally, 2003; Bourgeois & Eisenhardt, 1988). Conversely, postponing decisions may undermine effective decision-making in a more dynamic environment and negatively impact corporate performance (Baum & Wally, 2003; Judge & Miller, 1991).

Consistent with this view, Downey and Slocum (2022) find that entrepreneurs in effectuation perform better than those in causation under high perceived uncertainty. They attribute this to the fact that decision-makers in causation try to resolve uncertainty and get bogged down by considering too many options. Decision-makers who use effectuation easily handle affairs in fast-paced industry environments because they rely on simple decision rules and conventions and accelerate decision-making based on intuition. At high levels of uncertainty, relying on simple decision rules enhances decision-making accuracy instead of considering and weighing all options (Gigerenzer & Gaissmaier, 2010). For this reason, in industrial dynamics, the facilitating effect of causation on enterprise performance is weakened. Effectuation, on the other hand, speeds up the decision-making process by using more direct and heuristic approaches, enabling it to capitalize on the new opportunities emerging in the market. Hence, the inhibiting effect of effectuation on enterprise performance is weakened. Based on this, the following hypotheses are proposed:

H6: Industrial dynamics weakens the positive correlation between causation and enterprise performance.

H7: Industrial dynamics weakens the negative correlation between effectuation and enterprise performance.

The research model is shown in Figure 5-1. Entrepreneurial vision affects enterprise performance through the mediating effects of causation and effectuation. Further, industrial complexity and dynamics influence the effects of causation and effectuation on enterprise performance.

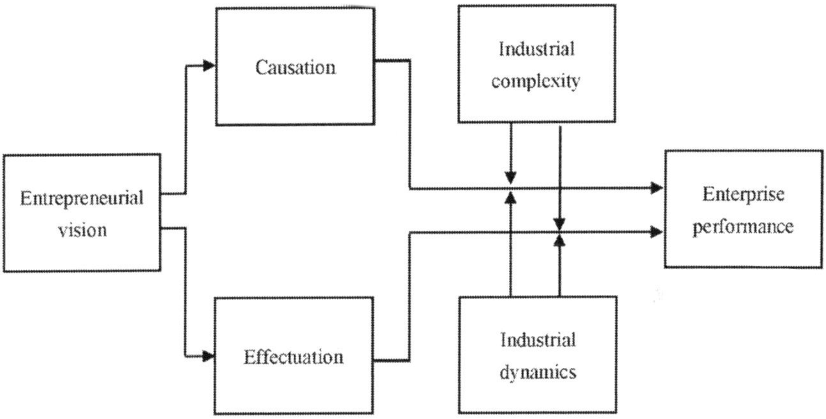

Figure 5-1 Research Model

Source: Organized by the author

Chapter 6
Research Design and Data Collection

This chapter mainly introduces the research methodology, data sources and variable measurements, and the data acquisition and measurement methods in detail. At the same time, the corresponding test model is designed according to the theoretical hypotheses in the previous section.

Research Methodology and Process

The research on questionnaire-based data sources in management literature is mainly conducted through multivariate statistical and econometric methods. We mainly use the multi-variate analysis method and STATA 14.0. Specifically, the research analysis process includes the first step: the content analysis of the scale. The sources of the survey scales are mainly divided into two parts. The research team mainly develops the scale of entrepreneurial vision. Decision logic, industrial complexity, industrial dynamics, and enterprise performance are mainly based on the mature scales developed by foreign researchers. It should be noted that the mature scales from abroad are revised as follows:

The first step is to design the initial questionnaire. Firstly, the foreign scales were validated using the "two-way translation" method to ensure the equivalence of the variables' meanings (Brislin, 1980). Specifically, we first translated the foreign scales into Chinese and then contacted English researchers in related fields to translate the Chinese scales into English. The scales were modified appropriately through comparison, and the initial research questionnaire was finally obtained. Secondly, we asked scholars in returnee entrepreneurship research to revise the scale. At the same time, we interviewed the top management of the sample companies to modify the scale further. Finally, we distributed and pretested the scale with some research samples. Specifically, item and exploratory factor analyses were used to delete the relevant items from the scale. The items with high explanatory power in the scale were selected based on the analysis results. The items with high commonality and high factor loadings were selected by exploratory factor analysis. At the same time, the items with ambiguous meanings were adjusted or deleted.

The second step is to analyze the validity. Validity is generally divided into three categories: content validity, construct validity and criterion validity. Factor analysis measures construct validity, mainly exploratory factor analysis (EFA) and confirmatory factor analysis (CFA). By exploratory factor analysis, we collect a portion of the total sample to analyze sub-level or latent variables to determine a conceptual framework based on the theories and concepts. The conceptual framework must also be validated by analyzing another sample portion.

The third step is to conduct a reliability analysis. Reliability refers to the consistency, stability and reliability of the test results. Generally, internal consistency is used to measure the level of reliability. That is, items at each level of the construct or scale are examined to collectively measure the consistency of the items within the same construct and the extent of the effects of random error. The higher the reliability coefficient, the more consistent, stable and reliable the test results. In factor analysis, the internal consistency α coefficient is generally used as the reliability coefficient of each construct or each level.

The fourth step is to perform a multivariate regression analysis. Based on the above research work, we finally analyzed the data to test our research hypotheses through multivariate regression analysis.

Questionnaire Design

Items are used in questionnaires to measure constructs or variables. Multiple items improve reliability over single items when the measurement items of the variables are consistent (Shattuck, 2006). Hence, it improves the reliability and validity of the questionnaire data. Multiple-item scales generally refer to scales consisting of three or more measurement items. Theoretically, it also includes scales consisting of two items. However, scales with three or more items help researchers to avoid problems that might be less recognized. Bagozzi and Richard (1994) suggested that a scale consisting of three to five items might be ideal. The scales selected for this paper are based on well-established and heavily practiced scales in China and abroad. In particular, the scale has been widely used in studying relationships in China. Other scales in China and abroad were analyzed and modified to some extent.

Principles of Questionnaire Design

The questionnaire should be designed to be as concise as possible so that it can be easily understood and completed by the respondents. Questions that are vague and potentially difficult to answer should not be asked (Li, 2004). It is essential to avoid inducing questions and double-break statements. The researcher should not involve his or her values in the questions and must maintain a scientific and rigorous attitude that is objective and neutral. In any social state, the public widely accepts ethical standards and behavioral norms (Li, 2011). Respondents will likely activate their self-protection mechanisms if a questionnaire asks about these standards or norms. Because of this, respondents may fill out the questionnaire based on social expectations rather than their true thoughts. It may result in social desirability response bias.

Paulhus (1991) found two types of expressions in the scale that are distorted to satisfy such social desirability response bias. One is exaggerating positive self-presentation; the other is impression management, i.e., intentionally changing behaviors and behavioral tendencies to please others. Regarding how to avoid the influence of possible unfavorable factors, Li (2011) argued that, in terms of scale selection, we should use the existing scales repeatedly applied in the literature and have high reliability and validity. Therefore, given the limitations of existing scales in terms of culture, language, and time and space, the principles of applicability, feasibility, and completeness of existing scales should be emphasized as much as possible in questionnaire design. In this study, the questionnaire design follows the principles proposed by the above scholars. The scales were further modified and adjusted based on the existing mature scales to improve the reliability of the data and the research conclusions.

Questionnaire Design Process

A rational questionnaire design process is an important prerequisite to ensure the reliability and validity of questionnaire measurements. Churchill (1979) argued that, under the condition of ensuring consistency, multi-items can improve the reliability of questionnaire data more than single items. Therefore, multiple items were used to measure the variables in this study. In addition, the questionnaire design process is based on the research results of Li (2003) and Peng (2009).

In addition, all questions in the questionnaire are based on the recent operations of the new businesses to avoid any bias due to the inability of the respondents to recall the relevant information for the required answers. In this way, the negative impact of memory bias can be prevented. Second, the questionnaire is filled in by entrepreneurs. They are very familiar with the business situation of their enterprises to prevent the one-sidedness of the respondents' judgments and perceptions. Moreover, all the questions are set to be straightforward, so they will not have difficulties understanding and answering them accurately. Finally, the first page of the questionnaire stated that the data collection was for purely academic purposes and used relative indicators rather than absolute ones to measure performance so that respondents would not be reluctant to answer the questions for fear of revealing information.

Measurement of Variables

Independent Variable: Entrepreneurial Vision

Entrepreneurial vision, as the core independent variable in this study, was measured using the Entrepreneurial Vision Scale developed in Chapters 3 and 4. The Entrepreneurial Vision Scale was measured following a strict scientific approach to scale development. First, the grounded theory was used to summarize the different dimensions of entrepreneurial vision. Second, the entrepreneurial vision scale was further developed through a large-scale questionnaire survey and tested for reliability and validity. Finally, the entrepreneurial vision variables that passed the rigorous reliability and validity tests were applied to measure entrepreneurial vision.

Dependent Variable: Enterprise Performance

Measurement of business performance in existing studies is divided into two main categories. One is performance measurement scales, which measure corporate performance through respondents' supervisory ratings. Existing mainstream studies mainly draw on the scales of Walton (1985), Huselid (1995) and Gray (1998). The other research category measures corporate performance by inquiring about objective financial indicators. A growing body of research suggests that corporate performance can be more accurately reflected through the direct setting of subjective financial indicators than the first category of measures of corporate performance (Hu et al., 2014; Bruton et al. (2010). Therefore, we draw on Li and Atuahene-Gima (2001) to measure corporate performance by inquiring about the growth rates of total assets, operating revenues, and net profits in the past three years (2019, 2020, and 2021).

Mediator: Decision Logic

Decision logic is generally measured by the effectuation scale (four-dimensional), the causation scale (one-dimensional) (developed and validated by Chandler et al. (2011)) and the differentiation scale between effectuation and causation (by Gabrielsson and Politis (2011) based on Prof. Sarasvathy's theory). This paper focuses on the mediating effects of different decision logic (goal orientation and measures orientation). Instead of exploring the structural dimensions of effectuation versus causation, it is sufficient to distinguish which decision logic is more frequently used by entrepreneurs in their decision-making process. According to Gabrielsson and Politis (2011), different measurement items distinguish entrepreneurs' preferences for effectuation and causation in the decision-making process, as shown in Table 6-1.

Table 6-1 Decision Logic Scale

Variable	No.	Item	Source of scale
Causation	1	I prefer to have predetermined goals and work hard to achieve them	Gabrielsson & Politis (2011)
	2	I avoid uncertainty to a large extent	
	3	I prefer budgeting and detailed competitive analysis when investigating market demand for our products or services	
	4	I prefer strategic, long-term, goal-oriented relationships with stakeholders	
Effectuation	5	I prefer flexible goals and can change the direction of the business based on results	
	6	I appreciate casual and informal relationships with my stakeholders	

Variable	No.	Item	Source of scale
	7	I prefer to investigate market demand for our products or services using informal methods	
	8	I embrace uncertain events and want to capitalize on these events	

Moderators: Industrial Complexity and Industrial Dynamics

Industrial complexity and industrial dynamics mainly reflect the market competition in the enterprise's industry. Industrial complexity refers to the heterogeneity in industry players' enterprise size and market power, where greater heterogeneity represents more complex industry conditions. The calculation of industrial complexity is mainly based on the research method proposed by Connelly et al. (2013). First, the Herfindahl-Hirschman Index (HHI) for different industries is calculated by the two-digit code classification of listed companies in the China Securities Regulatory Commission (CSRC). Second, the value of 1-HHI represents the degree of complexity of the industries in which different enterprises are located.

Industrial dynamics is measured via the perceived dynamics of the entrepreneur's business environment, using the scale of Jansen et al. (2006) (Table 6-2). Industrial dynamics has two main dimensions: market dynamics and technology dynamics. Market dynamics reflect the changes in the enterprise's market, while technology dynamics reflect the rate of technological progress in the enterprise's industry.

Table 6-2 Industrial Dynamics Scale

Variable	Dimension	No.	Item	Source of scale
Industrial dynamics	Market dynamics	1	Customers' needs and preferences change rapidly	Jansen et al. (2006)
		2	Customers' needs and preferences are highly unpredictable	
		3	New customers' needs for products and services are significantly different from those of regular customers	
		4	Industry products and services are becoming more and more diversified	
		5	Competition between enterprises and their peers is becoming more and more intense	
	Technology dynamics	6	Technologies in the industry in which the enterprise is located change frequently	
		7	Enterprises have difficulty in predicting the trend of technological change in the next five years	
		8	Technological changes present significant opportunities for the industry	
		9	Technological changes facilitate the generation of new products and services	
		10	Technological changes in the industry greatly affect the business activities of enterprises	

Control Variables

In addition, based on the existing research, we mainly control for the following variables. The individual-level variables are: entrepreneurs' gender, age, and education level. Specifically, (1) gender is coded as a dummy variable, with males assigned a value of 1 and females assigned a value of 0. (2) Age is examined as the actual age of the entrepreneur. (3) Educational levels of entrepreneurs are coded by the highest degree obtained (primary school=1, junior high school=2, high school=3, junior college=4, university (college)=5, master's degree=6, doctorate and above=7).

Enterprise-level control variables include (1) enterprise age, measured by the length of time from the date of incorporation of the enterprise to the time of the survey. (2) The natural logarithm of the number of enterprise employees in the year represents enterprise size. (3) Shareholding concentration. (4) Size of the board of directors. (5) Debt ratio of the enterprise. (6) Duality, 1 for the duality of chairman and general manager and 0 otherwise. (7) Institutional shareholders' ownership ratio. In addition, industry dummy variables are controlled according to the industry classification of enterprises.

Data Collection and Sample Statistics

In this round of data collection, we selected private enterprises in the Guangzhou Development District (four national economic zones (Guangzhou Economic and Technological Development Zone, Guangzhou High-tech Industrial Development Zone, Guangzhou Bonded Zone, Guangzhou Export Processing Zone), and the Sino-Singapore Guangzhou Knowledge City. The Guangzhou Development District has built a platform structure of "four zones and four centers" in the Guangdong-Hong Kong-Macao Greater Bay Area with the support of four major industrial clusters (the Knowledge City, the Science City, the Huangpu Port and the Bio-Island). At the same time, it promotes the construction of the Guangzhou-Hong Kong Special Co-operation Zone for Intelligent Manufacturing and the Guangzhou-Hong Kong Science and Technology Co-operation Park to enhance industrial agglomeration and clustering continuously. Guangzhou Development District insists on international cooperation and opening up to the outside world. It gathers more than 200,000 private enterprises and 4,200 multinational enterprises, including 207 projects invested by the world's top 500 companies. The district has made great efforts to introduce investments from multinational enterprises, especially to build a world-class biomedical park.

For this reason, it won the United Nations Investment Promotion Award in 2019, becoming the only winner in China that year. From 2019 to 2021, it was awarded China's Outstanding Investment Promotion Organization Award and Outstanding Investment Promotion Project

Award for three consecutive years. With a strong manufacturing industry, Guangzhou Development District has eight pillar industries (automobile, electronics, energy, high-end chemical, food and beverage, electrical machinery, integrated circuit, automobile manufacturing, green energy, new materials, biomedicine, high-end equipment, beauty and health). Guangzhou Development District aims to become a trillion-dollar industrial district. Five companies were listed in Guangzhou in the 2021 Fortune Global 500 list, two of which are headquartered in the Guangzhou Development District.

The data were collected for five months, from June 1, 2022, to November 13, 2022. During the data collection process, the survey was well organized. First, to ensure the data's quality, the respondents were trained and exchanged to clarify the meanings of the questionnaire items and to avoid the errors caused by ambiguity. Second, a pre-survey and on-site interviews with entrepreneurs were conducted at a training session for private enterprises in Foshan City organized by the United Front Work Department of the Guangdong Provincial Party Committee. Forty-five pre-survey questionnaires were distributed on-site, with 30 questionnaires recovered. Twelve entrepreneurs were interviewed. On-site interviews lasted 25 minutes per person, of which four entrepreneurs were followed up twice for 120 minutes per person. The questionnaire items were adjusted and modified according to the feedback results of the pre-survey. Third, a large-scale questionnaire survey was conducted after revising and refining the questionnaire. Table 6-3 below shows the questionnaires' distribution and recovery.

Table 6-3 Questionnaire Distribution and Recovery

Questionnaire distribution and recovery method	The number of questionnaires distributed	The number of questionnaires recovered	Recovery rate	Number of valid questionnaires	Validity rate
On-site distribution and recovery	190	161	84.73%	122	58.94%
Mobile phone distribution and recovery by Wenjuanxing	330	187	56.66%	117	35.45%
Distribution and recovery by e-mail	115	78	67.83%	59	51.31%
Total	635	426	67.08%	298	46.93%

A total of 635 questionnaires were distributed in this survey, and 426 questionnaires were recovered, with a recovery rate of 67.08%. One hundred twenty-eight invalid questionnaires were eliminated, and 298 valid questionnaires remained, with a valid recovery rate of 46.93%. The relevant staff of Guangzhou Export Processing Zone Administrative Committee, Guangzhou Economic and Technological Development Zone Administrative Committee and Guangzhou High-tech Industrial Development Zone Administrative Committee provided a list of the companies and their contact information. We contacted the entrepreneurs in advance to confirm whether they were willing to participate in the survey, explain the content of the survey, and determine the time, place, and participants. We distributed 190 questionnaires on-site and collected 161 of them. There were 122 valid questionnaires, with a validity rate of 58.94%.

In the same way, we communicated with entrepreneurs by phone and explained the terminology in advance. Then, we distributed 330 electronic questionnaires designed by Wenjuanxing APP through mobile WeChat. One hundred eighty-seven questionnaires were recovered. There were 117 valid questionnaires, with a validity rate of 35.45%. We used the same method of prior telephone communication and terminology clarification with the entrepreneurs. After that, we distributed 115 questionnaires by e-mail, and 78 were recovered. Fifty-nine questionnaires were valid, with a validity rate of 46.93%. Generally speaking, the distribution and recovery of questionnaires are relatively satisfactory and meet the basic requirements for statistical analysis.

The descriptive statistics of the research sample (Table 6-4) show 225 male entrepreneurs, accounting for 75.50% of the total. There are 73 female entrepreneurs, accounting for 24.50%. The gender distribution of entrepreneurs in this survey is also consistent with the ratio of male to female entrepreneurs in the latest 2021 National Survey of Private Enterprises conducted by the All-China Federation of Industry and Commerce. The ratio of male entrepreneurs is much higher than that of female entrepreneurs. Regarding the age distribution of entrepreneurs, only 6.38% are under 30 years old, 17.79% are 30-34 years old, 29.87% are 35-39 years old, 23.83% are 40-44 years old, and 22.15% are 45 years old and above. The education of entrepreneurs indicates that they are highly educated. 34.56% of the entrepreneurs have a bachelor's degree or below (only 7.39% without a bachelor's degree), 54.03% have a master's degree, and 11.41% have a doctoral degree. The vast majority of entrepreneurs have received a master's degree.

Table 6-4 Descriptive Statistics (N=298)

Item		Frequency	Percentage %	Cumulative Percentage %
Gender	Female	73	24.50%	24.50%
	Male	225	75.50%	100.00%
	Total	298	100.00%	
Age	Under 30 years old	19	6.38%	6.38%
	30-34 years old	53	17.79%	24.17%
	35-39 years old	89	29.87%	54.04%
	40-44 years old	71	23.83%	77.87%
	45 years old and above	66	22.15%	100.00%
	Total	298	100.00%	
Education	Bachelor's degree and below	103	34.56%	34.56%
	Master's degree	161	54.03%	88.59%
	Doctor's degree	34	11.41%	100.00%
	Total	298	100.00%	
Company age	Less than 5 years	52	17.45%	17.45%
	5-10 years	147	49.33%	66.78%
	11-15 years	59	19.80%	86.58%
	More than 15 years	40	13.42%	100.00%
	Total	298	100.00%	
Company size	Fewer than 20 employees	29	9.73%	9.73%
	20-50 employees	47	15.77%	25.50%
	51-80 employees	88	29.53%	55.03%
	81-110 employees	102	34.23%	89.26%
	More than 110 employees	32	10.74%	100.00%
	Total	298	100.00%	
Industry	Food manufacturing	17	5.70%	5.70%
	Furniture manufacturing	12	4.04%	9.74%

Item		Frequency	Percentage %	Cumulative Percentage %
	General equipment manufacturing	61	20.47%	30.21%
	Electronic devices and equipment	35	11.74%	41.95%
	Software and IT services	21	7.05%	49.00%
	Internet and related services	58	19.46%	68.46%
	Arts and culture	37	12.42%	80.88%
	Catering	22	7.38%	88.26%
	Others	35	11.74%	100.00%
	Total	298	100.00%	

From the distribution of enterprise characteristics, 17.45% of the enterprises are within 5 years old, and 49.33% are between 5 and 10 years old. It can be seen that most of the enterprises are in the growth period. It also conforms to China's current economic situation to a certain extent. Since the central government introduced "mass entrepreneurship and innovation" in 2013, the policy subsidies granted to entrepreneurs by various levels of government have stimulated entrepreneurship. From the perspective of enterprise size, small and medium-sized enterprises with more than 50 employees dominate, accounting for 74.50% of the total. B, the top three industries are general equipment manufacturing, Internet and related services, and culture and art, accounting for 20.47%, 19.46% and 12.42%, respectively.

Overcoming Common Method Variance of Data

Despite data analysis at the firm level, all data were obtained from team members, which to some extent causes a potential problem of common method variance (Podsakoff et al., 2012). However, the following approaches were attempted in this study to minimize the potential common method variance. First, regarding research design, this study is part of a larger data collection program. Therefore, as Podsakoff et al. (2003) suggested, the independent, dependent and moderating variables were placed in different questionnaire sections. Thus, a psychological gap was created for the respondents, thus reducing the problem of common method variance due to the psychological synchronicity of the respondents.

Second, in terms of research implementation, most of the questionnaires were collected on-site. Therefore, respondents were able to communicate freely with the research team members. Before distributing the questionnaires, the research team members gave a business card and a gift to each respondent who filled out the questionnaire. The team members then informed the respondents that the questionnaire was purely for academic purposes and had no business interests involved. No other than the research team members would have access to the recovered questionnaires, and the final data would only be analyzed and disclosed to the extent of corporate data. Then, the research team members promised anonymity to all respondents and gave each participant a copy of the instructions for completing the questionnaire. The instructions make it clear that there is no right or wrong answer to any questions. After reading the questions, participants were only required to complete the questionnaire based on their first impression. The above careful research design can also alleviate the concern of common method variance to a certain extent.

Third, Harman's one-factor test was used to analyze the common method variance of the returned questionnaires. All the items of 298 valid questionnaires were put together for factor analysis. The first principal component was obtained when the data were not rotated, and its loading was 12.057%, not a majority. It shows that the common method variance is not serious in this research data, and the data are reliable for further data analysis and hypothesis testing.

Chapter 7
Empirical Analysis and Hypothesis Testing

This chapter presents the data analysis based on the previous theoretical analysis, research hypotheses and research design. Firstly, the construct variables of the sample will be analyzed for reliability and validity. Secondly, descriptive statistics and correlation analysis are conducted for the overall sample. Finally, the research hypotheses are tested using stepwise regression analysis.

Reliability and Validity Tests

Reliability Test

Reliability analysis emphasizes the stability and internal consistency of the measurement items. Stability means that respondents use the same criteria when filling out the questionnaire. Internal consistency refers to how the items correlate and whether the items represent the same construct (Revelle & Zinbarg, 2009). Based on the method proposed by Fornell and Larcker (1981), reliability can be assessed using Cronbach's alpha and combined reliability (CR). When Cronbach's α coefficient and the CR value are greater than 0.7, the measurement scale has high reliability. Corrected Item-Total Correlation (CITC) has also been used to assess the reliability of individual measurement items. When the CITC value is greater than 0.4, it indicates high internal consistency between the measurement items and the overall construct of the scale and high reliability (Kerlinger, 1986). Based on this, the three approaches are simultaneously used to test the reliability of the variables.

(1) Reliability test of entrepreneurial vision

Entrepreneurial vision has 18 items in total. The CR of the overall scale was 0.939, and Cronbach's α coefficient was 0.913, higher than the cutoff value of 0.7. The CITC values of the 18 items ranged from 0.486 to 0.622, higher than the cutoff value of 0.4, and the Cronbach's α coefficient did not increase after the deletion of any item. It indicates the high reliability of the measurement scale of entrepreneurial vision (Fornell & Larcker, 1981). Specific reliability indicators of entrepreneurial vision are shown in Table 7-1.

Table 7-1 Reliability Analysis of Entrepreneurial Vision

Variable	**No.**	**Item**	**CITC**	**Alpha if the item deleted**
Entrepreneurial vision	1	I want to make the world a better place through my business	0.618	0.831
	2	I believe that there is always scope for improving the quality of our business	0.619	0.821
	3	I always reflect on my shortcomings and stay alert to complacency	0.549	0.802
	4	I am very tolerant of my friends, family, colleagues and subordinates	0.596	0.813
	5	I am receptive to criticism and do not resent it	0.547	0.825
	6	I am genuinely delighted by the success of my colleagues and subordinates, and I never worry about them surpassing me	0.486	0.736
	7	I can bring most of the team members together to work towards a set goal	0.495	0.799
	8	I am pleased to share the results of my cooperation with my colleagues and subordinates	0.539	0.815
	9	I believe in "one for all, all for one"	0.543	0.823
	10	I act on what I say	0.565	0.804
	11	I believe that reputation is the foundation of an enterprise, and an enterprise that loses its reputation will never have a bright future	0.614	0.836
	12	I would rather lose money than keep my credit when cooperating with other companies	0.622	0.825
	13	I have confidence in my professionalism	0.556	0.834
	14	I am confident in my ability to cope with unexpected situations	0.581	0.825
	15	I adapt to change flexibly	0.582	0.856
	16	I hope my company can go global as an	0.602	0.799

Variable	No.	Item	CITC	Alpha if the item deleted
		influential Chinese brand.		
	17	In my opinion, entrepreneurs must take on more social responsibility after achieving personal enrichment	0.557	0.863
	18	I consider entrepreneurs' moral integrity more important than their ability to make money	0.518	0.842

(2) Reliability test of causation

Causation has 4 items in total. The Cronbach's α coefficient for the total scale was 0.835, and the CR was 0.879, higher than the cutoff value of 0.7. The CITC values of the four items ranged from 0.68 to 0.71, much higher than the cutoff value of 0.4. Moreover, deleting any of the items did not increase the Cronbach's α coefficient value of the overall scale. It indicates that the causation scale is highly reliable, and all items consistently reflect the meaning of causation. The specific reliability test results are shown in Table 7-2.

Table 7-2 Reliability Analysis of Causation

Variable	No.	Item	CITC	Alpha if the item deleted
Causation	1	I prefer to have predetermined goals and work hard to achieve them	0.683	0.815
	2	I avoid uncertainty to a large extent	0.678	0.823
	3	I prefer budgeting and detailed competitive analysis when investigating market demand for our products or services	0.676	0.804
	4	I prefer strategic, long-term, goal-oriented relationships with stakeholders	0.709	0.836

(3) Reliability test of effectuation

Effectuation has 4 items in total. The Cronbach's α coefficient for the total scale was 0.827, and the CR was 0.922, higher than the cutoff value of 0.7. The CITC values of the four items were between 0.60 and 0.70, much higher than the cutoff value of 0.4. Furthermore, deleting any of the items did not increase the Cronbach's α coefficient value of the overall scale. It indicates that the reliability of the causation scale is high, and all items consistently reflect the meaning of effectuation. The results of the reliability test are shown in Table 7-3.

Table 7-3 Reliability Analysis of Effectuation

Variable	**No.**	**Item**	**CITC**	**Alpha if the item deleted**
Effectuation	1	I prefer flexible goals and can change the direction of the business based on results	0.679	0.834
	2	I appreciate casual and informal relationships with my stakeholders	0.701	0.825
	3	I prefer to investigate market demand for our products or services using informal methods	0.654	0.853
	4	I embrace uncertain events and want to capitalize on these events	0.602	0.806

(4) Reliability test of industrial dynamics

Industrial dynamics has a total of 10 items. The Cronbach's α coefficient for the total scale was 0.846, and the CR was 0.885, higher than the cutoff value of 0.7. The CITC values for the ten items ranged from 0.55 to 0.71, much higher than the cutoff value 0.4. Moreover, deleting any of the items did not increase the Cronbach's α coefficient value of the overall scale. It indicates that the reliability of the causation scale is high, and all items consistently reflect the meaning of industrial dynamics. The results of the reliability test are shown in Table 7-4.

Table 7-4 Reliability Analysis of Industrial Dynamics

Variable	Dimension	No.	Item	CITC	Alpha if the item deleted
Industrial dynamics	Market dynamics	1	Customers' needs and preferences change rapidly	0.582	0.83
		2	Customers' needs and preferences are highly unpredictable	0.685	0.78
		3	New customers' needs for products and services are significantly different from those of regular customers	0.711	0.76
		4	Industry products and services are becoming more and more diversified	0.655	0.87
		5	Competition between enterprises and their peers is becoming more and more intense	0.652	0.81
	Technology dynamics	6	Technologies in the industry in which the enterprise is located change frequently	0.605	0.87
		7	Enterprises have difficulty in predicting the trend of technological change in the next five years	0.575	0.85
		8	Technological changes present significant opportunities for the industry	0.604	0.79
		9	Technological changes facilitate the generation of new products and services	0.550	0.77
		10	Technological changes in the industry greatly affect the business activities of enterprises	0.611	0.82

Validity Analysis

In this study, confirmatory factor analysis was used to test the structural soundness of the measurement model. That is, only after the reliability and validity of the constructed variables are ensured is it meaningful to draw conclusions based on the statistical relationships between the latent variables (Li, 2009). Measurement reliability and validity can be determined by examining the reliability and validity of the measurement items. Confirmatory factor analysis involves a variety of model fit indicators. Therefore, it is prudent to refer to some stable indices to report the measurement results of multiple items rather than relying on one index type. Therefore, based on the existing research literature, the following indices were used to test the validity of the measurement model.

(1)χ^2 or χ^2/df. χ^2 is a differential fit index. A significant value of χ^2 obtained at some degree of freedom represents a misfit between the observation matrix and the theoretical estimation matrix, and its value is quite sensitive to the sample size. That is, the larger the sample size, the easier it is for the χ^2 value to become significant, leading to the rejection of the theoretical model. To minimize the impact of sample size on the fit test, most scholars suggest using χ^2/df as a measure. For a reasonable range of values, it is generally believed that the model fits better when χ^2/df is less than 2.0. A value between 2.0 and 5.0 is also acceptable (Peng, 2009). In this study, the model is considered acceptable when χ^2/df is no greater than 5.0.

(2) RMSEA, i.e., Root Mean Squared Error of Approximation, is used to compare a model's degree of goodness of fit. The closer the RMSEA is to 0, the better the fit of the model is. Steiger (1990) found that an RMSEA below 0.1 indicates a good fit, one below 0.05 indicates a very good fit, and one below 0.01 indicates an excellent fit. In this study, 0.1 was used as the criterion for judging the goodness of fit of RMSEA.

(3) NFI, or Normed Fit Index, is used to judge the model by comparing the X^2 value between the independent model and the set model, and an NFI greater than 0.9 is acceptable. The closer the NFI is to 1, the better the fit is.

(4) IFI, i.e., corrective fit index, reduces the dependence of the mean value of the index on the sample size and takes into account the effect of the degrees of freedom of the set model. It is generally recognized that an IFI greater than 0.9 is acceptable. The closer it is to 1, the better the model's fit.

(5) CFI, i.e., Comparative Fit Index, indicates that the model is fitted to the non-central X^2 distribution with non-central parameters, thus overcoming the variability of the indicator. Again, a NFI greater than 0.9 is generally considered acceptable. The closer it is to 1, the better the model fit is.

(6) GFI, i.e., Goodness of Fit Index, indicates a non-statistical measure. It shows how much the model can explain the variation and covariance in the observations, with a range of values between 0 and 1. Again, a GFI greater than 0.9 is acceptable. The closer it is to 1, the better the model's fit.

The confirmatory factor analysis of the key variables (entrepreneurial vision, causation, effectuation and industrial dynamics) is shown in Table 7-5. The results show that the measurement model has good fit validity. The loadings of all factors were above 0.5, which met the reference standard and were significant at the P=0.01 level. Meanwhile, the average variance extracted (AVE) values of the above variables were greater than 0.5, and the CR values were greater than 0.8. It conformed to the reference standard. Therefore, it indicates that the measurements of the variables have good convergent validity (Hair et al., 2010).

Table 7-5 Validity Analysis of Variables

Variable	Index						
	χ^2	df	CFI	NFI	GFI	RMSEA	RMR
Entrepreneurial vision	149.207	96	0.976	0.949	0.982	0.046	0.051
Causation	119.351	78	0.932	0.993	0.951	0.062	0.056
Effectuation	146.707	101	0.940	0.964	0.958	0.053	0.065
Industrial dynamics	150.311	103	0.961	0.993	0.994	0.047	0.045

Hypothesis Testing and Result Analysis

To avoid the influence of multicollinearity on the regression results, we checked each regression model's variance inflation factor (VIF). In all models, the VIF values of explanatory variables were lower than 5, and the VIF values of single variables were lower than the critical value of 10. Hence, there was no severe multicollinearity in the regression models. According to the theoretical hypothesis testing model designed in the previous section, the relationship between variables was empirically analyzed in this paper using the least squares regression equation model. First, the main effect test was conducted to test the effect of entrepreneurial vision on enterprise performance. Second, we tested the mediating effect of decision logic in the relationship between entrepreneurial vision and enterprise performance. Finally, we tested the moderating effects of industrial complexity and industrial dynamics.

Descriptive Statistics of Variables

Table 7-6 shows the descriptive statistics of the variables. The descriptive statistics show that on the seven-point scale of entrepreneurial vision, the average score for entrepreneurial vision was 6.368. The mean value of enterprise performance was 0.216, but there was a big difference in performance between different enterprises. The mean values of causation and effectuation were 3.652 and 4.375, respectively, with some differences. The mean of industrial complexity was 0.342, while that of industrial dynamics was 2.638.

Table 7-6 Descriptive Statistics of Variables (N=298)

Variable	Observation	Mean	Standard error	Min.	Max.
Enterprise performance	298	0.216	0.451	-2.206	13.638
Entrepreneurial vision	298	4.368	0.422	1	7
Causation	298	3.652	1.591	1	6
Effectuation	298	4.375	1.712	2	7
Industrial complexity	298	0.342	1.493	0.131	0.731
Industrial dynamics	298	2.638	1.067	1	7
Entrepreneur gender	298	0.755	0.301	0	1
Entrepreneur age	298	35.354	7.754	18	64
Entrepreneurs' education	298	4.353	0.3469	2	7
Enterprise age	298	7.293	2.847	3	21
Enterprise size	298	3.746	1.731	0.693	3.738
Ownership concentration	298	0.630	0.141	0.372	1
Board size	298	5.739	1.299	0	11

Variable	Observation	Mean	Standard error	Min.	Max.
Enterprise debt ratio	298	0.426	0.210	0.104	2.358
Duality	298	0.822	0.383	0	1
Institutional shareholding	298	0.174	0.413	0	0.633

Correlation Analysis

Table 7-7 reports the correlation coefficients between the variables. The preliminary results of the correlation coefficient table show a significant positive correlation between entrepreneurial vision and enterprise performance ($r=0.22$, $p<0.05$). Causation positively and significantly correlates with enterprise performance ($r=0.06$, $p<0.05$). Effectuation significantly negatively correlates with enterprise performance ($r=-0.14$, $p<0.05$). The directions of the correlation coefficients are consistent with the hypotheses, initially indicating that the hypotheses have strong rationality.

Table 7-7 Descriptive Statistics of Variables (N=298)

Variable	1	2	3	4	5	6	7	8	9	10	11	12	13	14	15	16
1. Enterprise performance	1															
2. Entrepreneurial vision	0.22	1														
3. Causation	0.06	0.02	1													
4. Effectuation	-0.14	-0.04	-0.04	1												
5. Industrial complexity	-0.16	-0.08	-0.03	-0.00	1											
6. Industrial dynamics	0.11	0.02	-0.02	0.07	0.08	1										
7. Entrepreneur gender	0.17	-0.07	0.01	-0.03	0.01	-0.00	1									
8. Entrepreneur age	0.06	0.02	-0.02	0.06	0.03	-0.04	-0.05	1								
9. Entrepreneurs' education	0.07	0.01	0.01	0.06	-0.06	0.03	0.06	0.28	1							
10. Enterprise age	0.10	0.01	0.07	-0.12	-0.03	-0.01	0.11	0.04	0.08	1						
11. Enterprise size	0.04	-0.00	-0.02	0.09	0.05	0.01	0.08	0.01	-0.03	-0.12	1					
12. Ownership concentration	0.04	0.03	0.00	-0.02	-0.07	-0.03	0.01	0.01	-0.01	-0.01	-0.03	1				
13. Board size	0.03	-0.06	0.02	0.05	0.00	-0.11	0.05	-0.19	-0.08	0.09	-0.03	0.05	1			
14. Enterprise debt ratio	-0.16	0.06	-0.03	0.11	0.07	0.12	-0.04	-0.17	0.12	-0.11	0.04	-0.08	-0.23	1		
15. Duality	0.02	0.04	0.01	-0.00	0.01	-0.05	-0.09	-0.07	0.00	0.02	0.02	0.13	0.23	0.10	1	
16. Institutional shareholding	0.01	-0.01	-0.01	-0.14	0.47	0.04	0.11	-0.03	-0.09	0.04	0.04	-0.34	0.21	-0.33	-0.05	1

Note: $p<0.05$ if the absolute value of the correlation coefficient is greater than 0.05.

Relationship Testing between Entrepreneurial Vision, Decision Logic and Enterprise Performance

Table 7-8 tests the relationships between entrepreneurial vision, decision logic and enterprise performance. Enterprise performance is measured using the average three-year total assets growth rate. The mediating effect of decision logic involved in the research model is tested by the classical research method proposed by Wen and Ye (2014). Model 1 in Table 7-8 is the baseline model, containing all control and independent variables. The results of Model 1 show a significant positive correlation between entrepreneurial vision and causation (b= 0.2063, $p<0.01$). The results of Model 2 indicate a significant positive correlation between entrepreneurial vision and enterprise performance (b= 0.1051, $p<0.01$). That is, the broader the entrepreneurial vision, the better the enterprise performance. Hence, H1 is supported. The correlation between entrepreneurial vision and enterprise performance no longer holds after the mediator variable of causation was added to Model 3. However, a significant positive correlation exists between causation and enterprise performance (b= 0.3046, $p<0.01$). This result suggests a complete mediating effect of causation in the relationship between entrepreneurial vision and enterprise performance. Therefore, H2 is supported.

Model 4 in Table 7-8 is the baseline model, covering all control and independent variables. The results of Model 4 show that there is a significant negative correlation between entrepreneurial vision and effectuation (b= -0.0987, $p<0.01$). The results of Model 5 show a significant positive correlation between entrepreneurial vision and enterprise performance (b= 0.1338, $p<0.01$). That is, the broader the entrepreneurial vision, the better the enterprise performance. After adding the mediator variable of effectuation to Model 6, the correlation between entrepreneurial vision and enterprise performance remains unchanged. However, a significant negative correlation exists between effectuation and enterprise performance (b=-0.4451, $p<0.01$). It suggests that causation partially mediates the relationship between entrepreneurial vision and enterprise performance. So, H3 is supported.

Table 7-8 Relationship Testing between Entrepreneurial Vision, Decision Logic and Enterprise Performance (N=298)

Variable	Causation	Enterprise performance	Enterprise performance	Effectuation	Enterprise performance	Enterprise performance
	Model 1	Model 2	Model 3	Model 4	Model 5	Model 6
Entrepreneurial vision	0.2063*** (0.0011)	0.1051*** (0.0011)	0.1451 (0.1011)	-0.0987*** (0.0287)	0.1338*** (0.0304)	0.1977** (0.0577)
Causation			0.3046*** (0.0123)			
Effectuation						-0.4451*** (0.0993)
Industrial complexity	-0.0049*** (0.0009)	-0.0041*** (0.0009)	-0.0041*** (0.0009)	-0.0047*** (0.0009)	-0.0042*** (0.0009)	-0.0047*** (0.0009)
Industrial dynamics	-0.0441*** (0.0032)	-0.0383*** (0.0032)	-0.0383*** (0.0032)	-0.0382*** (0.0032)	-0.0389*** (0.0032)	-0.0387*** (0.0032)
Entrepreneur gender	0.0028* (0.0015)	0.0021 (0.0015)	0.0020 (0.0015)	0.0021 (0.0015)	0.0020 (0.0015)	0.0020 (0.0015)
Entrepreneur age	-0.0610* (0.0336)	0.0064 (0.0341)	0.0064 (0.0341)	0.0046 (0.0341)	0.0032 (0.0341)	0.0019 (0.0341)
Entrepreneurs' education	0.1991*** (0.0200)	0.1993*** (0.0198)	0.1983*** (0.0198)	0.1998*** (0.0197)	0.1967*** (0.0198)	0.1965*** (0.0197)
Enterprise age	0.2220*** (0.0231)	0.2286*** (0.0231)	0.2292*** (0.0231)	0.2269*** (0.0231)	0.2306*** (0.0231)	0.2295*** (0.0231)
Enterprise size	0.7409*** (0.0361)	0.7402*** (0.0363)	0.7405*** (0.0363)	0.7403*** (0.0363)	0.7395*** (0.0363)	0.7397*** (0.0363)
Ownership concentration	-0.2404*** (0.0342)	-0.2424*** (0.0345)	-0.2416*** (0.0344)	-0.2420*** (0.0345)	-0.2409*** (0.0344)	-0.2398*** (0.0344)
Board size	0.0381*** (0.0042)	0.0347*** (0.0042)	0.0347*** (0.0042)	0.0350*** (0.0042)	0.0332*** (0.0042)	0.0335*** (0.0042)
Enterprise debt ratio	-0.0080*** (0.0014)	-0.0083*** (0.0015)	-0.0083*** (0.0015)	-0.0084*** (0.0015)	-0.0085*** (0.0015)	-0.0086*** (0.0015)
Duality	-0.0025* (0.0014)	-0.0033** (0.0013)	-0.0033** (0.0013)	-0.0036*** (0.0013)	-0.0035*** (0.0013)	-0.0038*** (0.0013)
Institutional shareholding	0.0063*** (0.0011)	0.0056*** (0.0011)	0.0055*** (0.0011)	0.0056*** (0.0011)	0.0057*** (0.0011)	0.0057*** (0.0011)
Constant	-4.3488*** (0.2161)	-4.1179*** (0.2165)	-4.1177*** (0.2163)	-4.0990*** (0.2162)	-4.1006*** (0.2159)	-4.0780*** (0.2158)
Industry	Control	Control	Control	Control	Control	Control
Log-likelihood	-14450.27	-14191.65	-14188.43	-14187.46	-14184.33	-14177.72
Wald test	1733.65***	2303.69***	2315.99***	2294.87***	2277.82***	2276.37***
R-squared	0.2547	0.2716	0.3718	0.2319	0.3321	0.3425

Note: *p<0.1, **p<0.05, ***p<0.01, standard error in parentheses.

To further test the mediating effect of decision logic between entrepreneurial vision and enterprise performance, we tested the mediating effects of causation and effectuation using the nonparametric and percentile Bootstrap method and the SPSS macro developed by Hayes et al. The logic of the test is to observe whether the confidence interval of the indirect effect of entrepreneurial vision on enterprise performance through causation and effectuation contains 0. If the confidence interval contains 0, the mediating effect does not exist. The mediating effect is significant if the confidence interval does not contain 0. The sampling was set to 5,000 times by Bootstrap, and the results are shown in Tables 7-9. The effect value of entrepreneurial vision on enterprise performance through causation was 4.758, with a 95% confidence interval of [7.426, 11.443]. The effect value of entrepreneurial vision on enterprise performance through effectuation was 3.629, with a 95% confidence interval of [-1.202, -0.571]. Their confidence intervals do not contain 0, indicating that entrepreneurial vision affects enterprise performance through the mediating effects of causation and effectuation, respectively.

Table 7-9 Mediating Effect Testing of Decision Logic (N=298)

	Effect value	SE	95% confidence interval of Monte Carlo simulation	
			LLCI (lower limit confidence interval)	ULCI (upper limit confidence interval)
Entrepreneurial vision—Causation—Enterprise performance	4.758	1.335	7.426	11.443
Entrepreneurial vision—Effectuation—Enterprise performance	3.629	1.064	-1.202	-0.571

Moderating Effect of Industrial Complexity and Industrial Dynamics

Table 7-10 examines the moderating effects of industrial complexity and industrial dynamics on the relationship between decision logic and enterprise performance. Model 7 is the baseline model, and the results of the model indicate a significant positive correlation between causation and enterprise performance (b=0.1933, p<0.01). The results of Model 8 show that the interaction term between causation and industrial complexity has a significant positive correlation with enterprise performance (b= 0.0168, p<0. 01). It suggests that causation contributes more significantly to enterprise performance in more complex industries. Therefore, H4 is supported. The results of Model 9 show that the interaction term between causation and industrial dynamics has a significant negative correlation with enterprise performance (b= -0.0452, p<0. 01). It suggests that causation's contribution to enterprise performance decreases in industries with higher industrial dynamics. Therefore, H6 is supported.

Model 10 is the baseline model, and the results of the model show that there is a significant negative correlation between effectuation and enterprise performance (b=-0.0954, p<0. 01). The results of Model 11 show that the interaction term between effectuation and industrial complexity has a significant negative correlation with enterprise performance (b= -0.0421, p<0.05). Thus, in more complex industries, the inhibiting effect of effectuation on enterprise performance is strengthened. Based on this, H5 is supported. The results of Model 12 show that the interaction term between effectuation and industrial dynamics is significantly and positively correlated with enterprise performance (b= 0.0265, p<0. 01). The inhibiting effect of causation on enterprise performance is mitigated in more dynamic industries. Consequently, H7 is supported. The moderating effects of industrial complexity and dynamics are plotted in Figures 7-1 to 7-4 by simple slope analysis to visualize these effects more intuitively.

Table 7-10 Moderating Effect Testing of Industrial Complexity and Industrial Dynamics (N=298)

Variable	Enterprise performance					
	Model 7	**Model 8**	**Model 9**	**Model 10**	**Model 11**	**Model 12**
Causation	0.1933*** (0.0087)	0.0929*** (0.0087)	0.1026*** (0.0087)			
Causation × Industrial complexity		0.0168*** (0.0024)				
Causation × Industrial dynamics			-0.0452*** (0.0091)			
Effectuation				-0.0954*** (0.0292)	-0.1237*** (0.0302)	-0.1268*** (0.0302)

Variable	Enterprise performance					
	Model 7	Model 8	Model 9	Model 10	Model 11	Model 12
Effectuation× Industrial complexity					-0.0421** (0.0183)	
Effectuation× Industrial dynamics						0.0265*** (0.0071)
Industrial complexity	0.5533*** (0.1787)	0.8891*** (0.1241)	0.5524*** (0.1780)	0.5608*** (0.1781)	0.8506*** (0.1244)	0.8927*** (0.1001)
Industrial dynamics	-0.0022 (0.0015)	-0.0022 (0.0015)	-0.0076*** (0.0013)	-0.0022 (0.0015)	-0.0074*** (0.0013)	-0.0042*** (0.0009)
Entrepreneur gender	-0.0178*** (0.0063)	-0.0178*** (0.0063)	-0.0183*** (0.0063)	-0.0362*** (0.0044)	-0.0370*** (0.0045)	-0.0389*** (0.0032)
Entrepreneur age	0.0035 (0.0023)	0.0035 (0.0023)	0.0036 (0.0023)	0.0035 (0.0023)	0.0035 (0.0023)	0.0020 (0.0015)
Entrepreneurs' education	0.1900*** (0.0562)	0.1896*** (0.0562)	0.1879*** (0.0562)	0.1857*** (0.0563)	0.1838*** (0.0563)	0.0032 (0.0341)
Enterprise age	0.2817*** (0.0316)	0.2807*** (0.0316)	0.2830*** (0.0315)	0.2794*** (0.0316)	0.2799*** (0.0315)	0.1967*** (0.0198)
Enterprise size	0.1569*** (0.0381)	0.1577*** (0.0381)	0.1525*** (0.0381)	0.1595*** (0.0382)	0.1556*** (0.0382)	0.2306*** (0.0231)
Ownership concentration	0.7306*** (0.0605)	0.7309*** (0.0606)	0.7306*** (0.0606)	0.7294*** (0.0606)	0.7295*** (0.0607)	0.7395*** (0.0363)
Board size	-0.2169*** (0.0578)	-0.2160*** (0.0578)	-0.2184*** (0.0578)	-0.2144*** (0.0578)	-0.2152*** (0.0578)	-0.2409*** (0.0344)
Enterprise debt ratio	0.0256*** (0.0064)	0.0256*** (0.0064)	0.0261*** (0.0064)	0.0255*** (0.0065)	0.0261*** (0.0064)	0.0332*** (0.0042)
Duality	-0.0091*** (0.0027)	-0.0091*** (0.0027)	-0.0090*** (0.0027)	-0.0092*** (0.0027)	-0.0092*** (0.0027)	-0.0085*** (0.0015)
Institutional shareholding	-0.0059*** (0.0020)	-0.0059*** (0.0020)	-0.0057*** (0.0020)	-0.0060*** (0.0020)	-0.0059*** (0.0020)	-0.0035*** (0.0013)
Constant	0.0043** (0.0020)	0.0043** (0.0020)	0.0041** (0.0020)	0.0045** (0.0020)	0.0042** (0.0020)	0.0057*** (0.0011)
Industry	Control	Control	Control	Control	Control	Control
Log-likelihood	-14450.277	-14191.654	-14188.431	-14187.464	-14184.336	-14177.726
Wald test	1733.65***	2303.69***	2315.99***	2294.87***	2277.82***	2276.37***
R-squared	0.1541	0.2516	0.2691	0.1319	0.1456	0.2901

Note: *p<0.1, **p<0.05, ***p<0.01, standard error in parentheses.

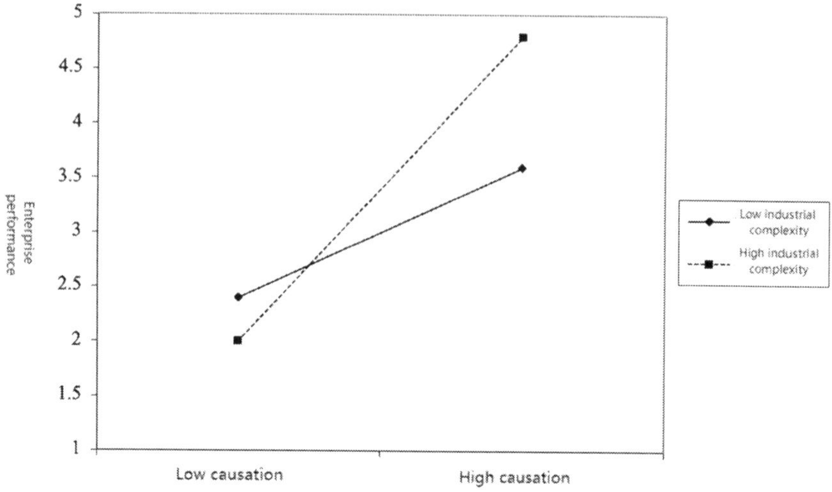

Figure 7-1 The Moderating Effect of Industrial Complexity on the Relationship Between Causation and Enterprise Performance

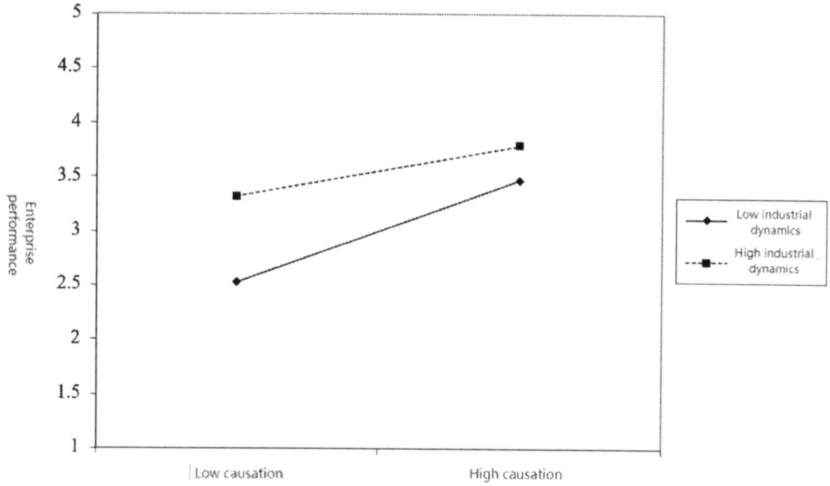

Figure 7-2 The Moderating Effect of Industrial Dynamics on the Relationship between Causation and Enterprise Performance

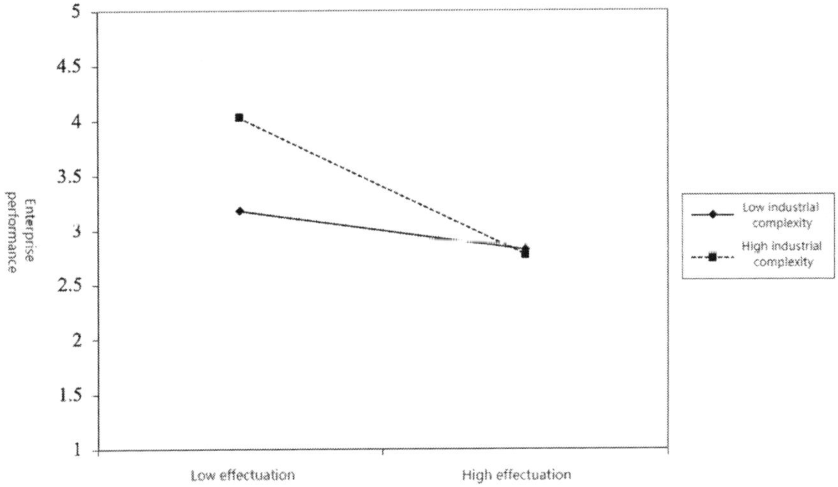

Figure 7-3 The Moderating Effect of Industrial Complexity on the Relationship between Effectuation and Enterprise Performance

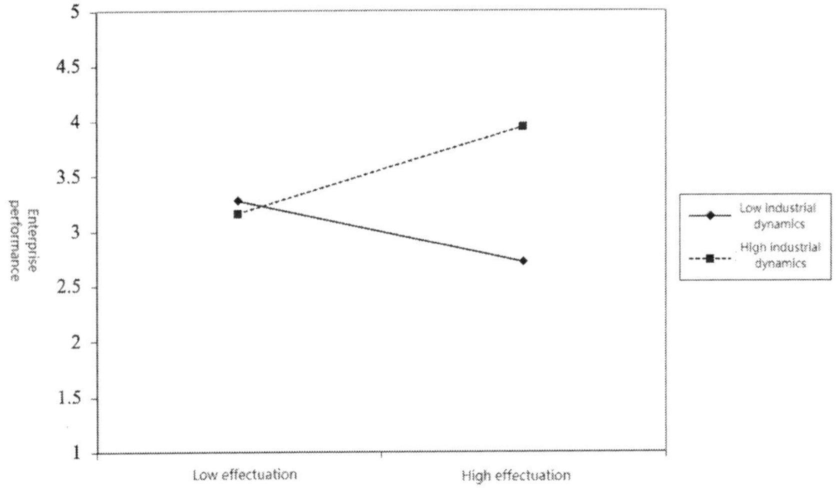

Figure 7-4 The Moderating Effect of Industrial Dynamics on the Relationship between Effectuation and Enterprise Performance

Robustness Test

Robustness tests are conducted to ensure the research results' stability. Robustness tests were conducted through alternative measures of enterprise performance. In the previous analysis, we mainly measured the performance by using the enterprise's average total assets growth rate in the last three years. In the robustness test, we used the enterprise's sales revenue growth rate in the last three years to measure the performance. The results of the robustness test are shown in Table 7-11 and Table 7-12. The results of Model 14 in Table 7-11 show a significant positive correlation between entrepreneurial vision and enterprise performance (b= 1.0429, p<0. 01). That is, the higher the entrepreneurial vision, the better the enterprise performance. Thus, H1 is supported. After the mediator variable of causation was added to Model 15, the correlation between entrepreneurial vision and enterprise performance no longer holds.

In contrast, causation was significantly and positively correlated with enterprise performance (b = 0.0087, p<0.01). It suggests that causation has a fully mediating effect between entrepreneurial vision and enterprise performance. Therefore, H2 is supported.

The results of Model 17 in Table 7-11 show a significant positive correlation between entrepreneurial vision and enterprise performance (b= 1.1477, p<0.01). The higher the entrepreneurial vision, the better the enterprise performance. After the addition of effectuation as a mediator variable in Model 18, the correlation between entrepreneurial vision and enterprise performance remained unchanged, and there was a significant negative correlation between effectuation and enterprise performance (b=-0.2794, p<0. 01). It shows that causation partially mediates the relationship between entrepreneurial vision and enterprise performance. Therefore, H3 is supported.

Table 7-11 Robustness Test of the Relationship between Entrepreneurial Vision, Decision Logic and Enterprise Performance (N=298)

Variable	Causation	Enterprise performance	Enterprise performance	Effectuation	Enterprise performance	Enterprise performance
	Model 13	Model 14	Model 15	Model 16	Model 17	Model 18
Entrepreneurial vision	0.2350*** (0.0459)	1.0429*** (0.0460)	0.0773 (0.0463)	-0.6993*** (0.0188)	1.1477*** (0.0495)	1.0350*** (0.0459)
Causation			0.0087*** (0.0023)			
Effectuation						-0.2794*** (0.0316)
Control variable	Control	Control	Control	Control	Control	Control
Constant	-3.6900*** (0.4222)	-3.6938*** (0.4221)	-3.4533*** (0.4181)	-3.5650*** (0.4185)	-3.3234*** (0.4159)	-3.6900*** (0.4222)
Industry	Control	Control	Control	Control	Control	Control
Log-likelihood	-3309.091	-3308.242	-3305.876	-3306.635	-3302.740	-3309.091
Wald test	925.65***	978.93***	1039.41***	1023.92***	1154.41***	925.65***
R-squared	0.1823	0.2126	0.2437	0.1033	0.1384	0.2315

Note: *p<0.1, **p<0.05, ***p<0.01, standard error in parentheses.

Table 7-12 examines the moderating effects of industrial complexity and industrial dynamics on the relationship between decision logic and enterprise performance. Model 19 is the baseline model, and the model results show a significant positive correlation between causation and enterprise performance (b= 0.2427, p<0. 01). The results of Model 20 show that the interaction term between causation and industrial complexity has a significant positive correlation with enterprise performance (b= 0.1461, p<0. 01). It suggests that causation contributes more significantly to enterprise performance in industries with higher industrial complexity. Hence, H4 is supported. The results of Model 21 show that the interaction term between causation and industrial dynamics has a significant negative correlation with enterprise performance (b=-0.0354, p<0. 01). It suggests that the facilitating effect of causation on enterprise performance decreases in industries with higher industrial dynamics. Thus, H6 is supported.

Model 22 is the baseline model, and the results of the model show that there is a significant negative correlation between effectuation and enterprise performance (b=- 0.0407, p<0. 01). The result of Model 23 shows that the interaction term of effectuation and industrial complexity is significantly and negatively correlated with enterprise performance (b= -0.2931, p<0. 01). It suggests that the inhibiting effect of effectuation on enterprise performance is further strengthened in industries with higher industrial complexity. Therefore, H5 is supported. The results of Model 24 show that the interaction term of effectuation and industrial dynamics has a significant positive correlation with enterprise performance (b= 0.0419, p<0. 01). It suggests that the inhibiting effect of causation on enterprise performance decreases further in industries with higher industrial dynamics. Because of this, H7 is supported.

Table 7-12 Robustness Test of Moderating Effects of Industrial Complexity and Industrial Dynamics (N=298)

Variable	Enterprise performance					
	Model 19	**Model 20**	**Model 21**	**Model 22**	**Model 23**	**Model 24**
Causation	0.2427*** (0.0268)	0.2438*** (0.0267)	0.2392*** (0.0267)			
Causation× Industrial complexity		0.1461*** (0.0219)				
Causation× Industrial dynamics			-0.0354*** (0.0048)			
Effectuation				-0.0407*** (0.0040)	-0.0406*** (0.0040)	-0.0399*** (0.0041)
Effectuation× Industrial complexity					-0.2931*** (0.0397)	
Effectuation× Industrial dynamics						0.0419*** (0.0040)
Control variable	Control	Control	Control	Control	Control	Control
Constant	0.0043** (0.0020)	0.0043** (0.0020)	0.0041** (0.0020)	0.0045** (0.0020)	0.0042** (0.0020)	0.0057*** (0.0011)
Industry	Control	Control	Control	Control	Control	Control
Log-likelihood	-10803.14	-10797.72	-10795.95	-10792.89	-10783.08	-10803.14
Wald test	1897.21***	1911.14***	1886.59***	1866.72***	1867.30***	1897.21***
R-squared	0.2701	0.2766	0.2913	0.2054	0.1778	0.3015

Note: *p<0.1, **p<0.05, ***p<0.01, standard error in parentheses.

Summary of Hypothesis Testing Results

For the hypotheses formulated, hypothesis testing was conducted through the designed empirical study. The results of the hypothesis testing are summarized as shown in Table 7-13. All the research hypotheses are supported.

Table 7-13 Summary of Hypothesis Testing Results

No.	Hypothesis	Results
H1	For an enterprise, the higher the entrepreneurial vision, the better the enterprise's performance.	True
H2	Causation mediates the relationship between entrepreneurial vision and enterprise performance.	True
H3	Effectuation mediates the relationship between entrepreneurial vision and enterprise performance.	True
H4	Industrial complexity reinforces the positive correlation between causation and enterprise performance.	True
H5	Industrial complexity reinforces the negative correlation between effectuation and enterprise performance.	True
H6	Industrial dynamics weakens the positive correlation between causation and enterprise performance.	True
H7	Industrial dynamics weakens the negative correlation between effectuation and enterprise performance.	True

Chapter 8
Conclusion and Discussion

Conclusion

The study of entrepreneurial strategic leadership has been the focus of attention in strategic management research since the 1980s. Researchers have extensively addressed the critical impact of entrepreneurial strategic leadership on enterprise performance (Hambrick & Quigley, 2014; Quigley et al., 2017; Withers & Fitza, 2017). However, most studies are based on Western management contexts, and there is no research on entrepreneurial strategic leadership in China's unique institutional and cultural contexts. Strategic leadership roles and motivations differ across institutional contexts (Aguilera & Jackson, 2010). They also differ greatly in the impact on corporate strategic decisions and competitive advantage (Crossland & Hambrick, 2007; Krause et al., 2019). Thus, this study focuses on entrepreneurial vision as a unique type of strategic leadership and explores the dimensions of entrepreneurial vision and its measurements.

Moreover, it examines the mechanism of the impact of entrepreneurial vision on enterprise performance. Three key scientific questions are answered: first, what is entrepreneurial vision? Second, how can entrepreneurial vision be measured? Third, how does entrepreneurial vision affect enterprise performance?

Based on the qualitative and quantitative data analysis, this study draws the following conclusions:

(1) It identifies the Chinese context's characteristics and constitutive dimensions of entrepreneurial vision. It is widely recognized in Chinese Confucian traditional culture and Chinese management practices that entrepreneurial vision has a crucial impact on organizational management practices. However, entrepreneurial vision has not been clearly defined. It draws on research on strategic leadership combined with an analysis of entrepreneurs based on the grounded theory. Then, it extracts the nine

dimensions of entrepreneurial vision (modernity, calmness, promise-keeping, vision, courage and insight, profound research, aspiration, win-win cooperation, and patriotism).

(2) It develops and tests a scale for entrepreneurial vision in China. In this study, the initial scale of entrepreneurial vision was constructed by combining the strategic leadership research literature with the entrepreneurial vision construct dimensions extracted from the grounded theory. The initial scale was used for the questionnaire survey and exploratory factor analysis. The scale was further optimized into 18 items in six dimensions (aspiration, modesty, win-win cooperation, promote-keeping, calmness and patriotism). Confirmatory factor analysis was conducted with the new scale. The study's results revealed good construct validity and reliability and satisfactory discriminant validity of the new scale.

(3) It explores the mechanism of entrepreneurial vision affecting enterprise performance. Entrepreneurial vision is an important embodiment of entrepreneurial strategic leadership in the Chinese context. Although management practices have observed the significant impact of entrepreneurial vision on organizational management, no systematic and rigorous evidence supports this speculation. A survey of 298 SMEs in this study found that entrepreneurial vision promotes enterprise performance, mainly through two different decision logics: causation and effectuation. This study is the first to confirm the critical impact of entrepreneurial vision on enterprise performance in the Chinese context through rigorous empirical analyses and its underlying mechanisms.

(4) It reveals the significant impact of industrial complexity and industrial dynamics on the relationship between entrepreneurial vision and enterprise performance. The industry environment is a critical condition for entrepreneurs to make decisions. The effectiveness of any given decision-making process or strategic initiative depends largely on its fit with the industry environment (Dean & Sharfman, 1996; Judge & Miller, 1991). This study found that the relationship between entrepreneurial vision and enterprise performance was also affected by industrial complexity and industrial dynamics. Industrial complexity strengthens the facilitating (inhibiting) effects of causation (effectuation) on enterprise performance, while industrial dynamics weaken these effects. By introducing the analysis of industry environment factors, we further

deepen the understanding of the boundary conditions of the relationship between entrepreneurial vision and enterprise performance.

Based on the above summary, the entrepreneurial vision scale was first developed and systematically tested in the Chinese context. We explored the mechanism and boundary of entrepreneurial vision influencing enterprise performance. This study deepens the understanding and knowledge of entrepreneurial vision in the Chinese context. It expands the analytical framework of strategic leadership to provide effective suggestions for improving management practices in the Chinese context.

Theoretical Contributions

This study systematically analyzes the characteristics of entrepreneurial vision and its influence on enterprise performance. It creatively confirms the value of entrepreneurial vision as an important strategic leadership for organizational management practice in China's unique institutional and cultural context. The theoretical contributions of this study are summarized in the following three aspects:

First, the grounded theory and scale development techniques were used to identify the meaning and dimensions of entrepreneurial vision. The localization of strategic leadership has long been a focus of academic research. The research on the localization of strategic leadership greatly expands the explanatory power of this topic for management practice, and more critically, it is an important channel for contributing to management knowledge in China. China has a long history of political, social, and economic management experience and various management and leadership models. With the rapid rise of China's economy, conducting an in-depth and systematic study of China's unique strategic leadership from a local perspective is significant. Compared with paternalistic leadership, a highly localized signature of leadership styles, there is little research on the characteristics of local strategic leadership (Cao & Li, 2010). Based on theoretical analysis and practical observation, this study developed the concept and connotation of entrepreneurial vision in the Chinese context. It has also systematically developed a scale of entrepreneurial vision, providing an important basic tool for local research on entrepreneurial vision. Existing research on entrepreneurial vision remains at the stage of theoretical discourse and conceptual presentation without the extraction and operation of theoretical constructs and the empirical testing of conceptual frameworks. Based on China's unique cultural and institutional background and the reality of corporate practice, a scale for measuring entrepreneurial vision was developed and validated. It provides a measurement tool for subsequent quantitative research on entrepreneurial vision.

Further, it lays the foundation for the comparative study of strategic leadership in cross-cultural contexts. It clarifies the entrepreneurial vision's structure and measurement scale in the local Chinese cultural context. Moreover, it reveals the differences in the focus of strategic leadership between Chinese and Western cultures, guiding the subsequent cross-cultural comparative research on strategic leadership.

Second, it reveals the dual mechanisms of entrepreneurial vision on enterprise performance. It is uncertain whether and how vision, as an important component of entrepreneurial strategic leadership, affects enterprise performance. The upper-echelon theory suggests that entrepreneurs' traits affect enterprise performance through information-seeking and decision-making. However, existing studies do not provide more evidence (Crossland & Hambrick, 2007). In this study, we introduced two types of decision logic, causation and effectuation, and confirmed the dual impact of entrepreneurial vision on enterprise performance through different decision logic. It confirms for the first time the impact of entrepreneurial vision, a localized form of strategic leadership in China, on enterprise performance, deepening and expanding the research on strategic leadership. More importantly, it reveals the dual influence mechanisms of causation and effectuation. This conclusion provides a deeper understanding of how entrepreneurial vision affects enterprise performance. Despite causation and effectuation being the most popular new theories in decision-making research in recent years, there has not been much comparative research on how they affect performance. It has been widely recognized that causation and effectuation positively affect enterprise performance (Brettel et al., 2012; Smolka et al., 2018). However, a comparison in this study reveals differences in the effect of the two types of decision logic on enterprise performance. It confirms the theoretical differences between the two types of decision logic. More importantly, it further deepens and expands the related research on causation and effectuation.

Third, it extends the research on the impact of entrepreneurial vision on enterprise performance from the perspective of industry dynamics. For a long time, there has been no consensus on how strategic leadership affects enterprise performance, leading to much criticism of strategic leadership research (Wangrow et al., 2015). The seemingly contradictory views of strategic leadership provide a new way of thinking, as the external environment may influence the way entrepreneurial vision affects enterprise performance. We introduced the perspective of industry dynamics and confirmed the speculation. The impact of entrepreneurial vision on enterprise performance depends to some extent on the dynamic industrial environment faced by the company. The industrial dynamic environment is a critical condition for companies to make decisions. The effectiveness of any given decision-making process or strategic initiative depends heavily on its fit with the industry environment (Dean & Sharfman, 1996; Judge & Miller, 1991). Industrial complexity and dynamics were introduced to portray the significant impact of the industry's dynamic environment on the relationship between entrepreneurial vision and enterprise performance. This conclusion partly bridges the paradox of the research on the relationship between strategic leadership and enterprise performance. That is, the effectiveness of any strategic leadership is not stable but is affected by the dynamics of the external industry environment. At the same time, the introduction of industrial dynamics further enriches the context of entrepreneurial vision-related research. It also responds to the current debate in strategic leadership research about the usefulness of simple mental models versus more complex mental models in strategic decision-making (Wooldridge & Cowden, 2020).

Practical Implications

The conclusion is of great significance to the management practice of Chinese enterprises. China's economy has maintained sustained and rapid growth over the past 40 years of reform and opening up. Even in the face of global uncertainties, such as the U.S.-China trade war and the COVID-19 pandemic, the Chinese economy has maintained its unique resilience, which is fundamentally attributed to the entrepreneurship of countless Chinese enterprises and entrepreneurs. Penrose defines the economic benefits that result from the growth of numerous enterprises as growth economies. One of the distinguishing features of growth economies, as opposed to economies of scale, is that these benefits depend on a particular set of productive resources of a specific enterprise.

Furthermore, the utilization of the opportunities offered by these resources can be little related to the size of the enterprise. Thus, the benefits of a growth economy are available to enterprises of all sizes. So, from the perspectives of both the enterprise and the entire economy, the growth of enterprises of any size can be attributed to the efficient use of resources (Penrose, 1959). Where, then, does the drive for growth come from? It may not be external competition and internal demand as emphasized in traditional economics, but rather a return to a focus on entrepreneurs. Based on the study of entrepreneurial vision, this paper seeks to present the critical role of entrepreneurial vision, a unique form of strategic leadership, in business growth. The value of entrepreneurial vision for management practice is summarized in the following two areas:

First, entrepreneurs should pay attention to cultivating vision. Entrepreneurs are the key to organizational decision-making. For China in the transition period, the government has long dominated the allocation of market resources. Because of this, most entrepreneurs in China are keen to establish close personal relationships with the government. Entrepreneur ability is often measured by overemphasizing the ability to build a network of relationships without cultivating the entrepreneur's moral qualities. A possible prediction is that, with the gradual deepening of market-oriented reforms and the improvement of the institutional environment, the government tends to play a more and more important role as an "effective market, competent government" in allocating market resources. Enterprises competition is increasingly a competition of entrepreneurship rather than a competition of personal relationships with resource allocators. At the same time, with the rise of anti-globalization and populism, the global economic situation may be subject to higher uncertainty. Hence, emphasizing the cultivation of entrepreneurial vision is crucial in improving business resilience and maintaining long-term competitive advantage.

Second, the selection of managers needs to consider the suitability of their competence to the industry environment. When selecting managers, many enterprises take the previous performance of candidates as the main reference index rather than the actual needs of the enterprise and the industry situation at the current stage. Thus, a problem arises that the winners may have had an impressive track record in the past, but their competencies may not match the current development needs of the enterprise. Numerous studies have shown that the development of an enterprise is closely related to the environment in which it operates. In different industry environments, there are differences in the requirements for managers' competence. When there is a dynamic combination of complexity, fecundity and dynamics in the industry environment, managers should act as creators, accelerators, maintainers and changers in different industry environments. Correspondingly, the requirements for managers' competence vary greatly. Hence, it is essential to consider the characteristics of the industry environment in screening managers.

Limitations and Prospects

This study portrays the characteristics of entrepreneurial vision and its mechanism and boundaries of influence on enterprise performance in China's unique cultural and institutional context. It is of great theoretical significance in deepening the study of strategic leadership in the Chinese context and guiding management practice in China. However, its limitations and shortcomings are as follows:

First, it expands the scope of sample selection and generalizes the conclusion. In this study, the sample selection criteria were formulated about the literature specification of similar research topics, generally meeting the needs of the research design for research samples and methods. However, the sample collection was limited by certain conditions in the actual research. From the research on feature recognition of entrepreneurial vision, the retrospective information of secondary data may involve some bias in selection. The selected enterprises for the case studies were all large-scale enterprises, without interviews with entrepreneurs from SMEs. However, there are some differences between the management model of large enterprises and SMEs. Because of this, the explanatory power of the entrepreneurial vision dimension, which was refined based on managers of large-scale enterprises, may be reduced in SMEs. Follow-up research needs to expand the sample selection scope and conduct more detailed and in-depth interviews with enterprises of different sizes. Based on this, the dimensions and connotations of entrepreneurial vision can be enriched. In addition, from the empirical sample, data were collected from both online and offline sources. However, due to the limitation of data collection time and epidemic prevention policy, there may be insufficient sample sources, and the empirical analysis is mainly based on cross-sectional data. Using various methods, we tried to minimize some possible econometric problems (e.g., endogeneity, common method variance). However, it cannot completely avoid or eliminate the interference of these problems with the study results. In future research, we can use large-scale tracking data to strengthen empirical findings further when conditions permit.

Second, it enriches the research methodology to analyze the black box of entrepreneurial vision's influence mechanism on enterprise performance from more dimensions. This study combines grounded theory and empirical research methods on questionnaire data, fulfilling the need for characterization and empirical hypothesis testing of entrepreneurial vision and enterprise performance. By combining more extensive research methods, future research can open the black box of how entrepreneurial vision affects enterprise performance. In future research, longitudinal single-case studies or multi-case studies can be further utilized (Yin, 1994). Longitudinal studies allow us to observe the effects of entrepreneurial vision on enterprise performance across enterprises of different sizes and development cycles to obtain more systematic and comprehensive conclusions. In addition, combining experimental studies can help to test the important causation of entrepreneurial vision affecting enterprise performance. Controlled experimentation isolates causal variables and allows for the robustness test of a theory.

Moreover, they provide compelling evidence for the theory (Pfeffer & Sutton, 2006). The use of diversified research methods can make up for the shortcomings of a single research method. It can further contribute to strategic leadership research in the Chinese context from a theoretical perspective.

Third, a cross-cultural comparative study can enhance the generalizability and validity of the concept of entrepreneurial vision. This study provides an in-depth and systematic investigation of the concept of entrepreneurial vision in China's unique cultural context. Although this study provides valuable insights into entrepreneurs' behavioral and psychological characteristics in this particular cultural group, it does not represent entrepreneurs in different cultures worldwide. Cross-cultural comparative research is essential to improve the validity of the concept and scale of entrepreneurial vision. Cultures have significant differences regarding values, religious beliefs, social structures, and economic systems. These differences may greatly affect entrepreneurial vision. Based on this, through cross-cultural comparative research, we can explore the similarities and differences of entrepreneurial vision in different cultural contexts. Thus, the diversity of entrepreneurial behaviors and psychological characteristics can be more comprehensively understood. Such cross-cultural comparisons can help identify the impact of cultural factors on entrepreneurial vision and provide more precise and effective guidance on how to strengthen and enhance entrepreneurial leadership. However, there are some challenges in cross-cultural comparative research. Cultures differ in language, values, and religion, so some adjustments may be required in the research design and data collection. In addition, cross-cultural research demands more time, resources, and cross-cultural communication to ensure the accuracy and reliability of the research results. It is also an important field for future research on entrepreneurial vision.

Afterword

As a management practitioner, I witnessed China's reform and opening up and the rapid development of the private economy. Seeing many private enterprises' rapid growth and sudden decline has interested me in exploring the mysteries determining enterprises' success or failure. During my study tour, I attempted to focus more on the research of entrepreneurs through systematic theoretical knowledge learning, mainly focusing on the significant theoretical and practical issues of entrepreneurial patterns.

This study systematically researched the development process of entrepreneurial spirit in China since the reform and opening up and its important position in the contemporary Chinese economy. Under China's unique cultural and institutional background, the entrepreneurial landscape profoundly impacts the enterprises' development and performance. Through this study, we have a clearer understanding that entrepreneurs are not only the operators but also the leaders of enterprises and are the fundamental driving forces of the enterprises' sustainable development. This study, for the first time in the context of China, clarifies the dimensions of the entrepreneurial landscape, providing us with a clear cognitive framework. By delving deeper into these dimensions, we have gained a better understanding of the qualities that Chinese entrepreneurs need to possess, such as being humble, being calm in times of change, keeping promises, having unique vision, having exceptional courage and vision, striving for excellence, having lofty aspirations, creating win-win situations together, and having a sense of patriotism. These qualities affect a company's internal culture and positively impact its external image and social responsibility.

Another highlight of this study is developing and validating the Entrepreneur Pattern Scale. Through systematic research methods, researchers have constructed a scientifically credible scale to measure the entrepreneurial landscape. This provides a powerful tool for future related research and a method for evaluating and cultivating the entrepreneurial landscape for the business community. More importantly, this study reveals how the entrepreneurial landscape affects corporate performance.

In the research, through extensive empirical analysis, researchers have confirmed that the entrepreneurial landscape significantly impacts corporate performance while also revealing the inherent logic of this impact. The entrepreneurial landscape not only influences the decision-making and execution of enterprises through causal logic and effect logic but also has varying degrees of influence in different industry environments. It provides valuable references for entrepreneurs and business managers, helping them better respond to challenges in different environments and formulate more scientific and reasonable strategies and decisions.

The metaphysical is the way, while the paranormal is the tool. This study analyzes the growth path of Chinese private enterprises during the transformation period from the perspective of the entrepreneurial pattern, providing us with a more comprehensive and in-depth understanding of the entrepreneurial pattern. It has important significance for academic research and provides a valuable reference for the sustainable development of Chinese enterprises. I hope that in the future, research in this area can continue to deepen and provide more beneficial insights and support for the healthy development of Chinese enterprises.

References

Acemoglu, D., García-Jimeno, C., & Robinson, J. A. (2015). State capacity and economic development: A network approach. *American Economic Review*, 105(8), 2364-2409.

Adner, R., & Levinthal, D. A. (2004). What is not a real option: Considering boundaries for applying real options to business strategy. *Academy of Management Review*, 29(1), 74-85.

Aguilera, R. V., & Jackson, G. (2010). Comparative and international corporate governance. *Academy of Management Annals*, 4(1), 485-556.

Aldrich, H. E., & Fiol, C. M. (1994). Fools rush in? The institutional context of industry creation. *Academy of Management Review*, 19(4), 645-670.

Alvarez, S. A., & Barney, J. B. (2014). Entrepreneurial opportunities and poverty alleviation. *Entrepreneurship Theory and Practice*, 38(1), 159-184.

Alvarez, S. A., & Busenitz, L. W. (2001). The entrepreneurship of resource-based theory. *Journal of Management*, 27(6), 755-775.

Alzamora-Ruiz, J., & Fuentes-Fuentes, M. M. (2021). Martinez-Fiestas M. Effectuation or causation to promote innovation in technology-based SMEs? The effects of strategic decision-making logics. *Technology Analysis & Strategic Management*, 33(7), 797-812.

Anand, S., Hu, J., Liden, R. C., et al. (2011). Leader-member exchange: Recent research findings and prospects for the future. *The Sage Handbook of Leadership*, 311-325.

Antonakis, J., Avolio, B. J., & Sivasubramaniam, N. (2003). Context and leadership: An examination of the nine-factor full-range leadership theory using the Multifactor Leadership Questionnaire. *The Leadership Quarterly*, 14(3), 261-295.

Arend, R. J., Sarooghi, H., & Burkemper, A. (2015). Effectuation as ineffectual? Applying the 3E theory-assessment framework to a proposed new theory of entrepreneurship. *Academy of Management Review*, 40(4), 630-651.

Ault, J. K., & Spicer, A. (2020). State fragility as a multi-dimensional construct for international entrepreneurship research and practice. *Asia Pacific Journal of Management*, 37(4), 981-1011.

Autio, E., Kenney, M., Mustar, P., et al. (2014). Entrepreneurial innovation: The importance of context. *Research Policy*, 43(7), 1097-1108.

Avolio, B. J., Gardner, W. L., Walumbwa, F. O., et al. (2014). Unlocking the mask: A look at the process by which authentic leaders impact follower attitudes and behaviors. *The Leadership Quarterly*, 15(6), 801-823.

Baker, T., & Nelson, R. E. (2005). Creating something from nothing: Resource construction through entrepreneurial bricolage. *Administrative Science Quarterly*, 50(3), 329-366.

Banerjee, A. V., & Duflo, E. (2007). The economic lives of the poor. *Journal of Economic Perspectives*, 21(1), 141-168.

Banks, G. C., McCauley, K. D., Gardner, W. L., et al. (2016). A meta-analytic review of authentic and transformational leadership: A test for redundancy. *The Leadership Quarterly*, 27(4), 634-652.

Baron, R. A.(2009). Effectual versus predictive logics in entrepreneurial decision-making: Differences between experts and novices: Does experience in starting new ventures change the way entrepreneurs think? Perhaps, but for now, "caution" is essential. *Journal of Business Venturing*, 24(4), 310-315.

Bartunek, J. M., Gordon, J. R., & Weathersby, R. P. (1983). Developing "complicated" understanding in administrators. *Academy of Management Review*, 8(2), 273-284.

Bass, B. M., & Bass, Bernard, M. (1985). Leadership and performance beyond expectations.

Benitez, J., Arenas, A., Castillo, A., et al. (2022). Impact of digital leadership capability on innovation performance: The role of platform digitization capability. *Information & Management*, 59(2),103590.

Berends, H., Jelinek, M., Reymen, I., et al. (2014). Product innovation processes in small firms: Combining entrepreneurial effectuation and managerial causation. *Journal of Product Innovation Management*, 31(3), 616-635.

Bergh, D. D., Aguinis, H., Heavey, C., et al. (2016). Using meta-analytic structural equation modeling to advance strategic management research: Guidelines and an empirical illustration via the strategic leadership-performance relationship. *Strategic Management Journal*, 37(3), 477-497.

Besharov, M. L., & Smith, W. K. (2014). Multiple institutional logics in organizations: Explaining their varied nature and implications. *Academy of Management Review*, 39(3), 364-381.

Beugelsdijk, S., McCann, P., Mudambi, R. (2010). Introduction: Place, space and organization—economic geography and the multinational enterprise. *Journal of Economic Geography*, 10(4), 485-493.

Blauth, M., Mauer, R., & Brettel, M. (2014). Fostering creativity in new product development through entrepreneurial decision-making. *Creativity and Innovation Management*, 23(4), 495-509.

Bian, Y. J., & Qiu, H. X. (2005). Social Capital of Enterprises and Its Efficacy. *Social Sciences in China*, 02, 87-99+207.

Boal, K. B., & Hooijberg, R.(2000). Strategic leadership research: Moving on[J]. The Leadership Quarterly, 11(4), 515-549.

Bock, A. J., Opsahl, T., George, G., et al. (2012). The effects of culture and structure on strategic flexibility during business model innovation. *Journal of Management Studies*, 49(2), 279-305.

Boddewyn, J. J., & Brewer, T. L. (1994). International-business political behavior: New theoretical directions[J]. *Academy of Management Review*, 19(1), 119-143.

Bouckenooghe, D., Zafar, A., & Raja, U. (2015). How ethical leadership shapes employees' job performance: The mediating roles of goal congruence and psychological capital. *Journal of Business Ethics*, 129(2), 251-264.

Bourdieu, P. (1986). The forms of capital. *Cultural theory: An anthology*, 1, 81-93.

Branstetter, L., Lima, F., Taylor, L. J., et al. (2014). Do entry regulations deter entrepreneurship and job creation? Evidence from recent reforms in Portugal. *The Economic Journal*, 124(577), 805-832.

Brettel, M., Mauer, R., Engelen, A., et al. (2012). Corporate effectuation: Entrepreneurial action and its impact on R&D project performance. *Journal of Business Venturing*, 27(2), 167-184.

Brews, P. J., & Hunt, M. R. (1999). Learning to plan and planning to learn: Resolving the planning school/learning school debate. *Strategic Management Journal*, 20(10), 889-913.

Brockman, P., El, Ghoul, S., Guedhami, O., et al. (2020). Does social trust affect international contracting? Evidence from foreign bond covenants. *Journal of International Business Studies*, 1-34.

Bromiley, P., & Rau, D. (2016). Social, behavioral, and cognitive influences on upper echelons during strategy process: A literature review. *Journal of Management*, 42(1), 174-202.

Brown, J. S., & Duguid, P. (1991). Organizational learning and communities-of-practice: Toward a unified view of working, learning, and innovation. *Organization Science*, 2(1),40-57.

Brown, M. E., Treviño, L. K., & Harrison, D. A. (2005). Ethical leadership: A social learning perspective for construct development and testing. Organizational Behavior and Human Decision Processes, 97(2), 117-134.

Busenitz, L. W., Gomez, C., & Spencer, J. W. (2000). Country institutional profiles: Unlocking entrepreneurial phenomena. *Academy of Management Journal*, 43(5), 994-1003.

Cardon, M. S., Gregoire, D. A., Stevens, C. E., et al. (2013). Measuring entrepreneurial passion: Conceptual foundations and scale validation. *Journal of Business Venturing*, 28(3), 373-396.

Carter, S. M., & Greer, C. R. (2013). Strategic leadership: Values, styles, and organizational performance[J]. Journal of Leadership & Organizational Studies, 20(4), 375-393.

Centola, D., & Macy, M. (2007). Complex contagions and the weakness of long ties. *American Journal of Sociology*, 113(3), 702-734.

Chan, S. C. H., Huang, X., Snape, E. D., et al. (2013). The Janus face of paternalistic leaders: Authoritarianism, benevolence, subordinates' organization-based self-esteem, and performance. *Journal of Organizational Behavior*, 34(1), 108-128.

Chandler, G. N., DeTienne, D. R., McKelvie, A., et al. (2011). Causation and effectuation processes: A validation study. Journal of Business Venturing, 26(3), 375-390.

Chatterjee, A., & Hambrick, D. C. (2007). It's all about me: Narcissistic chief executive officers and their effects on company strategy and performance. *Administrative Science Quarterly*, 52(3), 351-386.

Cao, Y. F., & Li, P. (2010). Study on the Localization of Leadership in China: Status Analysis and Suggestions. *Chinese Journal of Management*, 11, 1704-1709.

Chen, H., & Xu, Q. (2021). Synergy of Effectuation and Causation: An Emotional Complexity Perspective. *Frontiers in Psychology*, 12.

Chen, X. P., Xu, S. Y., & Fan, J. L. (2012). Empirical Methods in Organization and Management Research (2nd Edition). *Peking University Press*.

Chen, Y., Friedman, R., Yu, E., et al. (2011). Examining guanxi practices' positive and negative effects: A multi-level analysis of guanxi practices and procedural justice perceptions. *Asia Pacific Journal of Management*, 28(4), 715-735.

Cheng, B. S., Boer, D., Chou, L. F., et al. (2014). Paternalistic leadership in four East Asian societies: Generalizability and cultural differences of the triad model. *Journal of Cross-Cultural Psychology*, 45(1), 82-90.

Chiang, J. T. J., Chen, X. P., Liu, H., et al. (2021). We have emotions but can't show them! Authoritarian leadership, emotion suppression climate, and team performance. *Human Relations*, 74(7), 1082-1111.

Child, J. (1972). Organizational structure, environment and performance: The role of strategic choice. *Sociology*, 6(1), 1-22.

Chowdhury, F., Audretsch, D. B., & Belitski, M. (2019). Institutions and entrepreneurship quality. *Entrepreneurship Theory and Practice*, 43(1), 51-81.

Coviello, N. E., & Joseph, R. M. (2012). Creating major innovations with customers: Insights from small and young technology firms. *Journal of Marketing*, 76(6), 87-104.

Crossland, C., & Hambrick, D. C. (2007). How national systems differ in their constraints on corporate executives: A study of CEO effects in three countries. *Strategic Management Journal*, 28(8), 767-789.

Dean, J. W., & Sharfman, M. P. (1996). Does decision process matter? A study of strategic decision-making effectiveness. *Academy of Management Journal*, 39(2), 368-392.

Delmar, F., & Shane, S. (2003). Does business planning facilitate the development of new ventures?. *Strategic Management Journal*, 24(12), 1165-1185.

Dess, G. G., & Beard, D. W. (1984). Dimensions of organizational task environments. *Administrative Science Quarterly*, 52-73.

Dew, N., Read, S., Sarasvathy, S. D., et al. (2009). Effectual versus predictive logics in entrepreneurial decision-making: Differences between experts and novices. *Journal of Business Venturing*, 24(4), 287-309.

DiMaggio, P. J., & Powell, W. W. (1983). The iron cage revisited: Institutional isomorphism and collective rationality in organizational fields. *American Sociological Review*, 147-160.

Du, C. Z., & Guo, S. L. (2012). Analysis of influencing factors and their mechanisms of Chinese firms' growth in economic transition. *China Industrial Economics*, 11, 97-109.

Du, Y. Z., & Sun, N. (2022). Constructing a theoretical management system with Chinese features: Necessity, feasibility and ideas. *Chinese Journal of Management*, 19(06), 811-820+872.

Dutt, N., Hawn, O., Vidal, E., et al. (2016). How open system intermediaries address institutional failures: The case of business incubators in emerging-market countries. *Academy of Management Journal*, 59(3), 818-840.

Eckhardt, J. T., & Shane, S. A. (2003). Opportunities and entrepreneurship. *Journal of Management*, 29(3), 333-349.

Eisenhardt, K. M., & Bourgeois, III, L. J. (1988). Politics of strategic decision-making in high-velocity environments: Toward a midrange theory. *Academy of Management Journal*, 31(4), 737-770.

Elenkov, D. S., Judge, W., & Wright, P. (2005). Strategic leadership and executive innovation influence: an international multi-cluster comparative study. *Strategic Management Journal*, 26(7), 665-682.

Engelen, A., Gupta, V., Strenger, L., et al. (2015). Entrepreneurial orientation, firm performance, and the moderating role of transformational leadership behaviors. *Journal of Management*, 41(4), 1069-1097.

Erben, G. S., & Güneşer, A. B. (2008). The relationship between paternalistic leadership and organizational commitment: Investigating the role of climate regarding ethics. *Journal of Business Ethics*, 82(4), 955-968.

Eseryel, U. Y., Crowston, K., & Heckman, R. (2021). Functional and visionary leadership in self-managing virtual teams. *Group & Organization Management*, 46(2), 424-460.

Eyana, S. M., Masurel, E., & Paas, L. J. (2017). Causation and effectuation behavior of Ethiopian entrepreneurs: Implications on performance of small tourism firms. *Journal of Small Business and Enterprise Development*.

Faccio, M., Marchica, M. T., & Mura, R. (2016). CEO gender, corporate risk-taking, and the efficiency of capital allocation. *Journal of Corporate Finance*, 39, 193-209.

Ferrier, W. J.(2001). Navigating the competitive landscape: The drivers and consequences of competitive aggressiveness. *Academy of Management Journal*, 44(4), 858-877.

Fiedler, F. E. (1971). Validation and extension of the contingency model of leadership effectiveness: A review of empirical findings. *Psychological Bulletin*, 76(2), 128.

Fleishman, E. A. (1953). The description of supervisory behavior. *Journal of Applied Psychology*, 37(1), 1.

Fredrickson, J. W., & Iaquinto, A. L. (1989). Inertia and creeping rationality in strategic decision processes. *Academy of Management Journal*, 32(3), 516-542.

Fredström, A., Peltonen, J., & Wincent, J. (2021). A country-level institutional perspective on entrepreneurship productivity: The effects of informal economy and regulation. *Journal of Business Venturing*, 36(5).

Fan, J. L., & Zheng, B. X. (2000). Paternalistic leadership in Chinese organizations: An analysis of cultural perspectives. *The Research on Native Psychology*, 13(1), 127-180

Fu, P. P., & Tsui, A. S. (2003). Utilizing printed media to understand desired leadership attributes in the People's Republic of China. *Asia Pacific Journal of Management*, 20(4), 423-446.

Gabrielsson, J., & Politis, D. (2011). Career motives and entrepreneurial decision-making: examining preferences for causal and effectual logics in the early stage of new ventures. *Small Business Economics*, 36(3), 281-298.

Gao, R., Hu, H. W., & Yoshikawa, T. (2022). Attraction versus competition: A tale of two similarity effects in director selection of Chinese firms. *Asia Pacific Journal of Management*, 1-42.

Gardner, W. L., Cogliser, C. C., Davis, K. M., et al. (2011). Authentic leadership: A review of the literature and research agenda. *The Leadership Quarterly*, 22(6), 1120-1145.

Gardner, W. L., Fischer, D., & Hunt, J. G. J. (2009). Emotional labor and leadership: A threat to authenticity? *The Leadership Quarterly*, 20(3), 466-482.

Gibb, A. A. (1997). Small firms' training and competitiveness. Building upon the small business as a learning organization. *International Small Business Journal*, 15(3), 13-29.

Gigerenzer, G., & Gaissmaier, W. (2011). Heuristic decision-making. *Annual Review of Psychology*, 62(1), 451-482.

Gómez-Mejía, L. R., Haynes, K. T., & Núñez-Nickel, M., et al. (2007). Socioemotional wealth and business risks in family-controlled firms: Evidence from Spanish olive oil mills. *Administrative Science Quarterly*, 52(1), 106-137.

Graen, G. B., & Uhl-Bien, M. (1995). Relationship-based approach to leadership: Development of leader-member exchange (LMX) theory of leadership over 25 years: Applying a multi-level multi-domain perspective. *The Leadership Quarterly*, 6(2), 219-247.

Graf-Vlachy, L., Bundy, J., & Hambrick, D. C. (2020). Effects of an advancing tenure on CEO cognitive complexity. *Organization Science*, 31(4), 936-959.

Granovetter, M. (1985). Economic action and social structure: the problem of embeddedness. *American Journal of Sociology*, 91(3).

Greenwood, R., Díaz, A. M., Li, S. X., et al. (2010). The multiplicity of institutional logic and the heterogeneity of organizational responses. *Organization Science*, 21(2), 521-539.

Grégoire, D. A., & Cherchem, N. (2020). A structured literature review and suggestions for future effectuation research[J]. Small Business Economics, 54(3), 621-639.

Hambrick, D. C., & Finkelstein, S. (1987). Managerial discretion: A bridge between polar views of organizational outcomes. *Research in Organizational Behavior*.

Hambrick, D. C., & Mason, P. A. (1984). Upper echelons: The organization as a reflection of its top managers[J]. Academy of Management Review, 9(2), 193-206.

Hambrick, D. C., & Quigley, T. J. (2014). Toward more accurate contextualization of the CEO effect on firm performance. *Strategic Management Journal*, 35(4), 473-491.

Hambrick, D. C. (2007). Upper echelons theory: An update. *Academy of Management Review*, 32(2), 334-343.

Hannan, M. T., & Freeman, J. (1977). The population ecology of organizations. *American Journal of Sociology*, 82(5), 929-964.

He, J. X., Ge, J. Y., & Zhang, F. (2021). Global contributions of Chinese scholars to management research: International cooperation, frontier hotspots, and contribution path--A quantitative analysis based on thousands of English journal papers on management worldwide (2013-2019). *Management World*, 37(09), 36-67.

He, X. G., & Li, X. C. (2005). Entrepreneurial ability and firm growth: an empirical study based on China's experience. *Economic Research Journal*, 10, 101-111.

Hedberg, L. M., & Lounsbury, M. (2021). Not just small potatoes: Cultural entrepreneurship in the moralizing of markets. *Organization Science*, 32(2), 433-454.

Henderson, A. D., Miller, D., & Hambrick, D. C. (2006). How quickly do CEOs become obsolete? Industry dynamism, CEO tenure, and company performance. *Strategic Management Journal*, 27(5), 447-460.

Henisz, W. J. (2002). Politics and international investment: Measuring risks and protecting profits. *Edward Elgar Publishing.*

Hillman, A. J., & Hitt, M. A. (1999). Corporate political strategy formulation: A model of approach, participation, and strategy decisions. *Academy of Management Review*, 24(4), 825-842.

Hoang, H., & Antoncic, B. (2003). Network-based research in entrepreneurship: A critical review. *Journal of Business Venturing*, 18(2), 165-187.

Hofstede, G. (1980). Motivation, leadership, and organization: do American theories apply abroad? *Organizational Dynamics*, 9(1), 42-63.

Hollander, E. P., & Julian, J. W. (1969). Contemporary trends in the analysis of leadership processes. *Psychological Bulletin*, 71(5), 387.

House, R. J. (1971). A path-goal theory of leader effectiveness. *Administrative Science Quarterly*, 321-339.

Hu, W. B., Zhang, Y. L., & Yang, J. (2014). Homogeneity or heterogeneity: a study of the moderating effect of entrepreneurial orientation on the relationship between technical, entrepreneurial teams and new enterprise performance. *Management World*, 06, 92-109+187-188.

Hwang, H., & Powell, W. W. (2005). Institutions and entrepreneurship//Handbook of entrepreneurship research. Springer, Boston, MA, 201-232.

Inkpen, A. C., & Tsang, E. W. K. (2005). Social capital, networks, and knowledge transfer. *Academy of Management Review*, 30(1), 146-165.

Ireland, R. D., Hitt, M. A., & Sirmon, D. G. (2003). A model of strategic entrepreneurship: The construct and its dimensions. *Journal of Management*, 29(6), 963-989.

Jafari-Sadeghi, V., & Garcia-Perez, A., Candelo, E., et al. (2021). Exploring the impact of digital transformation on technology entrepreneurship and technological market expansion: The role of technology readiness, exploration and exploitation. *Journal of Business Research*, 124, 100-111.

Jansen, J. J. P., Van, Den, Bosch, F. A. J., & Volberda, H. W. (2006). Exploratory innovation, exploitative innovation, and performance: Effects of organizational antecedents and environmental moderators. *Management Science*, 52(11), 1661-1674.

Jenkins, W. O. (1947). A review of leadership studies with particular reference to military problems. *Psychological Bulletin*, 44(1), 54.

Jensen, S. M., & Luthans, F. (2006). Relationship between entrepreneurs' psychological capital and their authentic leadership. *Journal of Managerial Issues*, 2006, 254-273.

Jiang, C. Y., & Zhao, S. M. (2006). The relationship between social capital and corporate entrepreneurship and performance: the mediating role of organizational learning -- an empirical study of emerging firms in Jiangsu and Guangdong. *Management World*, 10, 90-99+171-172.

Judge, T. A., Bono, J. E., Ilies, R., et al. (2002). Personality and leadership: a qualitative and quantitative review. *Journal of Applied Psychology*, 87(4), 765.

Judge, W. Q., & Miller, A. (1991). Antecedents and outcomes of decision speed in different environmental contexts. *Academy of Management Journal*, 34(2), 449-463.

Katz, D., & Kahn, R. L. (1978). Organizations and the system concept. *Classics of Organization Theory*, 80, 480.

Katz, J., Gartner, W. B. (1988). Properties of emerging organizations. *Academy of Management Review*, 13(3), 429-441.

Kernis, M. H., Goldman, B. M. (2006). A multicomponent conceptualization of authenticity: Theory and research. *Advances in Experimental Social Psychology*, 38, 283-357.

Kerr, S., Schriesheim, C. A., Murphy, C. J., et al. (1974). Toward a contingency theory of leadership based upon the consideration and initiating structure literature. *Organizational Behavior and Human Performance*, 12(1), 62-82.

King, T., Srivastav, A., & Williams, J. (2016). What's in an education? Implications of CEO education for bank performance. *Journal of Corporate Finance*, 37, 287-308.

KirznerI. (1973). Competition and entrepreneurship. *Chicago: University of Chicago Press.*

Kiss, A. N., & Danis, W. M. (2010). Social networks and speed of new venture internationalization during institutional transition: A conceptual model[J]. Journal of International Entrepreneurship, 8(3), 273-287.

Kogut, B., & Zander, U. (1996). What do firms do? Coordination, identity, and learning. *Organization Science*, 7(5), 502-518.

Krause, R., Li, W., Ma, X., et al. (2019). The board chair effect across countries: An institutional view. *Strategic Management Journal*, 40(10), 1570-1592.

Laine, I., & Galkina, T. (2017). The interplay of effectuation and causation in decision-making: Russian SMEs under institutional uncertainty. *International Entrepreneurship and Management Journal*, 13(3), 905-941.

Li, G., Li, L., Choi, T. M., et al. Green supply chain management in Chinese firms: Innovative measures and the moderating role of quick response technology. *Journal of Operations Management*, 66(7-8), 958-988.

Li, H. (2001). Atuahene-Gima K. Product innovation strategy and the performance of new technology ventures in China. *Academy of Management Journal*, 44(6), 1123-1134.

Li, J. P., Wu, R., & Yang, D. L. (2020). Convergence of institutional and entrepreneurship research: Historical overview and future directions. *Management World*, 36(05), 204-219+19.

Li, S. W. (2021). Ethical leadership development and the construction of "gentlemanly" management in the context of Confucian culture. *Leadership Science*, 10, 61-63.

Li, T., Xu, X., & Sun, S. (2016). Inclusive finance and economic growth. *Journal of Financial Research*, 04, 1-16.

Li, W., &Au, K. Y., He, A., et al. (2015). Why do family-controlled firms donate to charity? The role of intrafamily succession intention, social status, and religiosity. *Management and Organization Review*, 11(4), 621-644.

Li, W. W. (2021). Corporate strategic leadership in China: Opportunities and challenges. *Quarterly Journal of Management*, 6(01), 36-48+163.

Li, X. C., Han, J., & Li, W. W. (2015). Inheritance or creating another territory? --The construction of authoritative legitimacy in the second generation of family business succession. *Management World*, 06, 110-124+187-188.

Li, X. C., He, X. G., & Zou, L., K. (2020). Family business research: theoretical advances and future perspectives. *Management World*, 36(11), 207-229.

Li, Y. Y., & Tang, N. Y. (2022). Research on responsible leadership: A comparative analysis of domestic and international studies based on knowledge mapping. *Journal of Management Sciences*, 35(04), 82-98.

Li, Z. W. (2003). Organizational learning and enterprise performance under dynamic environmental conditions. *Zhejiang University*.

Liu, D., Liao, H., & Loi, R. (2012). The dark side of leadership: A three-level investigation of the cascading effect of abusive supervision on employee creativity. *Academy of Management Journal*, 55(5), 1187-1212.

Locke, E. A., & Latham, G. P. (1990). A theory of goal setting & task performance. *Prentice-Hall*, Inc.

Lord, R. G., De, Vader, C. L., & Alliger, G. M. (1986). A meta-analysis of the relation between personality traits and leadership perceptions: An application of validity generalization procedures. *Journal of Applied Psychology*, 71(3), 402.

Lu, Y. D., & Sun, J. Y. (2013). New perspectives on the growth strategy of Chinese enterprises: the concept, connotation and methodology of the composite foundation perspective. *Management World*, 10, 106-117+141+187-188.

Luciano, M. M., Nahrgang, J. D., & Shropshire, C. (2020). Strategic leadership systems: Viewing top management teams and boards of directors from a multiteam systems perspective. *Academy of Management Review*, 45(3), 675-701.

Mackey, J. D., Frieder, R. E., Brees, J. R., et al. (2017). Abusive supervision: A meta-analysis and empirical review. *Journal of Management*, 43(6), 1940-1965.

Mahmood, I. P., & Rufin, C. (2005). Government's dilemma: The role of government in imitation and innovation. *Academy of Management Review*, 30(2), 338-360.

Mair, J, Marti, I., & Ventresca, M. J. (2012). Building inclusive markets in rural Bangladesh: How intermediaries work institutional voids. *Academy of Management Journal*, 55(4), 819-850.

Mair, J., & Marti, I. (2009). Entrepreneurship in and around institutional voids: A case study from Bangladesh. *Journal of Business Venturing*, 24(5), 419-435.

Makhija, M. V., & Stewart, A. C. (2002). The effect of national context on perceptions of risk: A comparison of planned versus free-market managers. *Journal of International Business Studies*, 33(4), 737-756.

Malhotra, S., & Harrison, J. S. (2022). A blessing and a curse: How chief executive officer cognitive complexity influences firm performance under varying industry conditions. *Strategic Management Journal*, 13(43), 2809-2828.

Mann, R. D. (1959). A review of the relationships between personality and performance in small groups. *Psychological Bulletin*, 56(4), 241.

Manolova, T. S., Eunni, R. V., & Gyoshev, B. S. (2008). Institutional environments for entrepreneurship: Evidence from emerging economies in Eastern Europe. *Entrepreneurship Theory and Practice*, 32(1), 203-218.

Martin, R., Thomas, G., Legood, A., et al. (2018). Leader–member exchange (LMX) differentiation and work outcomes: Conceptual clarification and critical review. *Journal of Organizational Behavior*, 39(2), 151-168.

Martinko, M. J., Harvey, P., Brees, J. R., et al. (2013). A review of abusive supervision research[J]. *Journal of Organizational Behavior*, 34(1), 120-137.

Mayer, D. M., Kuenzi, M., Greenbaum, R., et al. (2009). How low does ethical leadership flow? Test of a trickle-down model. *Organizational Behavior and Human Decision Processes*, 108(1), 1-13.

McFadyen, M. A., Cannella, Jr, A. A. (2004). Social capital and knowledge creation: Diminishing returns of the number and strength of exchange relationships. *Academy of Management Journal*, 47(5), 735-746.

McMullen, J. S., Bagby, D. R., & Palich, L. E. (2008). Economic freedom and the motivation to engage in entrepreneurial action. *Entrepreneurship Theory and Practice*, 32(5), 875-895.

Meuser, J. D., Gardner, W. L., Dinh, J. E., et al. (2016). A network analysis of leadership theory: The infancy of integration. *Journal of Management*, 42(5), 1374-1403.

Mintzberg, H., & Waters, J. A. (1985). Of strategies, deliberate and emergent. *Strategic Management Journal*, 6(3), 257-272.

Nadkarni, S., & Narayanan, V. K. (2007). Strategic schemas, strategic flexibility, and firm performance: The moderating role of industry clock speed. *Strategic Management Journal*, 28(3), 243-270.

Nahapiet, J., & Ghoshal, S. (1998). Social capital, intellectual capital, and organizational advantage. *Academy of Management Review*, 23(2), 242-266.

Nason, R. S., & Wiklund, J. (2018). An assessment of resource-based theorizing on firm growth and suggestions for the future. *Journal of Management*, 44(1), 32-60.

Neely, Jr, B. H., Lovelace, J. B., Cowen, A. P., et al. (2020). Metacritiques of upper echelons theory: Verdicts and recommendations for future research. *Journal of Management*, 46(6), 1029-1062.

Ng, T. W. H. (2017). Transformational leadership and performance outcomes: Analyses of multiple mediation pathways. *The Leadership Quarterly*, 28(3), 385-417.

Nickerson, J. A., Zenger, T. R. (2004). A knowledge-based theory of the firm—The problem-solving perspective. *Organization Science*, 15(6), 617-632.

Nunnally, J. C. (1978). An overview of psychological measurement. *Clinical Diagnosis of Mental Disorders*, 97-146.

Nunnally, J. C. (1994). Psychometric theory 3E. *Tata McGraw-Hill education.*

Nutt, P. C., & Backoff, R. W. (1997). Crafting vision. *Journal of Management Inquiry*, 6(4), 308-328.

O'Brien, D., Sharkey, Scott, P., Andersson, U. et al. (2019). The micro-foundations of subsidiary initiatives: How subsidiary manager activities unlock entrepreneurship. *Global Strategy Journal*, 9(1), 66-91.

Ocasio, W. (2011). Attention to attention. *Organization Science*, 22(5), 1286-1296.

Ocasio, W. (1997). Towards an attention-based view of the firm. *Strategic Management Journal*, 18(S1), 187-206.

Oliveira, T., Thomas, M., & Espadanal, M. (2014). Assessing the determinants of cloud computing adoption: An analysis of the manufacturing and services sectors. *Information & Management*, 51(5), 497-510.

Oliver, C. (1991). Strategic responses to institutional processes. *Academy of Management Review*, 16(1), 145-179.

Ostgaard, T. A., & Birley, S. (1996). New venture growth and personal networks. *Journal of Business Research*, 36(1), 37-50.

Palich, L. E., Cardinal, L. B., & Miller, C. C. (2000). Curvilinearity in the diversification–performance linkage: an examination of over three decades of research. *Strategic Management Journal*, 21(2), 155-174.

Pan, Y., Verbeke, A., & Yuanm W. (2021). CEO transformational leadership and corporate entrepreneurship in China. *Management and Organization Review*, 17(1), 45-76.

Park, S. H., & Luo, Y. (2001). Guanxi and organizational dynamics: Organizational networking in Chinese firms. *Strategic Management Journal*, 22(5), 455-477.

Pellegrini, E. K., Scandura, T. A., & Jayaraman, V. (2010). Cross-cultural generalizability of paternalistic leadership: An expansion of leader-member exchange theory. *Group & Organization Management*, 35(4), 391-420.

Peng, M. W., & Heath, P. S. (1996). The growth of the firm in planned economies in transition: Institutions, organizations, and strategic choice. *Academy of Management Review*, 21(2), 492-528.

Peng, X. B., Liu, Y. L., Jiao, Q. Q., et al. (2020). The nonlinear effect of effectuation and causation on new venture performance: The moderating effect of environmental uncertainty. *Journal of Business Research*, 117, 112-123.

Peng, X. M. (2009). A study of the mechanism of corporate networks on technological innovation performance: the mediating effect of exploitative-exploratory learning. *Zhejiang University.*

Penrose. (2007). The Theory of the Growth of the Firm. *SDX Joint Publishing Company.*

Perry, J. T., Chandler, G. N., & Markova, G. (2012). Entrepreneurial effectuation: a review and suggestions for future research. *Entrepreneurship Theory and Practice*, 36(4), 837-861.

Pfeffer, J., & Sutton, R. I. (2006). Hard facts, dangerous half-truths, and total nonsense: Profiting from evidence-based management. *Harvard Business Press*.

Podsakoff, P. M., MacKenzie, S. B., & Podsakoff, N. P. (2012). Sources of method bias in social science research and recommendations on how to control it. *Annual Review of Psychology*, 63(1), 539-569.

Reagans, R., & McEvily, B. (2003). Network structure and knowledge transfer: The effects of cohesion and range. *Administrative Science Quarterly*, 48(2), 240-267.

Reed, R., & DeFillippi, R. J. (1990). Causal ambiguity, barriers to imitation, and sustainable competitive advantage. *Academy of Management Review*, 15(1), 88-102.

Reymen, I. M. M. J., Andries, P., Berends, H., et al. (2015). Understanding dynamics of strategic decision-making in venture creation: a process study of effectuation and causation. *Strategic Entrepreneurship Journal*, 9(4), 351-379.

Reymen, I., Berends, H., Oudehand, R., et al. (2017). Decision-making for business model development: a process study of effectuation and causation in new technology-based ventures. *R&D Management*, 47(4), 595-606.

Rothaermel, F. T.,& Alexandre, M. T. (2009). Ambidexterity in technology sourcing: The moderating role of absorptive capacity. *Organization Science*, 20(4), 759-780.

Samuelsson, M., & Davidsson, P. (2009). Does venture opportunity variation matter? Investigating systematic process differences between innovative and imitative new ventures. *Small Business Economics*, 33(2), 229-255.

Sarasvathy, S. D., Dew, N., Read, S., et al. (2008). Designing organizations that design environments: Lessons from entrepreneurial expertise. *Organization Studies*, 29(3), 331-350.

Sarasvathy, S. D., Dew, N., Velamuri, S. R., et al. (2003). Three views of entrepreneurial opportunity//Handbook of entrepreneurship research. Springer, Boston, MA, 141-160.

Sarasvathy, S. D., & Dew, N. (2005). New market creation through transformation. *Journal of Evolutionary Economics*, 15(5), 533-565.

Sarasvathy, S. D. (2001). Causation and effectuation: Toward a theoretical shift from economic inevitability to entrepreneurial contingency. *Academy of Management Review*, 26(2), 243-263.

Schaubroeck, J. M., Shen, Y., Chong, S. (2017). A dual-stage moderated mediation model linking authoritarian leadership to follower outcomes. *Journal of Applied Psychology*, 102(2): 203.

Scheaf, D. J., Davis, B. C., Webb, J. W., et al. (2018). Signals' flexibility and interaction with visual cues: Insights from crowdfunding. *Journal of Business Venturing*, 33(6), 720-741.

Schriesheim, C. A., & Hinkin, T. R. (1990). Influence tactics used by subordinates: A theoretical and empirical analysis and refinement of the

Kipnis, Schmidt, and Wilkinson subscales. *Journal of Applied Psychology*, 75(3), 246.

Schumpeter, J. A., & Nichol, A. J. (1934). Robinson's economics of imperfect competition. *Journal of Political Economy*, 42(2), 249-259.

Shamir, B., & Eilam, G. (2005). "What's your story?" A life-stories approach to authentic leadership development. *The Leadership Quarterly*, 16(3), 395-417.

Shane, S. A. (2003). A general theory of entrepreneurship: The individual-opportunity nexus. *Edward Elgar Publishing*.

Shane, S., & Venkataraman, S. (2000). The promise of entrepreneurship as a field of research. *Academy of Management Review*, 25(1), 217-226.

Sheng, Z. H., Yu, J. Y. (2021). Complex systems management: a new field of management with Chinese features. *Management World*, 37(06), 36-50+2.

Shinkle, G. A., & Kriauciunas, A. P. (2012). The impact of current and founding institutions on strength of competitive aspirations in transition economies. *Strategic Management Journal*, 33(4), 448-458.

Siddique, C. M., Siddique, H. F., & Siddique, S. U. (2020). Linking authoritarian leadership to employee organizational embeddedness, LMX and performance in a high-power distance culture: a mediation-moderated analysis. *Journal of Strategy and Management*, 13(3), 393-411.

Simon, H. A. (1973). The structure of ill structured problems[J]. Artificial Intelligence, 4(3-4), 181-201.

Simsek, Z., Jansen, J. J. P., Minichilli, A., et al. Strategic leadership and leaders in entrepreneurial contexts: A nexus for innovation and impact missed? *Journal of Management Studies*, 52(4), 463-478.

Snowden, D. J., & Boone, M. E. (2007). A leader's framework for decision-making. *Harvard Business Review*, 85(11): 68.

Sonenshein, S. (2014). How organizations foster the creative use of resources. *Academy of Management Journal*, 57(3), 814-848.

Sørensen, J. B. (2007). Bureaucracy and entrepreneurship: Workplace effects on entrepreneurial entry. *Administrative Science Quarterly*, 52(3), 387-412.

Spence, M. (1974). Competitive and optimal responses to signals: An analysis of efficiency and distribution. *Journal of Economic Theory*, 7(3), 296-332.

Spigel, B. (2017). The relational organization of entrepreneurial ecosystems. *Entrepreneurship Theory and Practice*, 41(1), 49-72.

Stam, D., Lord, R. G., Knippenberg, D., et al. (2014). An image of who we might become: Vision communication, possible selves, and vision pursuit. *Organization Science*, 25(4), 1172-1194.

Sternberg, H. S., Hofmann, E., & Roeck, D. (2021). The struggle is real: insights from a supply chain blockchain case. *Journal of Business Logistics*, 42(1), 71-87.

Stevens, S. S. (1971). Issues in psychophysical measurement. *Psychological Review*, 78(5), 426.

Stogdill, R. M. (1948). Personal factors associated with leadership: A survey of the literature. *The Journal of Psychology*, 25(1), 35-71.

Tepper, B. J. (2007). Abusive supervision in work organizations: Review, synthesis, and research agenda. *Journal of Management*, 33(3), 261-289.

Thomas, A. B. (1988). Does leadership make a difference to organizational performance? *Administrative Science Quarterly*, 388-400.

Thornton, P. H., & Ocasio, W. (2008). Institutional logics. *The Sage Handbook of Organizational Institutionalism*, 840, 99-128.

Tolbert, P. S., David, R. J., & Sine, W. D. (2011). Studying choice and change: The intersection of institutional theory and entrepreneurship research. *Organization Science*, 22(5), 1332-1344.

Townsend, D. M., Hunt, R. A., McMullen, J. S., et al. (2018). Uncertainty, knowledge problems, and entrepreneurial action. *Academy of Management Annals*, 12(2), 659-687.

Tsai, W., & Ghoshal, S. (1998). Social capital and value creation: The role of intrafirm networks. *Academy of Management Journal*, 41(4), 464-476.

Tsoukas, H., & Vladimirou, E. (2001). What is organizational knowledge? Journal of Management Studies, 38(7), 973-993.

Uzzi, B., & Lancaster, R. (2003). Relational embeddedness and learning: The case of bank loan managers and their clients. *Management Science*, 49(4), 383-399.

Venkataraman, S. (1997). Value at risk for a mixture of normal distributions: the use of quasi-Bayesian estimation techniques. *Economic Perspectives-Federal Reserve Bank of Chicago*, 21, 2-13.

Vera, D., & Crossan, M. (2004). Strategic leadership and organizational learning[J]. Academy of Management Review, 29(2), 222-240.

Waldman, D. A., Ramirez, G. G., House, R. J., et al. (2001). Does leadership matter? CEO leadership attributes and profitability under conditions of perceived environmental uncertainty. *Academy of Management Journal*, 44(1), 134-143.

Walumbwa, F. O., Avolio, B. J., Gardner, W. L., et al. (2008). Authentic leadership: Development and validation of a theory-based measure. *Journal of Management*, 34(1), 89-126.

Walumbwa, F. O., Mayer, D. M., Wang, P., et al. (2011). Linking ethical leadership to employee performance: The roles of leader–member exchange, self-efficacy, and organizational identification. *Organizational Behavior and Human Decision Processes*, 115(2), 204-213.

Walumbwa, F. O., & Schaubroeck, J. (2009). Leader personality traits and employee voice behavior: mediating roles of ethical leadership and work group psychological safety. *Journal of Applied Psychology*, 94(5), 1275.

Wang, A. C., Tsai, C. Y., Dionne, S. D., et al. (2018). Benevolence-dominant, authoritarianism-dominant, and classical paternalistic leadership: Testing their relationships with subordinate performance. *The Leadership Quarterly*, 29(6), 686-697.

Wang, C. L., Ahmed, P. K. (2007). Dynamic capabilities: A review and research agenda. *International Journal of Management Reviews*, 9(1), 31-51.

Wang, K. D., Tu, W. J., & Huo, B. F. (2022). Supply chain leadership: literature review and research prospects. *Foreign Economics & Management*, 44(06), 110-134.

Wang, L., Chu, X. P., Peng, C. D., & Yue, L. (2020). A study of the spillover mechanism of daily interactions of family roles on the development of paternalistic leadership - Empirical evidence based on TMT log traces of family firms. *Management World*, 36(08), 98-110.

Wang, M. S., Huo, N., & Zhou, X. (2021). Research on value co-creation mechanisms of digital brand communities - based on the perspective of experience-dominant logic. *Nankai Business Review*, 24(03), 92-103.

Wang, X. H. F., & Howell, J. M. (2010). Exploring the dual-level effects of transformational leadership on followers. *Journal of Applied Psychology*, 95(6), 1134.

Wangrow, D. B., Schepker, D. J., Barker, III, V. L. (2015). Managerial discretion: An empirical review and focus on future research directions. *Journal of Management*, 41(1), 99-135.

Webb, J. W., Khoury, T. A., & Hitt, M. A. (2020). The influence of formal and informal institutional voids on entrepreneurship. *Entrepreneurship Theory and Practice*, 44(3), 504-526.

Welter, C., & Kim, S. (2018). Effectuation under risk and uncertainty: A simulation model. *Journal of Business Venturing*, 33(1), 100-116.

Williamson, O. E. (2000). The new institutional economics: taking stock, looking ahead. *Journal of Economic Literature*, 38(3), 595-613.

Wiltbank, R., Dew, N., Read, S., et al. (2006). What to do next? The case for non-predictive strategy. *Strategic Management Journal*, 27(10), 981-998.

Wong, E. M., Ormiston, M. E., & Tetlock, P. E. (2011). The effects of top management team integrative complexity and decentralized decision-making on corporate social performance. *Academy of Management Journal*, 54(6), 1207-1228.

Wooldridge, B., & Cowden, B. (2020). Strategic Decision-Making in Business[M]//Oxford Research Encyclopedia of Business and Management.

Wu, J. B., Tsui, A. S., & Kinicki, A. J. (2010). Consequences of differentiated leadership in groups. *Academy of Management Journal*, 53(1), 90-106.

Xu, K., Hitt, M. A., & Miller, S. R. (2020). The ownership structure contingency in the sequential international entry mode decision process: Family owners and institutional investors in family-dominant versus family-influenced firms. *Journal of International Business Studies*, 51(2), 151-171.

Yang, D. (2013). Corporate governance and enterprise performance--a sociological analysis based on the Chinese experience. *Social Sciences in China*, 01, 72-94+206.

Yang, Q. J. (2011). Business growth: political relevance or capacity building. *Economic Research Journal*, 46(10), 54-66+94.

Yu, G. L., Yao, J. M., & Zhang, L. G. (2017). A study of the relationship between paternalistic leadership, employee trust and job performance. *Journal of Northeast Normal University (Philosophy and Social Sciences)*, 02, 125-129.

Yu, X., Tao, Y., Tao, X., et al. (2018). Managing uncertainty in emerging economies: The interaction effects between causation and effectuation on firm performance. *Technological Forecasting and Social Change*, 135, 121-131.

Yu, X. Y., Li, Y. J., & Tao, X. M. (2017). Literature Review on Entrepreneurial Bricolage and a Research Agenda. *Chinese Journal of Management*, 14(02), 306-316.

Zaccaro, S. J. (2007). Trait-based perspectives of leadership. American Psychologist, 62(1), 6.

Zhang, W., Zhao, W., Gao, Y., et al. (2021). How do managerial ties influence the effectuation and causation of entrepreneurship in China? The role of entrepreneurs' cognitive bias[M]//Corporate Performance and Managerial Ties in China. Routledge, 85-113.

Zhang, W. Y., Zhou, L. A., & Gu, Q. L. (2005). Growth of high-tech firms and its influencing factors: an application of quantile regression modeling. *Management World*, 10, 94-101+112+172.

Zhang, X. A., He, H., & Gu, F. (2009). The effect of paternalistic leadership behaviors on team performance: the mediating effect of team conflict management styles. *Management World*, 03, 121-133.

Zhang, Y. (2021). Strategic leadership research: progress in the last 20 years and future research directions. *Quarterly Journal of Management*, 6(01), 1-15+160.

Zhang, Y., Liu, R. H., & Chen, H. Q. (2020). Influencing factors of platform leadership in business ecosystems - an exploratory study based on the grounded theory. *Nankai Business Review*, 23(03), 28-38+131.

Zheng, B. X. (1995). Differential patterns and Chinese organizational behavior. *The Research on Native Psychology*, 3, 142-219.

Zhou, D. M., Chen, X. L., Yang, J., & Lu, R. Y. (2020). Entrepreneurship research review and outlook. *Management World*, 36(01), 206-225+243.

Zhou, J. K., & Huang, Z. X. (2014). Housing system reform, mobility constraints and entrepreneurial choice of "doing business"--a theoretical and empirical study in China. *Economic Research Journal*, 49(03), 158-170.

Zhou, W. (2017). Institutional environment, public-private hybrid forms, and entrepreneurial reinvestment in a transition economy. *Journal of Business Venturing*, 32(2), 197-214.

Zhou, Z. J., Wang, H. R., & Xiu, Z. F. (2021). Actively constructing a theoretical management system with Chinese features--an analysis based on the articles published in A-class journals of management science of NSFC (2013～2020). *Management World*, 37(09), 57-77.

Zhu, H. Q. (2021). Carrying on the Past and Creating the Future: Comment on Research on Strategic Leadership Summary of 20-Year Advancement and Future Research Directions. *Quarterly Journal of Management*, 6(01), 16-25+161.

Index

I

L

M

N

O

P

Q

R

S

T

U

V

W

Made in United States
Orlando, FL
05 November 2026

90229841R10151